Penguin Books
I am Ned Kelly

John Molony was born in Melbourne in 1927.
The author of several books, he is at present
Professor of History and head of the History
Department of the Faculty of Arts at the
Australian National University, Canberra. His
field of interest includes modern European
history and Australian history. This Kelly book
is the first of several on Australian mythology;
others will cover Eureka, the Anzacs, and
Australian nationalism, which Molony
believes was frustrated by federation.

I am Ned Kelly

John Molony

Penguin Books Australia Ltd,
487 Maroondah Highway, P.O. Box 257
Ringwood, Victoria, 3134, Australia
Penguin Books Ltd,
Harmondsworth, Middlesex, England
Penguin Books,
625 Madison Avenue, New York, N.Y. 10022, U.S.A.
Penguin Books Canada Ltd,
2801 John Street, Markham, Ontario, Canada
Penguin Books (N.Z.) Ltd,
182-190 Wairau Road, Auckland 10, New Zealand

First published by Allen Lane, 1980
Published by Penguin Books Australia, 1982
Copyright © John N. Molony, 1980

Typeset in Cairo Light by The Dova Type Shop, Melbourne
Offset from the Allen Lane edition
Made and printed in Hong Kong by
Colorcraft Ltd

CIP

Molony, John, 1927-
I am Ned Kelly.

Originally published: Melbourne: Allen Lane, 1980
Index
Bibliography
ISBN 014 006247 5

1. Kelly, Ned, 1855-1880. 2. Bushrangers — Biography.
I. Title.

364.1'55'0924

To my own four Australians
Damien, Michael, Leah and Justine

Contents

Acknowledgements

It is sometimes said by an author that without the assistance of so-and-so, this work would never have been written. In this case it is not true. I would have done it, but badly. The Australian Research Grants Committee made it possible for me to obtain the services of Robyn Carter as a research assistant. She made it easy for me to live with the boys in the mountains and on the plains near Greta. In the manner of Ned's beloved sister Maggie she brought me the supplies necessary for the story to survive. She also made the family tree which I had fled from in despair. My thanks are due also to Kevin Cowan of the Geography Department, Australian National University, who generously drew the map.

The major repositories of 'Kellyana' in manuscript are the La Trobe Library of the State Library of Victoria and the Public Record Office of Victoria. In New South Wales they are at the Mitchell Library of the Library of New South Wales and the New South Wales State Archives. Those whose task it is to preserve and make available

the records of the two colonies in respect of those outlawed by their authorities were most generous in time,
courtesy and forbearance. The same applies to the staff
of the *Mansfield Courier* where the files of the *Mansfield
Guardian* are held.

For the rest I can do no more than list their names and
all will know of my debt to them. Some are policemen,
others clerics. Many are of the Kelly 'clan' related by
blood and marriage to those who appear in these pages
and, that they spoke to me at all, is testimony to the
cleansing flow of the passing years. Others again were
interested in my work and with encouragement and
guidance they helped me: Dagmar Balcorek, William
Batchelor, Jean Batten, James Byrne, Ross Cranston,
Eddy Cully, Chris Cunneen, Gavan Daws, David
Denholm, Neville Drummond, Ian Fitchett, John
Graham, Mrs Griffith, Kevin Hannan, Cameron Hazle-
hurst, Frank Hickey, Frank Higgins, Ken Inglis, Ian Jones,
John Keaney, Irene Klingsporn, Thomas Linane, Tom
Lloyd, David MacDonald, Beth McLeod, John McQuil-
ton, Allan Mason, Eddie Meek, Maureen Mier, Michael
Moignard, Bill Morrison, Sean Murphy, Bede Nairn, John
Nolan, Barbara Payne, Alan Queale, Peter Quinn, Mark
Richmond, Ray Riordon, Michael Ryan, Catherine San-
tamaria, Geoffrey Serle, Bunny Storer, Frank Strahan,
the Tadaro family and George Taylor.

In the History Department, A.N.U., the question was
sometimes asked whether I proposed to remove to Glenrowan or Greta to set up a Department of Kelly studies.
For all the wit and banter, the sober advice and
generous patience, I can only say my thanks, and
especially to Barbara Hutchinson who typed up a first
draft from my byzantine script, and to all those who
helped with the finished copy. Gerry Walsh, John Ritchie

and Brian Molony read the manuscript and they will see their precious imprint on these pages. My beloved Dinny, mother of our four Australians, learnt more about Ned and his time than one could reasonably expect even of a sixth generation Australian. Doubtless she longed for the last word and it is hers.

Preface

A book, like a man, has a simple beginning. This one began with a reaction. Perhaps because of my own Irish-Catholic background I shared the half-embarrassed attitude to Kelly which regarded him as someone best forgotten. There were so many unpalatable aspects to his story and with almost a sense of wonderment I faced the fact of his acceptance as a national myth. Mentally it was something I withdrew from and in my Australian history courses I omitted any reference to Ned. A Tuesday evening in early summer 1976 changed all that.

My previous book had been about a political party in fascist Italy and I was half-heartedly researching a work on Governor George Gipps to fill in the time before returning to European history. Sitting on the lawn in Fellows Garden at University House, Canberra, on that Tuesday evening, a group of us were discussing the development of Australian historical writing. With obvious puzzlement, one of our group recounted how a decision had been taken at a meeting in Melbourne a day or so previously not to have any official recognition of the centenary of Kelly's execution by the State of Victoria. To me such a decision was incomprehensible despite my shyness in respect of Ned and my lack of knowledge of him. The myth had transcended the man and I was as surprised as if I had heard that Italy had decided to erase the name of Garibaldi from her official records. With the impetuosity characteristic of the Gael I declared that, Victorian officialdom notwithstanding, I would write a life of Ned.

It seemed to me that were we deliberately to set our faces against our past, personified in the unique legend that is Ned, we would be impoverished. Such of course will not happen because it is not the way of life. No act of repression or deliberate ignorance will prevent a people from drawing on the well-springs of its heritage.

In Ned's case this is especially so because in him the great dream of our birth and early development, born of a longing for freedom and land, was at the heart. Kelly, like so many of his kind, longed to possess the land in freedom. His land, our land, is still there. Today it is peopled by many who no longer remember him with shame. If my work helps to reveal the mystery of why Australians have chosen Ned as part of their common inheritance I will have spent my time well.

The deeper I went into the sources which laid bare the facts on Kelly, the more the conviction grew that his story was one of a people rather than of a mere person. I make no apology for the presence of the Catholic Church and Ireland in this book for the Kellys and their clan were both Catholic and Irish and to ignore such is not to know them. But Ned's story is one of Australia and her people, the physical grandeur of Victoria's northeast, the men and women who struggled to make their way there and for some, including the Kellys, the failure to succeed. The account of their failure of necessity contains a condemnation of many members of the Victoria Police of that time, but that need not imply a reflection on its present membership. Indeed it can be said that the realization of the need to have a competent, trustworthy and respected police force in Victoria resulted in part from the Royal Commission into the Kelly affair held in 1881. In that sense Ned, at least by opposition, made his own contribution to reform.

The historian, like the lawyer, holds a brief but his is for the dead whose lips are sealed. He is not compelled to pick up that brief but, once done, his task takes on its own sacredness. Only the mute records, the dusty files, the broken down buildings, the tombstones, the editorials of long forgotten newspapers can speak today. In this case the Kelly country with its wild beauty, and some of its people with their reticence and delicacy also helped to break the silence. In the end it all remained a matter of trying to understand, to unravel the tangled skein of a life over which legend cast its spell so that reality had become secondary. The fabric in which I have clothed the story of Ned, of his people, of his time and place was woven deliberately for I could not tell of these things in a broken stammer nor in the dry jargon of a courtroom. In the end it may be the case that in speaking of Ned something has been said of the Australia that made him and which he loved.

I finished my work on the balcony of the Mansfield Hotel looking out at the distant Strathbogies and down at the monument to the dead policemen at the crossroads below. It was fitting that it be so, for that very day I talked with a woman in whom runs the blood of the Kellys, the Byrnes and the Kennedys. In that place where they had all stepped it was her great courtesy to share with me her knowledge of the past and help confirm me in my own view of it. I went then to my brother's home at Ararat where we read the manuscript together at his kitchen table. That too was fitting for in the end he was able to say to me that somehow it came back to a great simplicity. Ned who has become a part of the land and its memories remains beyond the judgement of any one of us. With that I am content.

Kelly – Quinn Family Tree

N.B. only those family members who appear in the text are included here.

b = born. m = married. d = died.
Principal characters are underlined.

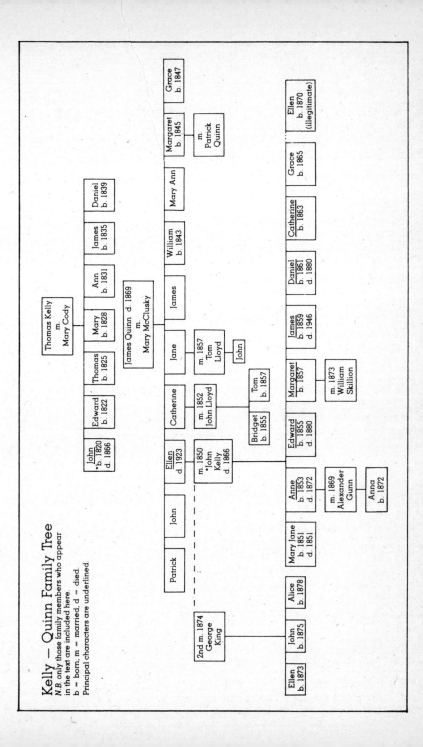

Map of Main Localities Mentioned in the Text

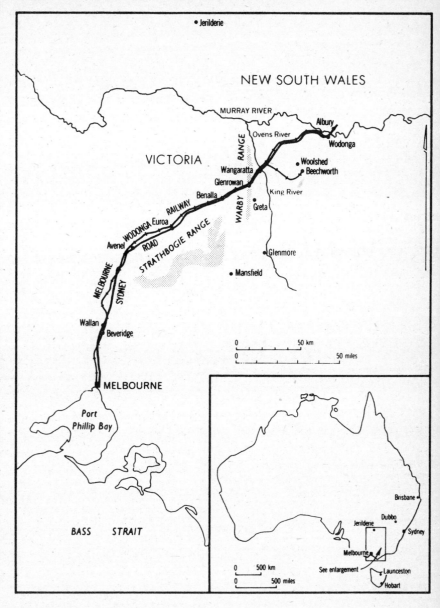

The Making of a Man   1

Far back in the ranges below the hump of Buffalo, and south-east beyond the origins of the Ovens, another river rises as a trickling vein, and begins its ever strengthening fall through the curving, dark valleys with their threatening crags, until it swells into a stream. Falling sharply from its bedded spaces the King opens quickly into a valley broken by cleaving mountains. Gradually their reaching arms recede, leaving the river to run its course in places where the land lies open to the step of man. After the quiet departure of the old ones who passed gently on that country another man, with purpose set of wresting a meagre pittance from that jealous land, came to reign beside the King on a station called Glenmore. His name was Quinn, his brood was plentiful, and turbulence was the mark in the eyes of those who now commanded in that stolen realm. A quick, dark haired boy with fluid, lidded eyes, guarded tongue, firming frame, sinewed hands and possessing a spirit untamed except by force, was numbered in that brood.

His name was Kelly but, unlike his grandsire Quinn of Glenmore, this one was native to the land, and thus his restless spirit, in the manner of the dark ancients who had gone before, was entwined with those ranges and valleys. To Kelly, as to those others, the land was ever kind and he, like them, left no mark upon it in his passing. But Kelly himself was marked, and not least by Old Quinn of Glenmore, who brought to his craggy domain the memories of woes of another place, lashed by foam and wind in a far north sea. It was as well for the black man to leave that country before these new ones came, because his cup of sorrow was already overfilled.

James Quinn was a Catholic of the maritime north, where the North Channel flows down from the Atlantic into the Irish Sea. His county was Antrim of the Glens with its streams called the Bann, the Main and the Bush, its Giant's Causeway of basaltic rock and its population of Presbyterians. In them the awful grandeur and rigidity of Calvin and Knox had blended with the sleet and whirling mists of Scotland, before they came across the Channel to colonize another's land. By 1804, when Quinn was born, the Irish of the old country and the old religion were as aliens, living in suffrance in a land that had once been theirs, and eking out an existence as cottagers and labourers. To them that act of usurpation, called a union, by which Ireland was shackled to Britain in 1800, meant nothing, because it merely canonized the religion and the property of the foreigner, and ensured that his dominion over the land and its people would be perpetuated. The earth that had once been luxuriant in corn and potatoes was given over in large part to pasturage, so that the Irish peasant saw the means of his own meagre subsistence taken from him by large landowners, who looked to flocks and herds for profit. The

Irish of Antrim had little else than their God and their children, and in the latter James Quinn and his wife Mary, née McClusky, were richly endowed, with their three sons and four daughters. Milk and potatoes, with the occasional bacon rind on festive occasions that James, a labourer, could provide, was sufficient to ensure survival, but little else. For the strong, emigration was the only alternative, while the weak soon found another with their decline and death in the potato famine of the mid-1840s.

In Ireland before the famine, only a few looked to the far distant southland for a haven. Some chance or quirk decided that they would leave forever their saints and sorrows on a journey to a land that no Irish mind could fully encompass. Not for them the quick passage across the Atlantic, with its promise of a welcome amongst their own in the ghettos of Boston, New York or Philadelphia. Instead, these others, a handful compared to the westward flood, set out towards the south along the coasts of Africa and other places of the heathen until they turned east at the Cape of Good Hope. After many weeks, landfall came, when first they saw Arthur's Seat and then Point Lonsdale beckoning welcome where it stood above the cave of Buckley. In 1841 that remnant of the brave, hardened now by fear and quickened by hope after the magnitude of that voyage, numbered Old Quinn and his family. He still wore his years lightly, as befits a man of thirty-seven, but no man could cross the world to an unknown destiny and look into the eyes of wife and children, where the one word of dependence was writ large, and not grow in gnarled wisdom. He was already amongst the old ones as he came through the Heads and up the bay; he would not pass that way again, yet through the years, beloved Ireland faded into

memory leaving her bitterness in his heart. Beside that
baggage in his spirit, the meagre chattels in the hold
belonging to Quinn were tokens only of the past. Distilled in sorrow, struggle and incomprehension it was
that inner baggage he would bequeath in the end.[1]

The *England*, of about 1,000 tons burthen, with Captain Thompson in command, had made a good passage
of 104 days from Liverpool, and of her complement of
349, eighteen were lost on the voyage. Sixteen were children, stricken by a wave of whooping cough, but the
Quinns remained untouched. The boys were named Pat,
John and James with Pat at fifteen the eldest while James
was a baby of six months. The daughters were Mary
Anne, eleven, Ellen, nine, who left in the end her legacy
to the new land, Catherine, seven and Jane, four. Their
mother Mary was aged at thirty-two by the continual
labour of childbearing begun at seventeen, but hope
could still be enkindled at the faint smudge of Melbourne town. The smoke of the settlement faded into the
darkness of strange ranges, etched by a pale blue that
no northern sky or sea had ever mirrored. According to
the documents left to the future, all the Quinns, including
baby James, could read, but not write, but it was ironical
that the first official record of that precocious one should
proclaim its indolent nonsense. Jimmy was to fall betimes
and often into the hands of officialdom, and all its records were not wrong.

Only four of those aboard the *England* had paid their
own passage. The rest, including the Quinns, were
bounty immigrants, come to supply a workforce for the
pastoral lands of Australia Felix. The government paid
£108 16s 6d for their carriage, and they joined 8,000
others who came to those parts in 1841. Port Phillip
prided itself prematurely on its freedom from the stains

of convictism, and the consequent dark inheritance of the mother colony. But many of those who held their heads high in Melbourne in 1841 had known the chain gang and the lash, the system of assignment and the ticket-of-leave, with all the other trappings of a civilization born in bondage. No free man could come to that shore and avoid daily commerce with others who had come as convicts. James Quinn came free, but none could tell on that winter morn the destiny of his brood.[2]

Melbourne on its pretty stream called the Yarra was barely four years in the making when Quinn and his family stepped ashore at nearby Sandridge on 17 July 1841. It was a miserable, wet Wednesday which at least helped to remind them that in some things the world was one. But other things were stranger, with streets that ran wide and straight, while bullock teams toiled in the mud that bogged the carriages and above in the sky flew the black cockatoos that screeched their welcome. Ramshackle buildings of brick and wood grew apace before their very eyes, and men with a firm look of conquest in their stride passed before them while in the shadows of the village moved men of a darker hue, who had bargained with Batman and lost an ancient patrimony. It was on their heritage that Melbourne was made, for its 8,000 inhabitants had become the sinews of a supply and commerce centre for those who had come with flocks and herds to occupy the lovely south lands of Australia Felix. They came from the settled districts of New South Wales, where pastoral expansion had already reached its limits by the 1830s and hundreds and thousands of cattle and sheep, with their owners and drovers, crossed the Murrumbidgee and the ancient, mother river called after an alien, Murray, on their way south. They came from Van Diemen's Land across a turbulent stretch of

sea in the wake of John Pascoe Fawkner. They were followed by bankers, merchants, priests, parsons and men
of the professions, publicans, prostitutes and pedlars,
for Melbourne was quickly marked as a metropolis of
tomorrow with all its glory and debasement. Finally they
came, like the Quinn, to be the hewers and drawers, the
masons and the carpenters, the grooms and servants.
It was up to James to find his place amongst them.[3]

One with whom he did not presume to rank was a
young and promising barrister, born from the same soil
as Quinn. Redmond Barry was a man of verve and spirit
who fought an uneventful duel with a fellow member
of the Melbourne Club in August 1841. Barry was a stick-
ler for the niceties of civilized behaviour and, on this
occasion he refused to take advantage of a helpless
opponent whose misfortune it was to shoot off his own
toe. Whether he would always remain like-minded only
the passage of years could foretell.[4]

As one who allegedly could read but not write, and
as a member of a rude and young society, Old Quinn
left little in the way of written records by which to trace
his movements in the next decade. Mary bore him three
more children. William was born in August 1843, and
his parents took him from their residence in Moonee
Ponds to St Francis Church where a priest called Daniel
MacEvey baptized him into the faith professed by his
ancestors. In June 1845 the family still lived in Moonee
Ponds where Margaret was born, but by November 1847
they had moved closer to the hub of the new municipality
of Melbourne to dwell in Spring Street and there, Grace,
the last of their children, was born.[5] For over twenty years
Mary had fulfilled the promise of that girlhood bridal
bed in Antrim. At thirty-seven she was still ready to return
to the life that she had known in Ireland as the wife of

a farm labourer. The difference was that, while James laboured as before, he did it now in his own right because he had rented a small farm at Wallan near the Sydney road, about thirty miles from Melbourne. By 1850 he had prospered and he was able to settle on 700 acres of land in the district, within a few miles of the same road, and there he bred horses and cattle and held in check that family which was now Australian and native, as well as Irish and alien.[6] To Quinn the new country had given the thing that Antrim never gave him: land with its pride of possession and independence from a driving land-lord. But the wild ones amongst the Quinns were already quickening with a strain of impatience and wilfulness that marked them from their more placid fellows. And up that artery between north and south, which linked Melbourne to the comely city of Australia's origin, another man came in late 1849. He was lithe and strong of build, with hands worn by toil, but with a spirit renewed again by freedom. His name was John Kelly.

On 20 February 1820 at the parish church of Killen-aule, in the diocese of Cashel and the county called Tip-perary, a son of Thomas Kelly and Mary Cody had been baptized with the name John.[7] He grew to manhood in that place and, as he grew, he took into himself the hard thoughts nurtured by so many against those foreigners who held authority in the land and against whom his grandfather fought at Vinegar Hill in 1798. By day he worked as a farm labourer, by night he sang, drank, danced and at times, with others, talked of freedom. But dreams of freedom can end in squalor and for John Kelly the end was both petty and perhaps plotted by others, because there were those in that land prepared to betray their own. A few weeks before his twenty-first birthday John, called by the police 'a notorious character', was charged with stealing two pigs, which those who held property sacred, even in the flesh of swine, looked upon as proof of deep-hued villainy. Sentenced to seven years transportation at the Cashel Quarter Sessions, John left his native glens with black and lasting bitterness rendered worse because of the fate of his friend and townsman, Philip Regan, who was also arrested, and at that on the word of an *agent provocateur*, for a crime of cattle stealing. Philip died, shot down by the police when allegedly attempting to escape, but possibly happy to see life ended because the beloved ash corner of Ireland was not easily left for the place called Van Diemen's Land.[8]

The *Prince Regent* sailed into the Derwent on 2 January 1841 and John Kelly spent the next two years in probation gangs. He was punished once for being absent from his station in 1842 and spent two months in chains. Later, as a ticket-of-leave man, he was fined 5s for being drunk and disorderly. Otherwise the period of felonry of John was quiet, but he learnt the singular lesson that a transgression against the law of property was paid for dearly in wasted and blighted years, loneliness and sometimes despair, and that those who fell from grace in such a manner carried the stigma for life. For two years more he served out his time as a ticket-of-leave man and on 11 January 1848, he was free to set his own course in life. Not yet thirty, he had the years of strength and hope ahead. As they had to so many others who had suffered the same fate as his own, the green lands across Bass Strait beckoned to John Kelly, known now as Red Kelly. It was a place that had not heard the curse of his kind, for the whip of the lash, the lacerated tearing of a back and the groaning of men had not been part of its past. To that land he sailed, for Tipperary was far in the past and pigs were not such a precious commodity in that new place.[9]

Red Kelly settled down near Wallan and, being both Irish and Catholic, and one who longed to work and be himself, he soon made the acquaintance of the Quinns. In so doing his eyes fell on young Ellen, now a girl of eighteen. Despite the twelve years difference in their ages, Red and Ellen became lovers, and by July 1850 Ellen knew that she was pregnant. Marriage was the only solution when a new life had quickened in a womb, so in mid-November they went down the road to Melbourne where the news of the separation of Port Phillip from New South Wales was being wildly proclaimed. On the eighteenth of that month Ellen, clearly pregnant, married Red at St Francis Church, in the presence of Father Gerald Ward. Words such as romance and elopement were absurd in such a setting because, though love was there, it intertwined with necessity of a kind Old Quinn back at Wallan was not the man to overlook. It was a hot summer for a young bride to be full of child, but by late February Mary Jane was born, and taken across the hills to Kilmore five days later for baptism. Ellen Kelly had set out young on the road of motherhood and in the next twenty-seven years she bore twelve children. Unlike her mother, to whom old James was ever mate, Ellen knew three men and bore them children. Nonetheless Red retained to the end his place in her heart, irrespective of those other shadowy occupants who followed him in her bed.[10]

At nearby Beveridge, Red built himself a dwelling of moderate proportions, according to the slender means he had available as a farm labourer. Work was plentiful for his father-in-law and others because Melbourne drew on any supplies, whether of vegetables or livestock, which the local countryside could supply. In any case a change had already swept over eastern Australia that spelt the end of the pastoral age, and the beginning of a new era. That very month of Mary Jane's birth saw Edward Hargraves, the consummate publicist, washing gold at Ophir in New South Wales, and by late May men were already leaving for the fields, hence draining the south, now called Victoria, of its manpower. Old Quinn kept his family about him, and Red Kelly had the sense to see that, even when gold was discovered soon afterwards in undreamt of quantities at Clunes, Ballarat, Sandhurst and Mount Alexander, a living was still to be made from the more immediate products of the earth. Hence they stayed on at the headwaters of the Merri Creek, with the occasional, but probably unprofitable foray to the golden fields.

In November 1853, another girl child was born to Red and Ellen to replace Mary Jane, whose feeble grasp on life had been tenuous from the start. This time the journey to Melbourne for the baptism was long and tedious, for with the great and incessant coming and going to the fields, even in mid-summer the track had become a nightmare stretch of pot holes, dust and broken-down conveyances. On 31 January 1854 Anne Kelly was baptized at St Francis, and they returned again to Beveridge where Ellen reared Anne, but only briefly at the breast, for she had started another child within three months.

In early January 1855 that child, a male called Edward, was born. Unlike the other major events of his life, and especially its end, the child's entry into this world was apparently unrecorded by the official agents of the society into which he was born. All Ellen Kelly's children were taken to the priest for baptism, and so assuredly was this first-born son. But no record survives of that event, and it is only his own youthful testimony, combined with the meticulous entry of a school inspector, that indicates the month of his birth. On 30 March 1865 Inspector Gilbert Wilson Brown spent the hours between 10.25 a.m. and 1.55 p.m. visiting Avenel School No. 8 where he wrote down the age of a boy in grade four, named Edward Kelly. He recorded his age as ten years and three months. At the end of the following year, the same Edward Kelly testified, to him whose interest it was in the colony of Victoria to record such matters, that his father was dead. He gave his age with some degree of precision as eleven and a half which means that on 29 December 1866 he was not yet twelve. If then both the boy and Inspector Wilson Brown are to be believed, Ned was born in January 1855.[11] His birth was within weeks of the creation of Australia's first legend, when some men in whom a spark of idealism burnt, struggled and died at Eureka. To that legend of a still-born republic the infant Edward was to add his mite. In the relatively brief span left to him before his manhood was snuffed out on a Thursday morning in November 1880, Ned also struggled against an officialdom as bent on the preservation of the values of a class structure within a dependent society, in the name of a distant crown, as it had been in Ballarat in December 1854. None of that, however, was either meaningful or apparent to Ellen Kelly as she replaced Anne with Ned at her breast. Whatever Red Kelly or old grandfather Quinn heard of Eureka in the wayside pubs of the Sydney road is not known. Red rejoiced in the man-child, and Old Quinn perhaps wondered how this new one would fit into the brood now gathering thick around him. Suffice to say that in so much, and not least in rebellion, he was to surpass them all.

The Gentle Years 2

On 14 December 1824 Hamilton Hume and William Hovell paused on their journey south at the foot of a volcanic hill which they proceeded to climb. From its summit they saw a pleasing plain stretching to the south, dotted with other hills of conical shape. The plain was unbroken except for the stands of gums which bowed to the east wind, while the bald hills lay mute like the stilled marbles of the gods. It was a place of great gentility in which, to both plain and hill, Hume gave the name Bland to honour one who had come to this land stained with blood, but who lived to bestow much life upon it. When John Batman bartered with the tribes, the land was called Mercer Vale after the English representative of those tradesmen who had associated together to replace the blackman. Gradually the land was given up to agriculture, so that by the late 1840s it had begun to resemble a huge English farm. By then the Sydney road was a busy thoroughfare and, soon after, the township of Beveridge was so named because Andrew Beveridge

had opened there The Tryste Inne for those who travelled that way. On the outskirts of the town stood the
slab home built by Red Kelly and there, near to that road
which became an artery of his passing existence, the
child, whom Ellen bore at her mother's home four miles
across the plain, grew to boyhood. From the door on the
east side looking up to the north, Ned could see the
mount called by Hume, Disappointment, because that
land, with all its quiet beauty, had a strength which at
times could conquer the brave.[1]

After a brief sojourn at the gold-fields, Red Kelly was
sufficiently confident of his own and Beveridge's future
as to commit himself to the purchase of three small allotments in the village.[2] The purchases were a gesture to
fortune as Beveridge was destined to a state of com-
placent tranquillity despite the fact that the road from
Melbourne north to Beveridge was completed in 1855.[3]
Its completion brought Melbourne within an easy day's
journey, but it was at the homestead a few miles to the
north-east that the new family born of Ellen and Red
found its focus in those years at Beveridge.

James Quinn was in the prime of his years when his
grandson, Ned, first lay in his arms in his home at Wallan
beside the Merri Creek. To that tranquil place with the
tall, strong gums, the rippling, nourishing creek, where
the platypus abounded, the fertile land where the mushrooms sprang after autumn's first rains, the dark blue
of Mount Disappointment where the whirling white of
the big cockatoos stood out in starkness, James had come
in hope in 1850. There he had bought land in extent
beyond the comprehension of those who had stayed
behind in the gloomy cottages of Ireland's north country,
and had built his home on a gentle slope of a folded
hill on the land, and from it the Quinn could survey all

he possessed.[4] The house James built was ample for himself, Mary and the family which, since their arrival in Australia, had increased to ten and its heart was the hearth where no hazelwood burnt but where the produce of moderate prosperity was prepared and shared. It was at that hearth, as much as at any other, that the boy who came the four miles from Beveridge across the paddocks listened, learnt and was seared in youth by a history that need never have been his, nor perhaps need never have been at all.

Here in the home of his grandparents Ned first heard the tales that bade fair to make him an alien in the new land in which his sinews had been moulded and quickened. No history in the conventional sense was ever taught by Old Quinn, nor by Red Kelly, as they talked in the lilting, soft tones of their people but in the tongue of a victorious invader, for the Gael was no longer theirs except in the brief greetings, Diaduit–'God be with you' – or the fleeting wheel of Mary's mysteries of the Rosary. The stories Ned heard were not about that recent Act of Union by which England wedded Ireland to a marriage of inconvenience, whose offspring were death and dishonour, but about that longer history when the Irish Catholics 'were persecuted, massacred, thrown into martyrdom and tortured'. The details filled the softness of the brogue with horror in the child's mind as he heard of the tortures of his people as they were rolled 'down hill in spiked barrels', of pulling out their 'toe and finger nails' and of their being stretched 'on the wheel'.[5] These stories included too, the massacre of Vinegar Hill and the other fruitless rebellions of Ireland while the name of Philip Regan, betrayed by his own and gunned to death less than twenty years before was often used by Red. It was a troubled child who slept under that shingle roof and stirred fitfully to the seeds of rebellion sown in his spirit, fertile both in imagination and memory, while James and Red sat on at the hearth never dimly perceiving the outcome of their reveries.

But the shaping of the child was not all in the manner of those gnarled gums that twisted and veered on the plains as they were driven by the east wind. There were the festivities connected with birth, for there was much springing of new life in the widespread clan which revolved around James Quinn. The Lloyds, John and Thomas, married Quinn girls, Catherine and Jane, and to the union between John and Catherine a child called Thomas was born on 5 November 1857, and baptized three weeks later at Coburg.[6] In that child much was also distilled of the dark spirits of Ireland's misery but he, and Ned, sang and played away the days of their childhood in the district of Beveridge while the cradles they quickly vacated were as quickly filled. In June 1857 Margaret was born to Red and Ellen Kelly, and two years later James, who was followed by Daniel in 1861.[7]

The small Kelly home sheltered five children by that latter year and it was as much as Red could do to make ends meet, with little to back him but odd jobs as a carpenter and the few cows he ran near the home. He had many more besides his own immediate ones to think of, for his apparent prosperity in the new land had attracted those whom he had left behind in Tipperary in 1841 to come also and join him at Mercer Vale. The ship *Maldon* carried a cargo replete with Kellys to Victoria in 1857 – aboard were Red's brothers Edward, Daniel and James together with his two sisters Mary and Anne, so that new and old intermingled using names that were passed on through the generations, but work and food had to be found to make of that valley

a haven.[8] The sustaining force of them all remained the
old patriarch close by, and while he could run cattle
and horses and sell both on good markets there was
no need to concern oneself unduly as to the future. The
only cloud was Old Quinn's nagging fear that 700 acres
would prove insufficient eventually to provide for that
burgeoning brood, and he knew in his heart that there
were temptations aplenty for ill-gotten gains amidst the
abundance that this new country offered.

The fears of Old Quinn were realized in 1860. The
beloved James, the prodigy the shipping records
alleged had been able to read at six months, wailing
infant held by his father as they came within the Heads,
was by the age of fifteen already 'an object of interest
to the police' although the why went unrecorded.[9] In
1856, at Kilmore over the range, young James was
charged with cattle stealing, to wit a bullock, but as the
evidence was not persuasive he was discharged.[10] The
important thing was his having come under notice, and
although he continued to live at home he was henceforth
under the watchful eye of both the parental and the civil
authority. James managed to contain himself until a mild
Sunday afternoon in the late winter of 1860. He betook
himself to the Star and Garter Hotel where he drank
deep and long with Francis Boulton. With the passage
of time and the inflaming of youthful spirits these two
fell to loud dispute whereupon their host ejected them.
Outside, words turned to blows, Boulton's horse bolted,
Boulton gave chase, James threw a stone which brought
Boulton down and the jury curbed James with a six-week
sentence.[11]

It was nineteen years since Old Quinn had come
ashore at Port Phillip, years during which he and his
clan had achieved passing respect and moderate toler-

ance. Sunday 19 August 1860 changed it all because one of the clan, Jimmy, the beloved who had consoled the patriarch in some measure for the loss of his first-born son Patrick – drowned crossing the big river at Echuca in 1850 – Jimmy was now a gaolbird. It was not that Jimmy alone had attracted the attention of the law for John, since Patrick's death the eldest son, had twice been charged with horse and cattle stealing respectively and twice discharged in 1860.[12] But Jimmy had passed beyond charge to bars and amongst them, only Red Kelly knew much of what that meant.

Out at the foot of Mount Disappointment in the home by the Merri Creek the note of keening was heard, as it had been for Patrick, because death has many forms. Ned was almost six and a new thing had come into his life, for Jimmy was spoken of in a whisper but it was not possible to conceal his absence because Jimmy, marked now as a recidivist, was no sooner out than he was in again. In February 1861 he was charged with horse stealing, convicted of illegal use of the steed, and sent to Pentridge for four months.[13] The clan now had an additional reason to visit Coburg besides baptisms, for St Pauls stood nearby to the prison. As for Ned, he now knew that his uncle Jimmy, the Jimmy who had grown as part of Australia, who had begun to teach Ned the way to handle a horse, who was quick with a fist, a drink and a laugh and generous to a little boy, Jimmy was a convicted criminal. The birth of Dan while Jimmy was away at 'college', as Pentridge was soon known amongst the clan, was some distraction to Ned, and no Irish crone cast shadows on that birth by twining baby hand to boy hand and looking down that future of the brothers.

The litany of clan criminality which began in 1860

became a tedious, oppressive and ever present factor
in the lives of the womenfolk and children. John Lloyd
was charged and acquitted of assault in 1860 at Donnybrook, while John Quinn was tried three times in 1860
and 1861 on various charges of horse and cattle stealing
and each time discharged. In March 1862 Jimmy was
back in court again, this time for violent assault, but the
charge was withdrawn. John Lloyd appeared for drunkenness on the same day but the case was withdrawn.
In May John was up for larceny; again nothing was
proven and the first stirrings of resentment began in the
clan when in the same year Red's brother James was
twice discharged for cattle stealing. Between 1860 and
the end of 1862, four members of the family had been
charged with a total of fourteen offences with only three
sustained against young Jimmy, whose most grievous
proven crime was that of illegal use of a horse.[14] To them
all, it had begun to appear that to be a Kelly, a Lloyd
or a Quinn was in itself as effective as branding a steer,
except that the brand claimed its recipient to be police
property, liable to any charge upon which the police
thought there was a chance of obtaining a conviction.
Resentment hardened to the first beginnings of rejection
of the new society; Red Kelly fed it with his memories
of Tipperary with its police informers and police brutality, while a little boy was starting to realize that he
belonged to a family to which a special stigma was
attached.

Ned was eight when he first appeared in court. With
his mother he went across the hills to Kilmore and the
silvered dew dripped from the trees as they rode
together on that early morning in the autumn of 1863.
They were on their way to attend a General Sessions
sitting in the Kilmore courthouse; all Ned could compre-

hend was that his uncle James Kelly was there to be charged with having stolen thirteen head of cattle belonging to Thomas Flynn, who followed the trade of blacksmith in Beveridge and made something on the side by running cattle on a local property. The crime had been witnessed by Agnes Flynn, the wife of Thomas, and she gave evidence to the effect that just after dark on 13 July 1862 she saw James Kelly and a companion, Cornelius Flynn, drive the cattle away. The court was not impressed when the small boy and his mother both attested to the presence of James Kelly in their home on the evening in question. Both James and Cornelius were sentenced to three years' hard labour.[15] The dew was dry on the branches as Ellen and Ned rode home to Beveridge and into Ned's soul a hardness had come, for he had either been taught to lie before the law, or he now knew that justice itself was a twisted fork that led some to freedom and others to thraldom. In either case the effect was the same. At the age of eight Ned had taken his first step outside the law.

Perhaps because neither Red nor Ellen were lettered they were determined that such would not be the case in respect of their children, and in 1861 Ned started in the first grade at the local school in Beveridge. It could scarcely be assumed that Red's house on the edge of the township was one in which education was fostered by example, for it possessed nothing in the way of reading matter except a prayer book and the occasional Melbourne newspaper. Nonetheless Ned learnt to read, write and do his rudimentary sums at Beveridge and learnt also something of the religion of his ancestors. With its awesome content of the sacred and its frail vestment of the human, it gave some minimal meaning to a life which, though set in the created beauty of Mercer's

Vale, had elements that gave point to the prayer of the
Rosary which spoke of Mary's children 'mourning and
weeping in this valley of tears'. In that home he prayed
the Rosary, and at the small but handsome bluestone
church in Beveridge, Ned heard first the blessed mutter
of the Mass intoned with the Roman-Irish accents of
Father Charles O'Hea who came up from Pentridge to
minister to the Irish of those parts. In 1863 Catherine was
baptized at Kilmore, the last of the Kellys born in Beveridge, and in that same year Ned first met the Master
in the meal at Mass because he had reached the age
at which he could know good from evil and bread from
sacramental presence.[16]

By the early 1860s, it had become evident to Red Kelly
that neither economically nor socially was life in Beveridge a desirable long-term prospect for himself or his
family. The long years of servitude had helped to break
both spirit and body, while mere toil at Beveridge had
not proved sufficiently rewarding to keep the family in
anything but precarious frugality, with too constant
reliance on the father-in-law on his broader acres at
Wallan.[17] More importantly, however, the constant
involvement of his relatives with the police had indicated the wisdom of a move to other parts, as even the
fact that Ellen was widely respected and accepted as
a midwife in the district did nothing to lessen that stain
of a convict past which Red carried with him from across
Bass Strait. His brother, James, was temporarily out of
the way doing three years, but the nearby presence of
the Quinns and Lloyds, with their tendency to trouble,
was a constant reminder to Red that Ned and Jim would
soon be at an age where family associations may begin
to outweigh paternal admonitions, and hence the possibility of his own sons coming before the courts. It was

with these things in his mind that Red took the Sydney road north, together with Ellen and their six children, in late 1863. They ranged from Anne, now nine, down to the new baby, whose Catherine was quickly made the diminutive Kate, with Ned eight, Maggie six, Jim four and Dan one. The Kelly family went up the road fifty miles and stopped at Avenel.[18]

Avenel was a village of about two hundred people situated on the Sydney road some seventy-five miles north-east from Melbourne. It straddled the Hughes Creek and lay on flat country surrounded on three sides by hills, with their prominence called Mount Barnard. It boasted two hotels, called the Avenel Arms and the Royal Mail, and two vineyards, and it had other minimum facilities required of a place where some men lived and others rested on their way to and fro the city and the fields.[19] Amongst these facilities there was a police station and a courthouse but, more importantly for the purposes of Red Kelly, there was also a school and with his growing family it seemed an ideal place to settle. Red had saved enough from the winding up of his affairs at Beveridge to rent a forty-acre dairy farm about two miles downstream from the village for £14 a year. The land belonged to Elizabeth Mutton, widow of William who had helped found the village back in 1840. Perhaps here was the new start Red hoped for, so the Christmas of 1863 was one of buoyancy, expectation and goodwill.[20]

Meanwhile, by the banks of the Merri Creek much goodwill had been dissipated by the renewed inability of young Jimmy Quinn to keep free of the law. He was long since the subject of the unremitting attention of the constabulary, and one of their number arrested him in mid-December 1863 as Jimmy was riding nonchalantly down the highway between Wallan and Donnybrook. Jimmy objected strenuously to his being detained, especially as the constable, Frederick Price, was lacking a warrant, which the family had begun to insist upon as a nicety requisite to the formality of arrest. Jimmy's recalcitrance was overcome with the use of a revolver, and as a result he idled away the time from 28 December to 19 February 1864 in the remand yard at Beechworth awaiting trial for horse stealing. It seems that in May of the previous year a gentleman named John Spicer had entrusted his grey racing mare into the care of the overseer of McCartney's station at a place called Greta, situated on the foothills near the eastern slopes of Mount Glenrowan. It was this horse Jimmy was found astride and, despite his producing a receipt for its purchase and a witness to attest to having been present at the transaction, despite also the plea of his lawyer that horse thieves normally refrained from publicly exhibiting themselves on the highway, Jimmy was found guilty. His peers were not convinced that the charge of actually stealing a horse could be sustained, but as someone had clearly committed a felony it was found convenient to convict Jimmy of illegal use. His Honour sentenced him to twelve months with hard labour. By the old patriarch out at the creek it was not regarded as an auspicious beginning to a new year. Indeed for some time the constant attention of the Kilmore police had begun to wear him down, and as early as 1860 he had contemplated a move and had tried to dispose of all his belongings by sale.[21] In the end, taking stock of all the relevant factors he decided to move further back and up to the north, beyond Mount Disappointment with all its portents and away from Mercer Vale with its own placid loveliness. The place he chose was Glenmore at the head of that valley down which flowed the King.

Glenmore was vast beyond the comprehension of men whose counting did not go beyond tens of acres, for its extent was 25,000. It had been taken up in 1843 by John Bond and passed to Jacob Vincent in 1845. The black-man and his dogs had resented the invaders, and by 1847 Vincent abandoned it so that for a time it passed back to those whose tenure of that ancient wilderness of mountain crags and swift streams was based on unity of spirit rather than domination for profit. Occupied again in 1851 it was further abandoned, and when Old Quinn took it up four white men had owned but never possessed it. According to those whose experience per-mitted them to make such fine judgements, over sixty acres of Glenmore were required to run a single head of cattle. It was scarcely a venture in mere profit-making James Quinn was engaged upon when he contemplated the buying of that run for £2,000.[22]

On 20 July 1864 the 700 acres at Wallan were sold to Thomas McDougall for £561 and James signed to that transaction with the cross of a marksman.[23] A month later Glenmore became his and he, his wife and their wild brood took up their residence at the foot of a dark moun-tain with the river to their front, the plain to the left and to their right the ranges ever flinging back into parts where no white foot had stepped. In those places the law was a distant symbol, with only young Jimmy's in-carceration to remind them all of its power, and in the evening when they gathered for the Rosary, they re-membered their wayward one, while Old Quinn tried to refrain from calling down curses instead of blessings as he prayed for the coming of another kingdom and the grace to be forgiven in like manner as he forgave those who trespassed against him. Perhaps he also

pondered on the possibility of maintaining those gathered around him on those vast acres where range
swallowed range, where cattle ran wild without fences,
where men could come and go in the night leaving a
herd depleted, and above all where there were no
boundaries to rein in those of his own blood whose feet
had already strayed and might do so again.

At precisely ten minutes past two on the afternoon of
30 March 1864, Ned, aged nine, underwent his first
public trial. The setting was that of Avenel School No.8
where he was enrolled in grade three. Before him stood
the recently appointed teacher, James Irving, a native
of Dumfries in Scotland, whose quickness of tongue was
oft and anon blurred by that fondness distilled in the
veins of his ancestors by their antidote to the sleet of
far northern winters.[24] James was flanked by his wife
Henrietta who had been Work Mistress under his charge
at Barrabool Hills and Breakwater, but who now occupied the stately position of Infant Mistress. A far more
awesome presence was that of Inspector Gilbert W.
Brown, representative of the Board of Education, who
had come in zeal and bristling efficiency to ascertain
whether the funds of the colony were put to good purpose
in the hall of learning at Avenel. Before him Brown saw
thirty-nine youngsters, ranging from those innocents of
six years and less to Margaret Burrows, blossoming into
maidenhood at fifteen, but still fruitlessly pursuing her
letters in the fourth grade.[25] Looking about he saw
slabbed walls lined with calico, a bark roof in great dis-
repair, two blackboards and a series of ten maps, including the old world and the new, with one of Palestine to
remind those tousled headed ones of a heritage they
still shared and its hope of a world beyond that depicted
before them. Brown sensed, by the attentiveness of his

audience, that the discipline exercised by James and Henrietta was good, but the examination upon which he embarked, of all those except the infants, revealed deficiencies which indicated that in some areas James' predecessor, Edwin Richardson, had lacked something as a pedagogue. Maggie Kelly was in the second grade at seven years and she passed in Reading and Writing, but failed in Arithmetic, as did her companions. Edward Kelly, with passes in Reading and Writing, did better than most of his fourteen classmates in third grade, but joined eleven who failed Arithmetic and all the class who failed in Grammar and Geography. Nothing stirred in the unfenced playground as the children underwent their ordeal, and even the scratching of the infants on their slates was temporarily stilled. Ned's eyes met Brown's briefly as he held out his written exercise, but there was nothing there to tell him that a few days earlier another little boy had come before the gaze of the inspector at the Woolshed Common School on the Ovens. His name was Joseph Byrne.[26]

In the evenings, after school, Ned helped Red with the milking, ran errands, cut firewood and sometimes opened his books. On the hills of Avenel he learnt to ride bareback and to feel the warmth of a horse and the softness of its nostrils, to love the sweetness of its sweat and the feed-laden odour of its breath as he caught it in the paddock, to sway with its movements, to guide it away from pot holes and to lie forward on its mane as together they rushed below hanging boughs. Back further in the ranges after strayed cattle, he learnt also to steady a horse on the rockface, to sit well back as it came swiftly down a slope and to love the sweep of the low country as it unfolded before him. His father, Red, was no horseman because he had come

from a land where those of his kind went on foot, and
the way with a horse which comes with youth could not
be learnt there. But the boy became part of his horse
and he knew that tenderness, firmness and softly spoken
commands made a unity of horse and rider. These ways
came also to Maggie, and Red and Ellen wondered what
forces which had shaped their own being were trans-
muted in the ones born of their union. To the physical
characteristics, the movement of hand and eye, the
brogue already harshening, other things were added
in the children that came from the new land, and the
parents knew that they were good and clean and strong
traits which spoke not of nation, but of country. At Avenel
the boy's identification with all that the map on the
school wall meant when it spelt out the simple word Australia began to shape and quicken.

The year 1865 began with life preserved. It was high
summer and the children of the township and its nearby
homesteads often swam in the creek which ran by the
town. A summer storm had swollen the Hughes and
young Richard Shelton, aged six, was swept away in
its rising waters. Ned was not exceptionally gifted as
a swimmer, but the struggle of the child to stay above
the water and the inevitable outcome of his predicament
without help urged him on and Richard was saved. It
was an act for which the people of the little town, and
particularly the Sheltons, were especially grateful, and
to Ned they gave an embossed sash as a memento of
the event.[27] At school the deed was talked about with
pride, but it did nothing to improve Ned's scholastic
ability. When Gilbert Brown again visited Avenel No.8
on 30 March 1865 he noted, amongst other things, that
the roof was still in bad repair, that the local committee
was divided amongst itself, that Maggie Kelly was still

in second grade though improving, but that Edward
Kelly, now aged ten years and three months, was in the
fourth grade and was still failing in his old weaknesses,
Grammar and Geography. When he returned to the
school in October there were no Kellys present nor were
there any on the roll for his two visits in 1866.[28] At the
age of ten Ned was educated insofar as that particular
refinement of human existence was understood or rendered possible out in the humpy on the forty acres.

William Campion was central to the ordered functioning of the township for he ran the general store, he was
the postmaster and in the name of the Colony of Victoria
he deputized for the official whose duty it was to record
that some were born and others died in that part of Her
Majesty's domain. On 3 October 1865 he duly registered
that on the tenth day of August a female child was born
to a dairyman named John Kelly. Her given name was
Grace and no one except the parents had been present
at the birth. It had taken Red seven weeks to get to the
point of registering his daughter, and although he was
still able to sign his name with a flourish to the capital
K, the firmness and confidence of four years previously
had gone from his hand and his heart.[29] All through the
years since he had left Van Diemen's Land, with so much
hope of a new life, he had determined to keep himself
forever free of further involvement with the law. Marriage to Ellen, the arrival of the children, recognition
by neighbours and friends, a place in a small community
with Kelly children at its school had all helped to keep
Red's sights on the concept of an ordered, decent life.
The year 1865 put paid to all that.

Ellen was the first of the family to appear in court, but
as complainant rather than defendant, and in the case
in question it was alleged that she had been assaulted

by her sister-in-law Anne Kelly who had inflicted injuries
which were estimated at £10. Although the case was dismissed, it brought the family into the public eye in a manner not conducive to uplifting the common estimate of
their general demeanour.[30] Red's own behaviour later
in the year did nothing to enhance that appraisal, for
he was charged with the illegal possession of a cow hide
belonging to his neighbour, Philip Morgan, found guilty
and fined £25 or, in default, sentenced to six months in
Kilmore Gaol.[31] It was Red's first appearance before a
court since he was granted his freedom and, although
the money to pay the fine was somehow raised, thus obvi-
ating the necessity of a return to prison, the old lag
charge was revived and the ex-convict was again
ranked in the criminal class. Perhaps pressing necessity
in the form of a family requiring to be fed, with a mother
about to give birth to her eighth child drove him to such
an act in the winter of 1865. Perhaps it was no more than
that the temptation of a strayed calf in the hills with a
faint brand had proved too much for an impecunious
breadwinner. Whatever the cause the consequence was
the same. Ned had a father who had spent a weekend
in the local lock-up, and in the minds of the young Cam-
pions, Sheltons and Muttons at school, it was a simple
matter to transfer parental guilt to the shoulders of a
small boy. Hercules Doxey was over a year older than
Ned, but he sat next to him in the fourth grade while
his younger sister Caroline sat with Maggie on the same
bench in the second.[32] Their father, Constable John
Doxey, had ridden out to the Kelly block between Avenel
and Tabilk where the young vines planted by Hugh
Glass lay dormant in expectation. Doxey had searched
the home and arrested its man. The Kelly children were
seen no more at Avenel No.8. The parents of the more

fortunate students bickered amongst themselves over school finances. Those less fortunate ones to whom nothing had been given except good fame found that it too passed away like dry grass before a fire.[33]

Red Kelly was still young enough to feel the strength of his manhood when the sun soaked up the glittering frosts from the early spring mornings of 1865. But deep in his being other elementary forces were at work and he added to their destructive powers by his weakness for brandy. In December John Doxey arrested him again with the charge of being drunk and disorderly, but this time he suffered no penalty except a Christmas overladen with debt, poverty and despair.[34] Throughout 1866 he and Ned struggled to keep the farm productive, but the winter was harsh and long and Red spoke more in the evenings of old Ireland and that southland to which he and others had been sent 'to pine their young lives away in starvation and misery amongst tyrants worse than the promised hell itself'.[35] All of the past was becoming jumbled in Red's mind and the days in Ireland's soft vales, where he was strong in 'true blood, bone and beauty'[36] were mingled now with the heartwrench of parting, the penury of Avenel, the half-averted glances of shy children who looked up in hopeful trust, and the unflinching strength of Ellen who begged him to lift up his heart. It was to no avail. In early December he took to his bed and, on the twenty-first, Doctor Healey examined him and departed from Avenel with that feeling which comes to one whose life is given to healing when he has left a bed from which there will be no arising. No carols were heard by the hearth of the Kelly homestead on Christmas Day, no oil soothed the hands and feet of that pilgrim as he passed beyond the touch of men on 27 December, and no priest

begged that his Redeemer would give John Kelly eternal
rest as they laid his body in the soil of Avenel. A boy
with a great void in his heart stood before William Campion to testify that Red was dead. It was fitting that in
signing himself as the son of his father Ned flourished
the K of Kelly for, in the land where Red finally became
one with its dust, he would live on henceforth only in
the fragile vessel of burgeoning manhood in that son.[37]

Greta by the Creeks   3

At certain times the whole countryside around Greta was clothed in green and thus the land itself gave lie to the reality that was existence for many who had settled in that place. The life they led depended on the vagaries of the weather, and it was a land in which no lip complained of rain, even when it came in proportions such as to flood the swamps of the Fifteen Mile Creek and to drizzle its wetness into all porous creatures. Other times would come, when the wind would blow and the swamps dry up, when the sun would shine relentlessly and the dust rise, so that the mountains were seen in a light that chilled more than the rain. In those days men looked to the heavens and felt expectation drain away as the high winds aborted the rain clouds in vain profusion over distant seas. Then men knew that drought had come upon the land, so that the grasses shrivelled in the heat and crows picked white the carcasses of the weak in the herds and flocks. In such times the bank managers tightened their lips over the mortgages, and the small shopkeepers in Benalla and Beechworth cast their eyes down as they filled orders which only hope could redeem. To some, perhaps, it seemed that the very vastness of those squatting runs of the northeast was itself an assurance of prosperity, but those who held the land did so in the knowledge of their precarious existence, and they feared in 1852 that their days were numbered, for they looked in awe at the thousands that poured across their runs in search of an element less reliable than the grasses of their pastures.

A man called Cropper passed through a valley twenty-five miles to the north-east of Greta in 1838. He was on his way to stock his run which lay between the King River and the Fifteen Mile Creek, but his ewes began to drop their lambs in that comely valley, so Cropper paused to build a woolshed and give a name to that place destined to draw men from myriad lands in search of the mineral that lay in abundance beneath its soil, and in the sparkling bed of its creek where the reeds rustled to the faintness of the wind.[1] It was thereabouts in 1852 that gold was first discovered in the northeast, and the rush was on for men spoke in awe of the quantities held in those ranges with their thin creeks, where the maddening metal lay in nuggets as profusely as stars in the Milky Way. Within a year 20,000 diggers were on the ground and the accents of the world were heard there, with voices ringing in exultation, or despair, or simple drunkenness, and they came and went in vast movements like armies disputing territories in the name of the god of greed.[2] Little Greta down the road felt the rumblings of this passage, as on foot and in all manner of carriage men went by in disjointed concourse, startling the ducks and geese of the peaceful swamps, and awakening the bitterns who boomed through the night like distant bulls.

Hence, through the years, great changes came over the northeast. Those ever flinging ranges saw the land of endless centuries heave and writhe as the seekers cut through and beneath it, while the ironbarks fell shattered to the ground, the birds and all creatures of the earth went back further towards the high country, and the waters of the streams coursed in dirty beds cut by man. Greta grew, with blacksmiths' shops, an hotel, a store, a school and a bakery, while that majesty created out of ancient and barbaric conflicts, imposing abstractions called rights and duties and christened law, came to be represented by a member of the Victoria Police, whose wont it was to ride along that awful bog called a road, from Benalla to Greta, in order to ascertain the state of the Queen's peace in the hamlet by the Fifteen Mile Creek.

But that reflected glory from a distant Crown, worn by the strong and upright woman across the seas, was paled by the tawdry character of many of those who wore her emblems in Victoria's northeast. During the great golden days it proved difficult to attract volunteers to the force because men had other forces pulling on their being. So it was that the lesser ones without drive, training, rudimentary learning or pity, brought, even upon the few who were otherwise, a reputation for brutality, venality, cowardice, revenge and corruption. It was never an onerous task to impose law and order on the fields in the days when the yields were immense, because the seekers themselves were compelled to adopt and uphold their own primitive code of justice and honour in order to preserve their livelihood. But when the surface gold ran thin in the 1860s and the companies took over in search of the deep leads, when the tent towns that had clustered like mushrooms after the first rains achieved structural stability, when commerce grew apace and all things settled to the tedium of normalcy, the role of the police was both strengthened and magnified, because now it encompassed the imposition of a stricter code which had to take account of all manner of infraction of the laws governing person and property. Were a horse or a beast missing, were a man's or a woman's character assailed, were a blow struck in anger, a property line infringed, perhaps through ignorance, or a bottle of hard spirits sold without due licence to the passerby, then into the fabric of communal interaction stepped one denominated constable. Abstraction the law may have been, but he gave flesh to that concept and his own strength or frailty, his own broad vision or narrow-mindedness, his propensity to tell the truth or his inclination to say with his tongue that which was not square with his mind, led him in the end to take sides, because all men, and especially those possessing little or nothing, could not have right on their sides. As a result of these matters, oft and anon, a constable would find himself confused, and the powerful were too frequently comforted in their sense of uprighteousness, while the patience of the poor perished with what little else they had.

Those same early 1860s, which saw the passing of the golden heyday, saw also the surge of another thrust towards acquisition of a more permanent source of frugal, economic viability by means of land possession. Thousands, it is true, wandered from field to field and eked out a living on the remaining scraps; others settled in the towns and devoted themselves to that high thing men call business; others left the colony and chased the golden rainbow to its source in distant places; others again went to fill the suburbs of the city, where they gazed upon the centres of financial strength and the mansions thrown up by the power of the very metal about which they could now only dream. But others said to themselves that the land itself was good, and on it they would establish their own dynasties of yeomen who would till, and tend, and reap the benefit of stability from the produce of their crops, herds and flocks. That hope became more and more urgent as the numbers departing the fields swelled, and down in Melbourne some visionaries who held power in the land thought deeply of those little ones and of the great squatters who held their vast runs. In the manner of dreamers who have awoken to reality, they tried their hands at law-making, and came up with things called Land Acts and their names of Nicholson, Duffy and Grant were enshrined in the legislative fancies their busy minds created. It pleased such men to think that their benevolence would curb the great squatters and increase the hold of the small farmers over a fair share of the common wealth. Assuredly their Acts were designed to allow access to those who had not, but whether through perversity or weakness, they also ensured continued possession to those who had, so that when the whole tortured process of alienation of the broad acres took place, seven-eighths of the land went to those who already had it – the squatters.[3]

Back on the vast runs like Bontharambo, the big ones played cricket, hunted kangaroos, and sighed with relief when it became clear that they would be able to remain as patriarchs over the land.[4] Great names there were amongst them, and huge squatters and mere speculators such as Hugh Glass, W. J. Clarke and the Dockers became legendary figures, while others were known only in passing, for the squatters too were subject to the vagaries of climate and prices, and their style of living fluctuated like the clouds gliding high beyond the mountains. Gold had come and was passing, so perhaps too the irritant called selectors, who strove for meagre parcels to stake a claim for another source of wealth, would pass.

To Greta and its district in those years the selectors came with names which recalled a common origin in those islands across the English channel: Dennett, Forge, McKenzie, Toakley, Harty, McNab and Quinn. Strong timber there was aplenty to construct their rude dwellings while the hills were clothed in stringybark trees which they stripped to form the roof. The furniture was homemade, rough but serviceable, while the heart of the home was the fireplace where a huge back log roared and provided warmth, for the winters in that country were often long and wet and dark. Gradually the land was cleared, and wheat and oats sown, while a bullock or a pig, and later a sheep, was slaughtered and often shared for meat.[5] But in those early years, the pioneers of the selector class struggled, as had their ancestors in feudal days and on miserable farmlets on the lands from which they had come in search of better times. Amongst those who came were the brothers John and Thomas Lloyd, who had selected a small parcel of land north of Greta bordering the run of J. W. Chisholm. Like the old patriarch Quinn, they had looked to the northeast as the new place in which to seek prosperity.

By 1865 Greta was in decline, and on 27 August of that year its few inhabitants were fascinated to see a party of police ride through their midst. It was not so much that they could claim that Greta and its environs were especially noted for adhesion to the forms of the law. Simply put, it amounted to wonderment that the constables from Wangaratta, and a detective from Melbourne, had decided that matters were so far awry in the neighbourhood as to warrant such undivided attention and in such strength. It was not however to the locals of the township, but to the farm of the Lloyd brothers, that the police contingent directed its steps. Arrived there, Detective Hudson chose a concealed position from which he and his fellows watched with interest a proceeding in itself of no unusual moment in the bush, the slaughter of a bullock. John and Thomas were assisted in this act by their employees, Jim Davies and one Ah Sam, and all were given pause for thought when the police rushed down and arrested the men on the charge that the young strawberry bullock they had despatched belonged to Mr Chisholm. Ah Sam was terrified, and showed himself prompt to assist the law in its enforcement, so that when the case came up for trial at Beechworth General Sessions in October, John and Thomas, and Jim Davies were charged with cattle stealing. Ah Sam testified against them, while John Quinn came down from Glenmore to swear that the beast in question was the property of the Lloyds. The jury was not impressed, nor indeed was the judge, who, in passing sentence, remarked that cattle stealing, given the difficulty of obtaining convictions, was much more dangerous than horse stealing. He did not indicate to whom the danger applied, but in this case the Lloyd brothers were clearly imperilled as his Honour was moved to sentence them to five years' imprisonment with hard labour. Jim Davies was acquitted, Ah Sam retired to obscurity, and when John Quinn arrived back at the home on the King the keening was heard again, for women were left without men, children without fathers and the land without tillers. The hoped-for new life for the clan in the northeast had begun on an inauspicious note.[6]

Down the road at Avenel a threshing of the spirit overtook Ellen Kelly after the loss of Red. The struggle to keep the little ones fed and clothed drove her to fits of imprecation, to the use of language which the court deemed abusive and threatening, to fear of assault to person and property, all of which saw her frail figure before the law with fines, dismissals and orders to keep the peace or forfeit liberty.[7] Meanwhile uncle Dan Kelly was reported in the Victoria Police Gazette in respect of a stolen horse, supposedly taken to Glenmore on the distant King, and Ned was said to be connected with the disappearance of a chestnut mare from a property near Avenel.[8] The boy had withdrawn within himself when the consciousness that Red would never guide him again became increasingly a clutch to the heart in the early months of 1867. Then he turned to the old ones of another civilization who were encamped by the creek nearby to his home. With them Ned, who had come to perceive dimly that his own being belonged in part to the holiness of place that the land held embraced, felt an empathy. He came to understand that the blackman's sense of freedom recognized no bondage imposed by an alien race, and that he had skills of survival honed by the centuries and perfected by his profound insight into the ways of the land and all its creatures. Of that quiet wisdom and of those uncanny abilities, by which broken twig and fallen leaf indicated the path of the hunt, the young, white Australian stood in awe, and he kept those things in his heart, for in that place he was strengthened and never threatened by those old ones.[9]

The winter of 1867 saw Ellen make the final and decisive move that guided her destiny. She needed the adult companionship of her own clan, as did her sisters Catherine and Jane, for they had lived alone with their children since the imprisonment of their husbands, John and Thomas Lloyd, two years before. The Kellys took to the road again, and came to Greta towards the end of the year. They travelled light on that road because they possessed little, and their spirits quickened at the thought of being once again amongst their own, for Greta brought them within an easy stretch to Glenmore, where Ellen looked to the comfort of her mother, while Ned spoke to his brother Jim of their grandfather who stood above them all. Through Euroa by the Strath-bogies, and Benalla on the Broken River, they passed and then they saw Mount Glenrowan on their left as they came down the gap at the end of the Warby Ranges. At their feet was a vast plain country, with tiny Greta at its edge, while to the south-east Buffalo bore its ancient cone, softened by time and clothed with timber. Beyond them rolled in wondrous glory all those ranges upon ranges which unfolded in a profusion of awesome splendour to reach their culmination in the Alps. Up there, they knew, ran the old river which Ned had seen on the map at Avenel, and beyond it lay the mother colony, where it had all begun in the counting of white man's time. It was much for a boy of twelve to see with the eye and encompass in the mind, and the dark hair lay quietly on the pillow that night, in a rough but warm bed with Jim and Dan. Ellen, Catherine and Jane talked far into the night, while the thirteen children slept in that broken-down old building that had seen better days as an hotel when Greta was young and the gold still held in the hills.

Christmas of 1867 had the clan united at Glenmore, and Ned walked for the first time in those gorges ringing with the raucous shrieking of galahs as they whirled through the trees, pitted with the holes of wombats in the acacia undergrowth, bedazzled by the gay profusion of parrots in winging flight; all the distances melted into a blueness above, for no greyness clouded that sky, which blackened only when the thunderclouds banked over the mountains and the storm rumbled down through the valleys. Grandfather Quinn's home was truly ancestral when compared with the humble dwellings Ned had known at Beveridge and Avenel. Along the length of the passage, bedroom followed bedroom and opened out onto a veranda which, running right around the house, was partly built-in to form a sleepout.[10] There was space aplenty for them all, and they could sit together at the huge table in the diningroom with its immense fireplace. Ned was almost thirteen and, as a man in the making, he was taken into the company of the men who knew that back in Greta it was he who would be responsible for women and children whose menfolk were gone where only God or the law governed their present being. His grandfather walked with him to the horse-paddock, and Ned noticed that his step was drawing in, his speech was slowing, and the frost of the winters had gathered about his temples. Nonetheless Old Quinn could still speak with steel of the past, tempered a little with hope in a future in which the acres of Glenmore would help sustain them. Up above them as they walked towered a prominence from which the whole valley of the King could be seen spreading below, and it all seemed enough to give warrant to hope.

January passed quickly, and it was time to return to

Greta to enrol the younger children at school, and look for some form of gainful employment for the older. They settled down in the house owned by the Lloyds and on the evening of 27 January 1868 James Kelly, Red's brother, slaked his thirst nearby in Laurence O'Brien's hotel. James was only recently released from Pentridge, and his ability to hold his drink had been much modified by lack of use. The children were in bed when the women heard a knocking, which heralded the arrival of a drunken James, demanding food and a bed. Never one to shirk confronting a nuisance, Ellen tongue-lashed her brother-in-law, and drove him from the house which James threatened, with drunken epithets, to burn down. The women knew that they were dealing with a man who, in drink taken, could do violence, so they sat up until one o'clock when, satisfied that James had departed, they retired. Shortly afterwards they awoke to the crackle of fire and, running outside, saw James with the hideous visage of a man whom drink had rendered maniac. The children were quickly awakened but within an hour the house lay in smouldering ashes while, grief-stricken, the women wailed at the total loss of all they possessed. Little Greta and its better ones, including the O'Briens, stood them in good stead for the night, and on the following day Detective Harrington arrested a sober and chastened James.[11]

In the weeks that followed mother and son forged bonds of love and loyalty that no test through the years could ever shake. Frail in body Ellen was, but her spirit remained unbroken by adversity, and she was determined, like her sire, to put down roots in the land and be her own woman, unencumbered by ties to those whom she knew could only degrade and infect her sons with the spirit of idleness which sneers at effort and

honour. To achieve that end, a home and a parcel of
land, however small, was imperative. Together Ellen
and Ned sought it, and across the gap in the ranges,
back along the road to Benalla, and four miles from
Greta, they found it. There, by the Eleven Mile Creek,
stood a selector's hut on eighty-eight thin and scrubby
acres. The hut was tiny but sturdy, with hewn log walls,
a dirt floor and a steady roof. The land was still under
bush which led back to low and infertile hills, but land
could be cleared, and the creek gave water, the timber
gave warmth.[12] They took it up and moved there soon
after the destruction of the communal home at Greta,
and Ellen was at peace, while Ned could rejoice with
that surge of strength which comes to the young when
the sap rises in their being, and around them all things
give promise of fulfilment. Mother and son talked long
as they looked about them on that first night at the Eleven
Mile, but their talk was of Red, the necessity of acquiring
more of the basic needs to provide some small measure
of comfort, and to what use, and with what means, they
would put the land. They did not know that a few miles
away, across the valley in the township of Beechworth,
another mother and son talked often long into the night,
as was the wont of Jews, as well as Irish, whose heritage
gave much food for the spirit after a meal was partaken.
The son was a few months younger than Ned and his
mother, like Ellen, was a woman driven by a restless urge
to leave a mark behind her. She was successful. Her son's
name was Isaac Alfred Isaacs.[13]

April 18 saw Ellen, Catherine and Jane in the Circuit
Court at Beechworth. Above them, on his bench, sat the
bewigged and scarlet robed figure of a judge who was
also a knight of the realm. It was not often that their sort
came into such a presence, and they were mindful of

their insignificance before one to whom their affairs
were a mere fading ripple on the surface of his greater
being. With a handsome and portly figure, a visage rendered tender by the passing of the years, and softened
by the love he bore his mistress and their children, the
judge was in the fullness of his mental and physical vigour. Sprung, as those before him in the courtroom, from
the peat mists of Ireland, Redmond Barry was fifty-five
years of age, and his greatest hopes had seen fulfilment
since his arrival in the colony thirty years before. In 1852
Barry had been appointed a judge of the Supreme
Court, and some older ones wondered at the seeming
ease with which one so young held power over life and
death, freedom or bondage. In the year of Ned's birth,
Barry, as Chancellor, presided over the opening term
of Melbourne University and he rejoiced at its existence
as a portent and assurance of stability in times that had
been rendered uneasy by his larrikin compatriots, with
motley and ill-assorted companions, at Eureka a few
months before. Though Barry always bade his friends
to cup deep with him on each anniversary of his arrival
in the colony, his heart was lonely until his eyes fell upon
the winsome figure of a woman who captured his attention, affection and devotion, and held him for life. In the
Victoria of the mid-nineteenth century, it was an alliance
at which even the broadminded winced, for the woman
in question had been wedded and bedded by another,
yet Barry remained convinced both of the probity of his
actions and of the necessity to express his need for
human companionship by a union with one whom, to
him at least, was a woman beyond compare.

Thus it was that Redmond Barry, K.B. and judge, book
lover and academic administrator, wine connoisseur
and master of Mrs Barrow, sat upon his bench in that

graceful courthouse of soft and golden coloured sand-
stone at Beechworth, and looked down upon these
women. He heard their story, he listened to the verdict
of the good and trusty ones called upon to balance up
the actions of their peer, and he turned to the worm of
a man trembling in the dock, and sentenced him to
death. It was verily an enormous and atrocious crime
of which James Kelly was guilty opined the judge, whose
whole being revolted at the thought of tender lives being
put in jeopardy by the action of a reckless maniac. James
stood and heard the verdict, though he was unfamiliar
with the jargon that forged arson from his drunken spree
at Greta. To him, a final sentence meant little, for if anything it was preferable to another term of ceaseless
drudgery in the Pentridge he abhorred. To the clan, it
was another proof of their impotency before a system
they were only beginning to comprehend, for they would
have been capable of meting out their own form of primitive and private justice to James. To the Executive Council it was all a little much: certainly a house had been
burnt, and perhaps lives had been endangered, but in
fact no souls had perished. They deliberated on the
matter, and with the full concurrence of Barry they com-
muted James' death sentence to another form of death,
ten years in prison.[14] His name and memory lingered
briefly in the thoughts and prayers of the family, but
James had passed into that greyness from which he was
heard of no more.

In all of that vast movement of men engendered by
the gold-rushes, some there were who remained behind
after the purpose of their coming was exhausted. They
eked out their lives on the fringe of the new society based
on agriculture then being developed apace in Victoria.
Amongst them were some of those who had left a life

of bondage to rapacious landlords and relentless
creditors in China, to pay their way to economic freedom
on the Australian gold-fields, and who preferred to stay
behind once the golden days were over. Such a one was
Ah Fook, whose new vocation was that of pig and fowl
dealer, and whose residence was Morse's Creek.

In mid-October 1869 while wending his way between
Greta and Winton, it being warm and the road dusty,
Ah Fook felt the need of refreshment. Whether he had
heard that stronger waters than those flowing in the
Eleven Mile Creek were available at Mrs Kelly's residence was never revealed, but the fact was that he came
to her doorstep, where he found Annie, now married to
a Scotsman, Alexander Gunn, sewing by the door. Ah
Fook declared his need, and Annie provided him with
a pannikin of creek water, which he promptly spat out,
and then proceeded to abuse her. Ned was splitting and
grubbing timber in the company of William Gray and
William Skillion not far from the house and, noticing the
altercation, he ran over to intervene. Despite his residence of more than a decade in the colony Ah Fook had
never acquired a command of the local language, which
possibly contributed to the confusion then ensuing. Ned
was growing to his manly stature, and he probably
administered more than a verbal rebuke to the Chinese
visitor, but Ah Fook carried no visible marks on his personage when he reported the incident at Benalla police
station later that evening, although Sergeant Whelan
asserted that there were abrasions on his legs and arms.
The pig and fowl dealer had money on his person, ten
shillings of which he alleged had been forcibly removed
by Ned, but he was unable to explain why Ned had not
taken the rest. The upshot of the fracas was Ned's arrest
for assault and robbery, and his being held in the

Benalla lock-up for twelve days, because justice demanded that Ah Fook's rights be preserved by the provision of an interpreter, and it took that long to acquire the services of one in the person of William Tze Hing. Although the law had for long prevaricated on permitting the first Australians to swear evidence in court, on the grounds that they were believed to know no god, Ah Fook was invited to open the proceedings at Benalla by blowing out a match, hence indicating that he was perfectly aware of the enormity of perjury in the tribunals of the white man's gods. Mr Wills, police magistrate, listened to the sorry little story of racial incomprehension, and concluded that it was scarcely more than tedious rubbish of no moment. Ned was discharged, but an ominous thing was said in that court-room in Benalla. Ah Fook pronounced in Cantonese, and Tze Hing put into English, words said to have been used by Ned. According to Ah Fook, Ned had said 'I'm a bushranger.'[15] And thus it was that in a dusty, fly blown courtroom at the other end of the world from which he had come, a Chinese pig and fowl dealer pronounced the first publicly recorded words said to have been uttered by the boy from the Greta hut.

Harry's Cub 4

Those years, in which the clan in the northeast shaped
its tortured destiny, etched out also the inexorable path
followed by others who quickened to that mountain air
and grew to another fulness. Across the plains at Chiltern an eager child rapturously watched the wattle
bloom and breathed in the heavy aroma of those golden
pods scenting the air of spring afternoons. She ran
beside the little lake near her home and rejoiced at the
spaciousness and openness of everything in this new
world, where all seemed fresh and young. But in the evenings her tiny being was caught by the chilled forebod-
ings of another's destiny, as she dimly perceived that
a twisted spirit was clutching at the inner core of her
father. The new land had been too immense a burden
for Walter Lindesay Richardson and, though he ten-
dered his medical care to others, he was rapidly moving
into that half world of lunacy from which there could
be no return. In the mind of his daughter the agony, the
hopelessness, the heroic devotion of her mother, the

enthralling rapture of the land itself, the drama of a
father's life unfulfilled and brought to nothing, caught
up with her creative urge which in woman's estate would
give the world and its literature the treasure of her *Fortunes.*

By the Greta hut across the valleys the wattle also
bloomed along the creek beds and the children ran
gladly and hungrily down the last few furlongs of the
track from school. Ellen clutched them proudly and felt
the new life quicken within her while she forced back
the memories of her husband Red and her father the
Quinn of Glenmore. In those very same weeks in which
James Quinn walked down the valley of death, and saw
the light fading on the great hills as winter closed in
about Glenmore, Ellen walked another path of crea-
tivity. What agony of loneliness or lust, what sense of
weariness with a burden beyond her frailty, what fear
of the intruder into that defenceless hut had moved her,
only Ellen knew, but as life slipped away from her father,
another life began in her womb. William Frost was a
boundary rider on a property near Greta and he
became a regular visitor to the hut on the Eleven Mile.
He too looked for companionship and the widow offered
that, so with promises of marriage he took his place
beside Ellen in that bed where Red's memory was faint
and ghostly.[1] The boy, Ned, turned his face away and
took to the hills of Glenmore, because the strong link
in his life with Ireland and its miseries was rapidly weakening as that figure, who embodied the last hope of the
clan, was stricken like the great gums of the high passes
when lightning shattered their core.

James Quinn's last days were filled with memories of
a far northern land filled with poverty and bitterness,
of this new land to which he had come in hope and

expectation when it was still part of the mother colony, the struggle of those early years at Moonee Ponds and Wallan before the golden days which made Glenmore possible. But it was all slipping away now with the twisting and thwarting of his hopes for respectability, dignity and even decency. His sons and sons-in-law were men marked before the law, his daughters lived in drudgery and grinding poverty, nor could any tell what would become of the new brood multiplying before him. Who could even tell of the future for which he had worked when he became the proud occupant of Glenmore. Would those wild ones hold those even wilder acres of tameless mountains and gorge, or would Glenmore pass from the Quinns as their good name and fame had passed? With these matters in his mind Old Quinn relinquished his hold on life, on Glenmore, on wife and on that brood sprung from them, and that mortal frame quickened in Antrim was laid to rest at Oxley on 25 August 1869. When they came to register the details of his death one small token of dignity was granted to his memory for the Irish cottar of Antrim was put down as the squatter of Glenmore although it went unmentioned that his domain was mostly barren and his assets almost nil.[2].

Up above Glenmore a runt of a man lived in a cave from which he rejoiced in looking out upon the loneliness of the world, breathing the air of the mountains and giving thanks for the freedom he enjoyed in those remote fastnesses. His liberty to do all this depended upon the goodwill of the family in their home below his lair, and the watchfulness of a peacock which, perched on the roof of the Quinn home, signalled in shrill and impetuous tones the passage of the stranger through that narrow valley. To Ned the climb up from his grandfather's home

was itself a source of exhilaration, because that rough
track through bush and over boulder was a challenge
to his sinews. But to be there was much more again,
because the stories told by the little man, in the accents
of Waterford, of transportation, freedom, horse stealing
and highway robbery were all of adventure, defiance,
chivalry, bravery and huge fun. But more than that was
the largeness of heart, soul, wit and native wisdom in
the slender frame of this one, gnarled by time and buf-
feted by a fate which had sharpened, but never twisted
his spirit. Harry Power was transported for seven years
in 1840 because, needing a pair of shoes to ward off the
chill of an Irish winter, and being without the means to
purchase them, he had stolen them. After a series of
vicissitudes in which it was his proud boast that he never
killed a man nor spoke in unbecoming terms to a woman,
Harry escaped from Pentridge in February 1869 by the
ingenious ruse of hiding himself in a rubbish cart and
waiting until they off-loaded him at the local tip. Glenmore became his base because the Lloyd brothers had
told him that he would be safe in its mountains, and from
his lookout he carried out his forays on mail coaches
and the odd, selected individuals whom Harry felt would
suffer little loss with the partial removal of their worldly
goods.[3]

The one thing the amiable scoundrel lacked was a
mate, if for no other reason than that he found it incon-
venient to hold his horse while he held up others. He
did not find it difficult to charm a fourteen-year-old boy
into providing him with the help he needed, especially
when that boy was already persuaded that he belonged
to a clan which held tenuous links with organized
society, and had nothing to lose by weakening those
links further. Old grandfather Quinn had followed Red

into the silence and it was useless for Ned to look for
advice to his Quinn or Lloyd uncles. Ellen was taken
up with the process of giving life and had little left to
give to Ned who found difficulty in accepting his
mother's pregnancy. Jim and Dan were too young to turn
to, while Maggie, who loved him fiercely, was herself
growing to womanhood and could share little abundance with Ned. Furthermore Ah Fook had pronounced
him a bushranger in the Benalla Court and he had spent
twelve days in confinement. Perhaps it was time to test
this new way of life and the apprenticeship with Harry
was open.

Whatever the complacency with which the clan
accepted Harry's presence in their midst, the Victorian
police were determined to put an end to the irritating
behaviour of the old lag, who had caused sufficient
inconvenience to the legal system by escaping twice
from Pentridge and now seemed able to rob at will in
his gentlemanly way. In mid-March 1870 Mr Robert
McBean of Kilfera Station rode into Benalla and called
at the police station. McBean was a squatter who knew
the clan well and he told a tale of having been relieved
of his horse, saddle, bridle and watch by two men, one
of whom he called Frost and the other he later identified
as Power. In such matters the agile minds of the Victoria
Police, especially in its upper echelons, were difficult
for the mere outsider to fathom, but the upshot of
McBean's story was that on 4 May a heavily armed dawn
patrol led by the redoubtable Superintendent Nicolson
surrounded the shanty on the Eleven Mile, and proceeded to the prompt arrest, not of Mr Frost but of the
youth Edward Kelly.

How Mrs Kelly, with the six-week-old Frost infant at
her breast, reacted to the arrest of her son and only

helper is not known but Ned looked exhausted, although
he was able to smile at old acquaintances on the road-
side as they carted him to Benalla. While awaiting trial
he smoked and sang like a bird in his cell, and, when
finally the fifteen-year-old lad was led into court a week
later, no one seemed to remember his juvenile years,
but only the way he irritated the worthy burghers there
assembled by his jaunty and nonchalant air. No one
even remarked on the possibility that his haughtiness
may have stemmed from his knowledge that he was innocent: the witnesses, including McBean, were unable to
sustain the charges that he had robbed in company and
that he had also robbed on the highway, using a firelock
to induce a certain Joseph Balwoski to yield up £5 10s
near Seymour on 20 April. Ned was discharged but
Superintendent Nicolson was not to be outdone in his
quest for old Harry so Ned was again hauled off, this
time to Kyneton to answer a further charge of Highway
Robbery Under Arms, alleged to have been perpetrated
at nearby Lauriston on 25 April 1870.[4]

The Irish were at home at Kyneton with its soft vales
and clean hills, its woodland and its wet mists and Ned
was at home in its prison. Indeed he may well have been,
for it was the pleasure of the prosecution to hold him
there for over three weeks until the police themselves
were induced to request his discharge, given that they
were unable to provide a shred of evidence against him.
Even the local paper expressed surprise at the oddness,
if not injustice, of their proceedings but it was pleased
to tell its readers that they could be sure that whatever
the police did in the matter, they could be certain was
done for good and upright reasons.[5] Ned of course was
not in prison in order that charges might be proved
against him, but because Superintendent Nicolson

thought that he would be able to induce this callow youth
to sing another song which would lead them to old Harry.
The worthy superintendent had forgotten that Ned was
already a gaolbird at the age of fifteen, in whose being
there was nothing of the traitor. On 3 June Power's cub
was out and on 5 June Power himself was in, for an
informant had sung the right song to the tune of £500
which was the reward for Harry's capture. Those stalwart
members of the Victorian police had set out for his lair
on 27 May, when Ned was still being remanded in Kyneton, and in the early morning they took Harry as he slept
beside his fire. At his courteous invitation they accepted
his hospitality of corned beef, bread and tea, although
Harry himself was disinclined to partake as his rude
awakening had considerably lessened his appetite.[6]
On 19 August 1870 the Chief Commissioner of Police,
being satisfied that Harry had been safely ensconced
in Pentridge to serve a fifteen-year sentence, wrote to
the Victorian Chief Secretary requesting that the reward
of £500 be paid to the informer who had led his officers,
Nicolson and Hare, to Harry's lookout. The name of the
man to whom the money was to be paid was Jimmy
Quinn. Thus the old vagabond was sold, but not by Ned,
and the clan numbered a police informer in its midst.[7]

While these stirring events were apace at the Eleven
Mile, on the King, and up and down the surrounding
roads, Captain Standish was exercising his mind in and
about the gaming boards and generous tables of the
Melbourne Club. Frederick Charles Standish had been
bred to the army, but horses were his early love and their
fickle performance the cause of his immigration to the
colonies in 1852. In April 1854 he became an assistant
commissioner on the gold-fields, joining those of his kind
whom that upright Quaker, William Howitt, regarded

as young, which they invariably were, 'insolent, imperious, useless, arrogant, incompetent, and empty headed'.[8] All of those things Frederick Charles may have been except for the last because by 1858, at the age of thirty-four he was appointed Chief Commissioner of the Victoria Police on a salary of £1,200, which afforded him the opportunity to indulge his tastes in gaming, food, wine and literature. Every now and then he was moved to repent of the doings of his companions in the legal system as, for example, when he told his intimate confidant, Curtis Candler, that a Crown Prosecutor had recently accepted £200 to stop legal proceedings in a notorious gambling scandal.[9] But by early 1869 the good Captain was minded to take in hand the problem of the mob of hellions in and around the Greta district, whom he regarded as a thoroughly disreputable lot and in need of a firm hand in order to curb their excesses. He bethought himself of Senior Constable Edward Hall, a young man whose superintendent regarded as hard working and intelligent, with a monomania for the formulation and application of his own form of bush law, and one who had a record of trouble-making in the Ovens area. It was this latter point which particularly impressed itself upon the mind of the chief of police; Hall had been accused of ill-treatment of a prisoner at Eldorado, of perjury and unnecessary interference in matters outside his ken, as a result of which he had so antagonized the people of the district as to cause the police magistrate to recommend his transfer. Hall had begged not to be disturbed in his comfortable billet, but Standish remained convinced that Edward was a man of hasty and injudicious conduct and were he inclined to continue so behaving it may as well be at Greta that he do so where the consequences, if resented by the inhabitants of that place, would be of little moment given the generally low estimate held by god-fearing people of the Greta people. It was a chastened young man who rode out from Benalla on 30 May 1870 bearing the special instructions of Standish as to how he was to conduct himself in the insalubrious locality of Greta.[10]

By July the local superintendent stationed at Benalla was so impressed with the peaceful state of affairs that had come upon the Greta district that he recommended the transfer of Hall elsewhere, but Captain Standish did not concur. He was the recipient of information from 'a private source' which gave him to understand that 'the Quinns, Kellys and all that disruptable gang' were still based on little Greta and so he decided to retain Hall there, at least until law and order could be strengthened by the establishment of a police station at Glenmore.[11] And so it came to pass that in 1870 Bismarck turned his mind to the unification of Germany, Pio Nono reflected on his own infallibility and the impending loss of his Roman state, the editor of the *Mansfield Guardian* was afraid that French vessels might shell Melbourne and Captain Standish concerned himself with the ravages wrought on society by the Greta 'gang'. They themselves were not unmindful of his concern, but there were more pressing matters to brood upon out at Ellen's hamlet. Thomas and John Lloyd had been released from Pentridge in 1869 where they had been reprimanded for such deviations as whistling and singing, taking soap, possessing pipes and tobacco and sundry such niceties not permitted in that institution.[12] Their return home meant at least a strengthening of the male workforce, as well as solace to Ellen's sisters and their families on the Fifteen Mile, especially as Ned had spent most of

the first part of 1870 in and out of the courts on the Power
affair, and Jim and Dan were still too young to offer much
assistance in clearing and scrubbing. One slight ray of
brightness penetrated the winter skies of the district for
it was known amongst the inhabitants that their Senior
Constable was contemplating marriage. But before that
blessed event could come to pass the intended groom
had to attend to the matter of an altercation between
Ned and his uncle Jimmy Quinn who, together with
Patrick Quinn, Ned's uncle by marriage, had set out to
do their nephew grave bodily harm, if not actual murder.

On 26 August in the evening, Hall was quietly atten-
ding his affairs in the barrack room when, hearing thun-
derous hoof beats, he looked out to see Ned rein in at
the veranda, leap from his horse and beg asylum on
the grounds that his uncle Jimmy was about to kill him.
Ned's point was given force by the fact that even then
Jimmy was alighting from his own horse to assault the
boy, so Hall intervened and demanded to know the
meaning of such conduct. James replied that, as he was
a gentleman of consistently good behaviour, his conduct
was of no consequence to the Senior Constable whom
he invited forthwith to place his nose in his posterior.
It does not appear whose posterior was specified in this
gentlemanly concourse, but Hall took umbrage, further
words were exchanged and the Senior Constable proceeded to seek the assistance of his coadjutor who
rejoiced in the name of Archdeacon, in order to effect
the arrest of James. Handcuffs, revolvers, stirrup irons,
swear words, oaths, much dust and noise all became
involved in the subsequent events, which Ned surveyed
from the safety of the barracks. One result of this was
the trial of Patrick on the charge of cutting and wounding
Hall who, nonetheless, was sufficiently recovered to

attend to his nuptials in Melbourne a fortnight later. Patrick himself was given ample time to consider the wisdom of brandishing a stirrup iron on or around the person of a constable, as his sentence was three years of hard labour at Beechworth.[13] James escaped with a three-month penalty and Ned was given a lesson in how to deal with a constable under provocation. Again it was a case of a family feud spilling over into the courts and served further to illustrate the increasing inability of the family to manage its own affairs. Finally it helped to alienate Ned from the older members of the clan, and Pat Quinn in particular never forgave his nephew for the affair, while Maggie Quinn and her infants mourned the absence of a husband and father.

Constable Hall returned to Greta with his bride at the end of September and determined that it and its surrounding districts would be tranquil and decent as befitted its status as the abode of newly-weds such as they. Violence, indecency, uncouth and unbecoming language and behaviour were all to be eschewed, but vigilance was required to ensure that all such manifestations of baseness be kept in check. Such was especially the case in respect of the lad Edward Kelly and all that ill assortment of vagabonds who lived in and about Mrs Kelly's shanty four miles away. The constable was wont to be up and about, and especially to listen to those whose tongues were loosened by drink at O'Brien's, and O'Brien himself was amongst such ones. In such a manner it came to the constable that Ned was planning a summer devoted to idleness and perhaps worse in the bush, accompanied by a certain Allan Loury, who also went by the surnames of Davis and Cook. To add further flavour to this tale it was rumoured that firearms were spoken of in connection

with the expedition to the bush, but whether it was intended that the two miscreants were to direct the same
against the local fauna or whether they were to breach
the Queen's peace in a more serious manner was not
known.[14] One thing was certain to the good constable.
Greta and even the bush would be better places were
young Kelly to find a more suitable residence during
the coming summer. The presence in the township of a
former policeman, Jeremiah McCormack, and his wife
Margaret, offered the possibility of arranging a respectable place for Ned to live.

It was so wet in the late spring of 1870 that the ground
in the swamp country became so sodden that, it was
claimed, the ducks were in danger of being bogged.[15]
McCormack, being a hawker and hence free from the
requirement of keeping strict appointments, decided to
wait it out in Greta while Ben Gould, another hawker,
had no option as he became so bogged near Mrs Kelly's
that he abandoned his waggon and retired to the shanty
in hope of 'finer or dryer weather'.[16] Things did not
improve and in desperation the Benalla paper took to
alliteration with 'more rain; more floods; more damage;
more destruction' and a good deal more of the same,
while out at Greta the mosquitoes waxed fat on the hides
of man and beasts, horses strayed on unfenced properties and tempers became more frayed.

It all ended up in a fracas with McCormack accusing
Ned of stealing his strayed horse, Ned striking McCormack who had doubted his word, Ben Gould devising
a deep meanness which covered the passing of a parcel
to Mrs McCormack in which the testicles of a calf lay
wrapped in a note of low and vulgar description. Ned's
involvement was peripheral to that of Gould, but it was
Ned whom Senior Constable Hall, mindful as ever of the

desirability of keeping the peace in Greta, hauled in
to Wangaratta charged with assault on the person of
Jeremiah and insulting behaviour to his wife Margaret.
The lad was fifteen, but was represented before the court
as being nineteen and as following the vocation of a
'tramp', although in respect of his place of origin it was
recognized that he was a 'native'. Though Ned claimed
extreme provocation, he admitted having struck McCormack, which brought him three months. Even in court
no one asserted that he had castrated the calf, written
the note or passed the parcel to Mrs McCormack; he had,
if anything, been unwilling to co-operate in the act, and
when given the parcel by Gould he had handed it to
a young Lloyd boy who had given it to Mrs McCormack.
Nonetheless even partial complicity in such indecencies
in a district where animals' testicles were as common-
place as ducks on the swamp was sufficient to excite
the disapproval of the law, especially were one a Kelly.
Another three months was added to the first charge and
Ned went off to spend the summer breaking stones in
that place where men had used the beauty of stone to
create a prison at Beechworth. The fact that he was not
then sixteen, and that he was serving time on his first
conviction was no cause for mitigating the severity of
his sentence, for Ned, in the minds of those who held
responsibility for good order in Victoria, was a criminal
and at that an incorrigible one.[17] Constable Hall for his
part went home to Greta rejoicing, not merely in the fact
that he could look forward to a Christmas of peaceful,
wedded bliss, but also for the £2 reward he had been
given for so expediting the detention of the lad from the
shanty on the creek. As for Ellen Kelly it was certainly
one less mouth to feed, but it increased her dependence
on others as well as on Jim and Dan.

While Ned whiled his time away and learnt the art
of survival in Beechworth, Superintendent Francis
Augustus Hare wondered when Senior Constable Hall
would redeem his promise not to let that particular
young rascal run long, wild and free in his native hills.
Riding with Superintendent Nicolson and Hall on their
way to a pleasant evening with squatter McBean, Hare
impressed upon Hall the need for something more to the
point than a mere bagatelle such as six months' recreation in Beechworth, and Hall gave his word to deliver
the lad safely up at the first possible opportunity after
his release.[18] The months went by and Ned was freed,
so Hare waited eagerly for further word from the custodian of the law in little Greta. Meanwhile he basked in
the affection and esteem of his superior and patron Captain Standish, and gave little thought to the days of his
own youth when, newly arrived from South Africa, he
had rejoiced in deceiving the gold-field's police as to
his non-possession of a licence. Since those days the
superintendent had become an upright member of
society, beginning with his own promotion to lieutenant
in the Victoria Police at the age of twenty-four and rising
ever since to prominence. Old Harry Power was safely
put away and it was high time to see to his cub. The
Superintendent did not have long to wait, for his Senior
Constable at Greta was an assiduous man whose word,
in relation at least to the detention of Ned, would not
lightly be broken.

South from Greta, Mount Samaria beside the Broken
River marked the high ridges of the Strathbogies, and
beyond them stood the township of Mansfield. In 1871
it still bustled with activity although the golden days
were gone; it boasted a doctor, a hospital, several pubs
and even a resident poet who declaimed the glories of

'sweet Mansfield' to an appreciative audience on
21 March of that year, and was able to read his verses
on the following day in the newly founded *Mansfield
Guardian*.[19] Over and above these attractions the town
lay claim to a resident yahoo of local fame named Isaiah
Wright.

Born in Dublin in 1850, Wright was a Protestant by
religion, a farmer by profession, a horseman by vocation
and an appropriator of others' steeds by inclination.[20]
But despite his weakness for horseflesh, his general row-
diness with drink taken, and his willingness to fight all
and sundry at the drop of a hat, Isaiah and his deaf
brother, known as Dummy, were well liked in and about
Mansfield where the inhabitants took a certain mild
pleasure in the flamboyant but harmless behaviour of
these rough but innocent young hoodlums. In March
1871 Isaiah chanced to pass by Maindample Park near
Mansfield and then his eyes happened to fall upon the
graceful figure of a white-faced chestnut mare in a paddock. The fact that she belonged to the postmaster at
Mansfield was a mere trifle to Isaiah who did not intend
to steal her, but merely to take a turn through the countryside with her and win the envy of his acquaintances by
the beauty of his steed. Thus horsed, Isaiah betook himself to the neighbourhood of Glenrowan and in due
course came to Greta to visit Ned's brother-in-law, Alexander Gunn, who held a small selection nearby to Ellen
Kelly. Being young, unemployed and full of good spirits,
Isaiah fell in easily with the local lads, amongst whom
was Ned, released from Beechworth after four months
of good conduct and rejoicing in his freedom, but aware
that he was still bound over to keep the peace for twelve
months. Ned and Isaiah struck up an immediate mate-
ship and spent a day looking for the chestnut mare which

had strayed away on the roads. Isaiah eventually decided that he was in a hurry to return home, so he asked Ned for a loan of a horse and it was agreed that Ned, thus rendered horseless, could have the use of the mare if he found her and Isaiah would eventually return to claim her. Isaiah made no mention of the fact that the mare was merely on 'loan', but back in Mansfield the postmaster had informed the police of his loss and hence she was advertised in the *Police Gazette* in order that the local constabulary could keep an eye out for her.[21]

The Senior Constable had devoted himself to the pursuit of young Kelly from the moment he appeared home. At hand he had an old lag named James Murdock who was happy to collaborate in the betrayal of the lad. Through Murdock, Hall was informed that Ned had ridden to Wangaratta on a mare in which the Senior Constable ought to take an interest, so a trap was laid for Murdock to hold Ned in conversation at the Greta bridge on his return home and thus facilitate his arrest by Hall. Meanwhile Ned enjoyed himself in Wangaratta. He put up at Peter Martin's Star Hotel and allowed the publican's daughters to ride the mare up and down the town, totally unaware that she was a wanted animal, because, as Ned said, she was branded 'as plain as the hands on a town clock' and it would have been senseless of him to have thus paraded the animal under the very noses of the police had he known her to be stolen. Hall was determined to bring in Ned himself, so did nothing to advise his fellow officers in the township while he thirsted expectantly for Ned's return. Murdock duly played his pretty part, Hall lied to Ned that he was required to come to the police barracks to sign fictitious documents and, upon Ned's refusal to dismount, Hall threw him to the ground and then attempted to shoot him dead three times with a revolver. The little town grew still as the shots rang in the street and a group of men watched while Ned thrashed the Constable with his spurs, but assisted Hall to manacle him while the constable pistol-whipped the boy about the head. Blood lay in the dust and Ned's clothes were caked in it, but he had not run for long, as Hall had promised his superior.

Barclay was an upright superintendent of police and he found the attempt by Hall to murder a sixteen-year-old boy somewhat alarming, while Captain Standish pondered the problem in Melbourne as he read Hall's account of the affair. He deemed it advisable to warn Hall not to cause medical expenses recklessly 'the next time he breaks the head of an Irishman' and contented himself with that. Nonetheless justice needed to be done and such a gross offender of the decencies of ordered society as Kelly had to be brought down by fair means or foul even though he would bear the marks of Hall's assault for the rest of his life. Hall was a perjurer as well as a uniformed thug, Murdock a paid informer (in this case £20 by Hall), and the Wangaratta bench compliant, because it had been borne upon the minds of many who possessed material things that those who threatened their peaceful holding of the same were a threat and a nuisance to be disposed of according to the law. The Beechworth General Sessions of 3 August 1871 processed as fine a travesty of justice as was likely to be seen in that solemn arena in any given year, for Kelly and Isaiah were brought up for trial, charged with stealing the lovely chestnut. It mattered little that Ned could call upon his former host, the governor of the prison, to testify that he could not have stolen the mare because he was a guest in that institution on the day she was stolen. It mattered less that Isaiah, spoken well of by some of the decent citizens of Mansfield, who admired their local boy, was given eighteen months, not for stealing but for illegal use of the mare. What then could it matter that, having heard out the perjured duo Hall and Murdock, and the jury having concluded that although Ned could not have stolen the mare, he had nonetheless received her feloniously, the judge spat out his foulness by giving Ned three years with hard labour? Could Hall add to all this? Yes, a little was left in the way of manhood out and about the hut at Greta in the person of Alexander Gunn: but he too, informed against and brought before the court on perjured evidence constructed by Hall, received three years' hard labour for the alleged theft of another horse. Across the oceans there were men dying because they were 'sworn to bring about a revolution that will regenerate the world' but at the Eleven Mile no one spoke yet of resistance to the authority they lived under.[22]

Down the Sydney road in the city Standish fawned upon his toady Hare, studied the racing form and totted up his gambling assets while he thought about the wisdom of transferring Edward Hall to another place in which to wreak his mischief. The Captain consoled himself with the thought that soon he would be within a day's comfortable journey of most of his men, because the tentacles of steel were already reaching out into the bush, to link all that world to Melbourne as the hub of the new civilization with its watchword of progress as befitted the capital of a colony of over 700,000 souls. At the home on the Eleven Mile it was spring, and the rains brought forth from the earth all things new, while the wattle bloomed again in gentle gold and scented the quiet air. In that shanty sorrow reigned, as women grieved fruitlessly for things that no spring could ever now renew. Out across the land in the evenings the plover was heard shrilling a call of defence of its young, but in the poor dwelling of Ellen Kelly it sounded as a mockery, for the ramparts of her home had fallen before triumphant powers.

The Passing of Boyhood 5

Williamstown was wedded to the waters of a calm and gentle sea which embraced her on all three sides as she reached out into the deeper parts, with her arm called Point Gellibrand. In that stately place, where civic pride and memories of her origins in the early days of the settlement had combined to give much grace and gentility, the winter of 1873 was as other winters. The fogs, as they rolled in from the bay, rendered mild and heavy the salted air, and the horns sounded in the distance with tones both of comfort and restrained authority. Through the mists off Gellibrand the ghostly figures of ships were seen, and to the upright citizens of the town they were a reminder that all men were not as they, with freedom, respect and dignity to clothe their inner selves, and warmth, sound food and gracious gardens to solace their mortal frames. The senses of the men of Williamstown, who knew the sea and her ways and who went upon her in their vessels, were affronted at the aspect of these ships. They were stunted and cut down, with the majesty of their masts struck from them, and over all bedecked in a hideous yellow, as befitted objects whose purposes had been thwarted to such an unholiness. Ships, to men who go in them, are places within a greater space in which there is the freedom of a universe to be explored and touched upon. Not so these ships – for they were hulks. Their purpose was to stay fixed, and confine within their narrow bellies the men to whom society had said that they were unworthy to come and go as others in the land. One of these ships bore the holy name of *Sacramento* and thus flung back at the centuries its pagan laughter, for it was no sign of man's freedom from an ancient curse, but rather it was a symbol of Caesar's state spelling bondage and never grace. To the *Sacramento* on 25 June in the winter of 1873 the person numbered 10926 came. In another world he was known as Edward Kelly.

Ned had spent two birthdays in the golden place at Beechworth. There life had not all been hard even though it was a prison because there were still the mountains with their crisp air and, at times, a visit from his family and friends. But in the summer of 1873, soon after his eighteenth birthday, it was decided to foster his education in a more advanced school of criminality. They sent him down to Pentridge, and after four months he went across the bay to the *Sacramento* and later, in August of that year, he was deposited on the shore at a place called, more appropriately, the Battery, for the boy who grew to manhood as the guest of Her Gracious Majesty bore more in his spirit than outwardly the signs from the battering he had taken from Constable Hall's revolver.[1] In these foul places of the metropolis there was much harshness, cursing, hatred and revenge. No woman walked there, no gentle word or soft caress was

heard or felt, no mother came to strengthen or comfort.
In the long nights a boy needed those things as he
struggled with the pangs of his own awakened individu-
ality and felt the surging of a sexuality that was denied
the normalcy of learning the ways of a man with a maid.
It became an existence of mechanical forbearance as
day followed day, and the day of release, in the natural
course of events, like the tides that lapped at the hulks,
would come in its turn.

Ned had learnt that to revolt was useless because the
law would win out in the end and even the passing of
two plugs of tobacco lengthened the period of servitude
by seven days.[2] Nonetheless docility had its own reward
for on 2 February 1874 he was free by remission, having
served two and a half years to expiate the crime of feloniously receiving the pretty mare of the Mansfield postmaster. The colony of Victoria paid him £2 10s 11d for
working fruitfully on the roads and in its prison work-
shops, but the price he paid for that which he cryptically
called 'experience' was known only to Ned, and perhaps
to the mother at the Eleven Mile to whom he went in February 1874. On this occasion he came home in the new
form of transport that ran beside the old road, for the
railway had come through to Wodonga on the river in
November 1873.[3]

During his absence there were many changes in the
district which had ramifications for the whole of the clan,
including those on the King. A police station had been
set up near Glenmore and from a safe distance of half
a mile, Constables Robinson and Boland had kept a
watchful eye on its inhabitants who were allegedly
engaged in constant thievery of horses and cattle.[4] The
two zealots did their best and even suffered the inconvenience of having their stables burnt down in the night,
but they failed to lay a single charge against the Quinns.

Life in that valley became so tedious that in April 1872 they professed it as their opinion that Glenmore did not need their presence for there was no crime there, nor even anything that required their interference whatsoever. This opinion was not pleasing to Captain Standish. He remained convinced that Glenmore was the rendezvous of a very troublesome section of what he was pleased to call 'the criminal class' and to his tidy mind and sense of propriety such a fact, based on mental association, weighed more heavily than the observation of his constables that this particular group did not appear to be behaving criminally.[5]

The clan however did number one in its ranks whose propensity to acts of violence, increasingly associated with drink which perhaps bordered on a sickness rather than a state, was more and more apparent. When the Captain thought of the Quinns, it was understandable that his mind would turn to Jimmy, who had followed his altercation with Constable Hall in 1870 with acts of chronic savagery in 1872, including an attack with an iron auger on a timber splitter called John Page and another of violent assault against the person of his own sister, Margaret. He received four and a half years on these charges and in the following year another two for an old charge of assault which had taken place at the Greta races in 1865. As a result James was safely put away for the ensuing several years, and, in institutions such as Beechworth, Pentridge and Geelong he incurred the displeasure of his mentors for such indiscretions as having a wool comforter around his neck, concealing chops and bread on his person and sitting improperly at supper.[6] When James entered the portals of Pentridge in May 1873, after a stint at Beechworth, the governor of that institution may have wondered whether he was presiding over a family residence especially set up for the benefit of the clan. Uncle James Kelly was there eking out his years on the arson charge, Ned was there in transit to the *Sacramento* and John Lloyd, now an old man at fifty, was a new arrival to do four years for an act that was a combination of revenge and hatred, and resulted in the killing of one horse as repayment for the impounding of six.[7] Finally there was a mere slip of a boy there and curiously, of them all, he was the only one doing time for the crime with which the whole clan was allegedly tainted in the mind of Captain Standish – cattle stealing.

Captain Standish had little difficulty in replacing Senior Constable Hall with a suitable person who would carry on the good work at Greta and ensure that the inhabitants of the shanty on the Eleven Mile were kept in good order. It mattered little that all those of man's estate were already disposed of because, with such a brood, it was inevitable that further trouble would brew, so a constable of determination and imagination had to be found. Across the valleys at Belvoir, Constable Ernest Flood had been giving the good Captain pause for thought, for were he to believe the whispers that came his way the Constable, although in all other respects a worthy member of his force, was a liar, a thief, a drunkard and perhaps other things as well. The Captain was loath to accept such accusations and the Constable quick to deny them, but it was probably wise to change his station, and were it indeed the case that Flood lacked something in respect of probity and sobriety he would, at all events, feel at home at Greta. It was not in the Captain's mind to set a thief to catch his fellows, but in such matters a realistic approach had to be taken, and, whatever else it was clear that the worthy Constable was wise in the ways of the world. And so it was that in August

1871 Constable Flood came to Greta with his wife and family, where he was instructed for a time in the intricacies of his impending charge by Hall, and a month later, promoted now to Senior Constable, he took command of that country, its swollen creeks, its flinging hills and its reputedly wayward people.[8]

It did not take long for the Senior Constable to get into his stride and within a few weeks he secured his first prizes in the persons of Jim and Dan. On 9 September he arrested them on a charge of the illegal use of a horse which he had caught them riding. The facts that they were little boys of ten and eleven, and that Jim was working on odd jobs for the owner of the horse, who made no claim that it was being illegally used, did not deter Flood from his fixity of purpose. The important thing was that they were Kellys, to be curbed at all costs, so off they were hauled to Wangaratta to spend two nights in the lock-up and then to be brought before a magistrate who summarily dismissed the charge as ludicrous.[9] To Flood it was, nonetheless, an important step as he had firmly established his authority, even over the children of the district.

The mother of all these scallywags, Ellen Kelly, was herself a source of irritation in that there was little doubt that she indulged in supplying the passerby with a sip of brandy if that was his fancy. But it was a charge that experience had proved hard to sheet home, as most customers were reluctant to admit to the identity of the vendor, and even magistrates were prepared to recognize that one so placed as Ellen had to eke out a miserable existence somehow. Flood noticed that there was another vulnerable target at the Eleven Mile. He was William Williamson, of English birth and known as Brickey because his trade was that of a layer of same.

Brickey was not especially adept at much else and it
was not hard to have him sent to Pentridge for an
eighteen month sojourn on the charge that he aided and
abetted an assault.[10]

Yet if the men and striplings of Greta were of interest
to Ernest Flood at least one of the womenfolk was of even
greater interest. Annie Gunn was a grass widow with
her husband languishing in prison since August 1871,
so that by the time of Flood's arrival she was alone, with
only Ellen to advise or protect her at the Eleven Mile.
By January 1872 Flood and Annie were so well
acquainted that Flood, concerned as to her wardrobe,
made out an open order to a seamstress for a black silk
dress for her, to cost about £5. In the home of the seamstress, Mrs Short of Benalla, he conducted himself in an
exceedingly familiar manner with Annie and so dis-
gusted Mrs Short and her husband James that the latter
saw fit to bring the matter to the attention of Standish,
who ordered Flood to be cautioned for his 'intimacy with
a notorious woman'. To what extent this advice was
accepted is unclear, except that on 9 November a child,
Anna, was born of Annie, and Alexander the Scot of
Edinburgh, still residing at Pentridge, was assuredly not
the father. Annie had eighteen hours after the birth to
repent of whatever misdemeanour had brought her to
this pass. The family buried her in the garden at Eleven
Mile Creek and thus Ellen Kelly, Annie's mother and
grandmother of the new Anna, was unable to present
herself in the Benalla Police Court on that day, 12 November. Flood had charged her with receiving a stolen
saddle, but the magistrate dismissed the case as worthless. Six years later Annie's brother, Ned, had not dismissed those matters from his mind for, when he stood
over the body of a policeman at Stringybark Creek, he

said that he would have liked Ernest Flood to be present in which case he would have roasted him on the fire.[11]

Out at Greta only one man was left by late 1872 – a young Australian-born labourer of twenty-three who came from Donnybrook near Beveridge and who had known the Kellys since childhood. Bill Skillion was his name and he stayed around the shanty because his fancy had been taken with the blossoming girlhood of young Maggie. Bill was to wait and indulge his fancy as he pleased, for in February 1873 Flood had bigger prey in his sights in the shape of another Kelly stripling, and hence Jim's turn had truly come.

Young Tom Lloyd had decided that, as his father needed legal advice to escape the charge levelled against him of horse killing, the simplest method of procuring the means to pay a lawyer would be by selling his father's cattle. He went a step further in that he included in the small herd two heifers belonging to George Chandler, a publican of Winton, and two steers, the property of James Cook who farmed in the same locality, and it is not all that unlikely that he thought they were strays because there were many such in the district. Thinking it unwise that he personally ought to involve himself in the sale, Tommy approached a seventeen-year-old youth named Thomas Williams to act on his behalf. Nothing loath Williams turned to young Jim Kelly, then aged thirteen, and asked him to help drove the cattle while he would attend to their sale. Here was the very chance Flood was expecting, and the two offenders faced the Beechworth Circuit Court where Judge Williams sat ready for action. It was Flood's imaginative twist to these events that put the two lads in even greater jeopardy, for he had decided that two atrocious acts of stealing had been perpetrated, on

which they had to be charged separately. Williams, the
offender, carefully explained to Williams on his bench
that he had led James Kelly into this enormity, and in
a scarcely broken voice James assented that such was
the case while James Dixon, a farmer who bought two
of the steers, testified that the older boy had transacted
the deal, while the younger had done no more than herd
the cattle. To the judge all this was mere quibbling.
Clearly he was dealing with a deep infection that was
festering in the land, and he could see no distinction
between the offenders, nor indeed was he minded to
take account of their tenderness of years, despite the
plea of the jury that he so do. He waxed eloquent on
the perversity that had led these criminals to go maraud-
ing throughout the countryside, stealing beasts with
reckless abandon, and he deplored the fact that the
legal system prevented his ordering them to be flogged.
Nevertheless he had another remedy at hand with which
to curb their youthful excesses and he proceeded to sentence each of them to five years of penal servitude.[12] Perhaps Senior Constable Flood went down to his house
satisfied, because in April 1873 the walls of Pentridge
held seven men of the clan in its embrace and Annie's
tongue was forever silenced. The blighted boyhood of
a thirteen-year-old certainly meant little to him and
there is poignancy in the fact that Jim's transgression
of greatest moment against the state during the long
years of his criminal apprenticeship was his possessing
paper with writing on it. For this the authorities added
a mere two days to his sentence, mindful perhaps that
his record stated that, while he could not write, he could
read just a little.[13]

  The arrest of young Jim, and thus the removal of the
only source of male strength, even though merely embry-

onic, left Ellen Kelly at the Eleven Mile bereft of support on a close family level. Flood had done his work with impunity and, as Ned later remarked, he was so competent that, unlike Hall and many other policemen, he did not have to 'hire cads' to achieve his objective.[14] His presence was a constant threat to the scattered remnants of the clan, and Ellen feared for the future because it was also apparent that the powerful squatting interests in the district were bent on her removal. Indeed McBean, the squatter of Kilfera, had gone so far as to try to rid the area of Ellen, whom he regarded as a 'head centre' in local mischief, by forcing her off the thin acres by the creek.[15] It was into this atmosphere of apprehension and dependence, which had been rendered even more painful to Ellen by the death of little Ellen, the daughter born of her passing union with the boundary rider, that George King stepped late in 1872 when Ellen was also grieving over Annie's death and there was another infant mouth to feed. George was a plausible Californian, young, healthy and ready to work, but with nowhere to go and Greta was as good as anywhere else provided he could get a feed and a warm bed with perhaps a drop of grog. A man was needed and George, in physical characteristics, was at least that, so by March 1873, when Jim was awaiting trial, Ellen was again with child. To the worthy and the upright such promiscuity was deplorable, but they could easily overlook the fact that here was a helpless woman with a full table of children to be fed, clothed and protected, olive branches whom God and man appeared to have forgotten and whom all fate derided, but for whom Ellen was, in this world, responsible.

Perhaps Ellen's or Annie's example was sufficient to persuade Maggie that marriage was a more desirable

form of union than a mere passing alliance. In any case
a bridal party set out from the Eleven Mile and rode into
Benalla on 17 September 1873. Ellen was there to give
her consent to Maggie's union with Bill Skillion but in
this, as in so much else, the bonds of the past were broken
for Ellen had heard her union rendered blessed in the
sonorous Latin tones of the old church of Ireland's centuries, while Maggie and Bill heard a new thing, as
William Gould pronounced them man and wife in a version wrought by the Primitive Methodists, who were
primitive indeed but scarcely in antiquity. Six weeks
later a child again wailed at the shanty, though it was
not of the new bride but of her mother that this infant
Ellen was born from her union with the Californian.[16]
These matters were all transacted as Ned was moving
from the *Sacramento* to the Battery by the quiet waters
of the bay to the south.

The homecoming in February 1874 was to a household
in which Bill Skillion added some stability, even if the
presence of a new half-sister indicated the continued
and heightened personal anguish of Ned's mother,
while the grave in the garden and little Anna in her cot
gave Ned much food for thought. Ned also noticed that
Flood's coming meant that his horses, 'thirty head of the
very best horses the land could produce', had been
reduced to one. The rest, according to Ned, had mostly
been stolen by Flood and sold 'to the navvies on the railway line' but the line had been completed and the men
were all gone, so redress was impossible. Gone also was
Flood who had found the police station an unfitting
dwelling for his family and also, having disposed of all
the available males in the clan, there was little to do,
so he asked to be transferred to Oxley where there was
a lot still to be done to clean up the district and win better

chances of promotion. He did not last long at Oxley, and
Ned gave it as his opinion that he had been removed
from the district because he took to horse stealing on
an equally grand scale there. A local squatter, John
Brown who had been for six years president of the shire,
presumably thought it sufficient to suffer the inroads
made on his horses and cattle by the local criminal
classes without the forces of the law adding to his discomfort. He petitioned for Flood's removal and Standish
was impressed enough to consider his dismissal, but
relented, so the Senior Constable remained in the
force.[17]

There was one useful thing Ned could do at the Eleven
Mile which was easily achieved as George King was
not the man to brush aside a demand that he make an
honest woman of Ellen. Again a wedding party set out
and William Gould again did his primitive thing in Benalla on 19 February 1874, with the result that Ellen Kelly
became Ellen King, though she was never to be known
as such except on official documents. George was now
twenty-five while Ellen was forty-two although she put
herself down as thirty-six. Of the four major participants
in the ceremony, the couple themselves, the son-in-law
Bill Skillion and the son Ned, only the latter could sign
his name, nor indeed could either bride or groom tell
the place where they were born. In thus wise was the
memory of Red honoured, for his son was not to stand
apart while the wife of Beveridge and Avenel bore
another's children without the other's name. No priest
entered into these transactions, not because the faith
was gone, but because the Irish shame was there, and
Mr Gould, who knew nothing of Roman niceties, did a
good and gracious thing for those of another flock in
his residence at Barkly Street, Benalla. They went forth

from his home to register the birth of Ellen, hitherto not
known officially to the colony of Victoria as a citizen, but
now able to bear her father's name. Back at Greta it
was immediately clear to Ned that, with a brother-in-law
and a stepfather in residence, young Dan would not
have to bear an ill-proportioned burden. He got on his
horse and went into the hills until he came to the neighbourhood of Mansfield. He thereby deprived the historian of indulging a whimsical fancy by having him
play with the Benalla Football Club, formed in April 1874
by 'lovers of this manly cold weather game'. They adopted the rules of the Carlton Club and played their first
game on Saturday 26 April.[18]

The years in prison had brought a calmness to Ned
that reflected his conviction, brought home to him by
sheer necessity, that the days of his hellion youth, such
as they had been, were over. It was clear that into the
distant future he was a marked man, and Flood had
been quick to remind him of that fact when they chanced
to meet at O'Brien's pub at Greta. Flood threatened that
if he transgressed again he would do him greater violence than Hall had done, which threat Ned would jus-
tifiably have interpreted as of murderous intent.[19] The
police had clearly won their battle against the clan,
which had been reduced to a mere remnant, and Ned
knew that to step outside the law now, even marginally,
was tantamount to sentencing himself to prison indefi-
nitely.

It was thus a chastened young man who applied for
work as a timber feller and bullock driver at a mill owned
by partners called Saunders and Rule. Later he worked
at another mill run by Heach and Dockendorff at
Killawarra, a few miles north-east of Wangaratta. He
was well spoken of by his workmates who regarded him

as 'warm-hearted, but rather impulsive, quiet, very
unobtrusive and an excellent axeman and very industrious'.[20] He met up again with Isaiah Wright who had married his first cousin Bridget Lloyd and something of the
old days returned. Wild Wright was a tall, strong, bony
man with a local reputation as a fighter of note and,
in August 1874, at Beechworth, a bout was arranged
between himself and Ned for the unofficial champion-
ship of the northeast. They went twenty rounds of bare
fisted barbarism and Ned won. Not surprisingly, the victor became the target of drunks who fancied themselves
as pugilists, and one such taunted Ned at the Killawarra
races. Ned took it quietly, even when struck twice by the
man, but warned him to desist. After the third blow Ned
turned and all the impetuosity of animal youth poured
out, so that in short order the man was scarcely recogniz-
able. After that he was left alone and local publicans
were grateful when he quelled disturbances on their
premises with the mere threat of interference.[21]

Towards the end of 1875 Ned returned to the Greta
district where he and Dan helped build a house from
granite quarried in the hills, and later Saunders and
Rule showed their trust in him by employment as their
overseer at another mill they had taken over, situated
not far from his mother's home. He was earning good
wages, never less than £2 10s per week, and gradually
he had become a well-liked, respected member of the
community. But work was not always easy to get and
when, in July 1876, the line from Wangaratta to Beechworth was completed the mill cut out and Ned was on
the loose. George King, father now of a second child
called John, was in the same position so he and Ned,
joined at the time by young Dan, took to prospecting
back in the hills, and in and around the King River. It

was a precarious existence dependent upon luck and some little skill and its very nature brought on the old wanderlust, the hand-to-mouth and devil-may-care attitudes which steady work since 1874 had helped to quell.[22] In the background lurked the ever present shadow of the police and Ned complained that he was still 'hounded down' and that if a bullock was missing in the district the constables would visit his mother's home, rousing its inmates in the middle of the night and generally making themselves obnoxious.[23]

Some of the Pentridge residents were back in the district although Alexander Gunn was heard of no more. Brickey Williamson returned to the Eleven Mile and old John Lloyd was discharged in April 1875 upon the authorization of 'His Excellency the Governor for special services rendered to the Police', but what precisely those services entailed was never clarified; young Jim came out in 1876 having grown to man's estate in prison and having earned £5 2s 11d for his three and a half years' work on behalf of the common good, while Dan had taken to riding the countryside with a group of young and generally harmless rascals who affected a kind of gear, with hat straps under their noses and bright sashes round their waists, and were known as the Greta mob.[24] The signs were not generally favourable and although things had been quiet at the Greta police station since Flood's departure in late 1873, Constable Hugh Thom, who arrived in August 1876, possibly wondered whether complacency was justified given the apparent tameness of the clan. He would have been even further justified in pondering on such matters had he been aware of a friendship which even then was being cemented by common bonds of felonry behind the walls of Beechworth prison.

From Clan to Mob 6

Back in March 1864 when Inspector Gilbert Brown rode down the slope of the hills out of Beechworth he came into a world which in the space of a few years had seen a transformation. The faint wind still sighed in the native pines and the warblers sang softly in the stringybark, but the people of the old tribes had gone, leaving only their drawings on cave walls and dim memories amongst the white men who succeeded them. Since 1852 thousands had poured in and out of those valleys, laying bare to the ribs the earth, stripping the slopes and hills and diverting streams. Towns had sprung up, fortunes had been made and often dissipated, and great visions dreamt. It was from there that Robert O'Hara Burke had left his police charge, and his unrequited love for an opera singer, to go off recklessly into the heart of the continent and walk upon its face to the northern point, before he lay down to die of hunger and frustrated hope. But at the Woolshed hope still held up, for it was a thriving place with 140 business houses of all kinds and

those scattered races of the earth were still represented
with the Chinese, who worked over the ground and took
the rich leavings of the whites, numbered amongst
them.[1]

A seven-year-old was in the second grade at the Catholic school when Gilbert Brown inspected it in March
and he passed in reading only, but when the Inspector
came back in October a great improvement had taken
place both in the boy and in the school, for Joseph Byrne
passed in all his tests, discipline was good, the books
were in adequate supply and Cornelius Donoghue, the
teacher, was happy with Brown's report. Young Byrne
progressed annually until the fifth grade in 1869, and
never failed to satisfy the examiners in every subject.
Other children came and went at the Woolshed whose
destinies were woven with that of Joe, for there were
Sherritts there, and Wicks, and a James Wallace who
was the best student of them all.[2] In the following year
Paddy Byrne, Joe's father, died, leaving a widow three
months pregnant with seven children to look after.

Nearby to the Byrne home on the Woolshed there was
a Chinese camp to which the quick-witted Joe often went
and listened, fascinated, to their tongue, so that in time
he acquired a modest mastery of its mysteries, and won
the trust of those who had learnt to fear the whiteman
since the riots on the Buckland in the golden days. He
learnt also that life on the fields, as the gold ran thin
and the towns wound down, was a matter of survival
as best one could and, unlike James Wallace who took
to teaching, as did Isaac Isaacs in Beechworth over the
hills, Joe took to the ranges, often accompanied by Aaron
Sherritt. Aaron was a year older than Joe and his father,
John, had a background that recurred often in Victoria
in the gold-rush period for he had been a member of

the feared Royal Irish Constabulary. Despite the difference in religion and outlook amongst their parents, the
two boys became close friends. They were not especially
particular as to their use of others' horses, and when
food ran short at home on the Woolshed a stray beast
could always be rounded up in a distant valley and
slaughtered for meat. They became expert horsemen
and knew their country as the larrikins of Collingwood
knew every inch of their alleys. To Joe and Aaron no track
was impenetrable and long days and cold nights in the
mountains made them as hardy as saplings growing
from a rockface. Joe had the Irish ballad blood in him,
and even in those early days he versified and sang as
they rode together in the ranges. They got to know also
the ways of the law, and how to evade them, so that on
the odd occasion that they appeared in the courts they
escaped with a fine or an acquittal. They soon discovered that in his own trade Mounted Constable Michael
Edward Ward was as clever as they were in theirs, and
in June 1876 Joe and Aaron had to answer a charge
brought by Ward. They were in the alleged unlawful
possession of the carcass of a cow, part of which Joe had
brought home to his widowed mother, Margaret Byrne,
who still resided on the Woolshed, although Joe now took
up residence wherever it suited him. The magistrate
quickly decided that a permanent abode for at least six
months would be more in order for these two young men,
so they learnt to break stones in Beechworth prison
where Joe passed notes to the free world requesting
tobacco, and Aaron found the toughness acquired in
the mountains helped him withstand the rigours of the
government establishment. In all respects they behaved
themselves, so that with one month's remission they were
out and free again well before Christmas.[3]

When Joe came out he met Jim Kelly and they rode
down to Greta together, where Joe made the acquaintance of Ned and young Dan. There was an immediate
recognition of kindred spirits between the two elder men
who shared a taste for more refined ways of dress,
behaviour and speech than the younger members of the
Greta mob although their dislike for the police was
mutual. It was indeed heightened by the story of the
death of Father Hely, which in late 1876 was on the lips
of many in the northeast, and in Catholic circles caused
widespread resentment. William Hely was an Irish priest
of about forty who wandered the world and came to
Wangaratta in April 1876. Unhinged perhaps in mind,
certainly afflicted with that weakness for alcohol that
no mark of ordination or Roman collar can disguise,
Father Hely rode off into the night on 24 May. He was
seen in and about the Riverina in the next few months,
still clutching to the tattered outward symbols of his
priesthood, until he came one night to the Belmore Inn
at Deepwater on the old road from Narrandera to
Wagga Wagga. It was 6 August and a few weeks before
a man bearing scarcely any resemblance to Hely had
stolen a quantity of tobacco and clothing from a sur-
veyors' camp nearby. Two zealous members of the New
South Wales Police went in search of the felon, and
being satisfied that Hely was he, they stood outside his
room at the inn and called on him to surrender. When
he failed to open the door, possibly because the name
they called out was that of Turner, the true thief in question, they broke in and shot him in the arm, side and
belly. He died, without medication, in the Wagga
Wagga lock-up sixteen hours later. The Attorney-
General of New South Wales, William Bede Dalley, com-
mended the policemen for their chivalry and they were

acquitted of manslaughter, despite the arrest of Turner
and the establishment of the true identity of Hely.[4] Such
indiscriminate slaughter of a man totally innocent of the
paltry crime involved, gave pause for thought to those
in the northeast, and especially those about Greta who
were given to infraction of the law. It was all one with
the pattern the clan had become accustomed to from
the early days of Kilmore, a pattern which hitherto had
not resulted in death, although Ned had narrowly
escaped at the hands of Hall. But it stood there as a
lesson and a grim warning, for who could suppose that
given a heated moment the Victorian police would be
less inclined to slaughter than their fellows across the
river?

The police were constantly vigilant of the doings of
the clan and Dan appeared in Beechworth at a General
Sessions hearing in February 1877 on a charge of stealing a saddle. The judge expressed surprise that he had
ever been brought before him, as a perfectly fair account
was given which satisfactorily proved that Dan had
bought the saddle. At the same time Aaron Sherritt and
Joe Byrne were charged with assaulting a certain Ah
On, but they claimed that the gentleman had first
chased and hit Aaron with a bamboo stick.[5] Both were
found guilty and it was becoming a little difficult to pur-
sue the policy of keeping the Greta mob in order,
especially when the local civil authorities clashed with
the custodians of the law in respect of the extent to which
the clan was actually engaged in nefarious pursuits, in
particular cattle stealing. Members of the Oxley Shire
Council thought that Mrs Kelly's home was the centre
of a cattle-stealing ring, and Captain Standish conferred on the matter with Mr Graves, the local member,
who confirmed his fears and thought the solution lay

in strengthening his force at Greta. All this came as a
surprise to Inspector Brooke Smith who was in charge
of the Beechworth district, and who thought there was
no cause whatever for alarm. He admitted that the
Quinns, Lloyds and Kellys were frequently seen 'riding
about the country', a form of behaviour he did not consider abnormal. He admitted too that there was the
possibility of Ned and Isaiah Wright engaging in 'mild
bushranging' given their 'intense vanity', but he firmly
rejected the cattle-stealing charge as there was no proof
of it, nor indeed was there any cause for precipitate
action. None of this calmed the fevered brow of the Captain at his Melbourne desk, who continued to fret about
these wild ones ranging their untamed hills so he sent
Constable James Hayes to Greta to aid Thom in his laud-
able but hitherto fruitless endeavours.[6]

A thorough investigation was clearly required, so the
Chief Commissioner sent Superintendent Nicolson out
to see for himself the woman who seemed to reign over
the mob from her castle beside the creek. He found her
surrounded by daughters and little children 'in poverty
and squalor' dwelling in a wooden hut divided by
blankets and rags into five partitions. The 'notorious' Mrs
Kelly told him that her sons were away working, but gave
no idea where they were engaged in such praiseworthy
efforts, and she further asserted that she was rarely visited by her relatives. None of this comforted Nicolson who
deemed it desirable to root the whole clan, stock and
branch, out of the district. He was uneasy at the fitness
of Constable Thom for such a task, especially if perchance any member of the clan were to fall into the
clutches of the law by a foolish act and be merely treated
in 'a very ordinary manner'. Far be it that anyone should
imagine that he wanted to oppress or worry the persons

in question. No, all Nicolson wanted was that whenever
they committed even 'a paltry crime', they should be
brought to what he was pleased in his mercy to call 'justice' and as a consequence to send them, not to that
pleasant place up at Beechworth, but to Pentridge itself.
Such a way of proceeding would serve to take the 'flashness' out of these people, and if anything irritated the
decency of this particular pillar of society it was 'flashness'. Nowhere is it evident how poverty, squalor, cloth
walls, hungry mouths, unemployment, inability to obtain
fertile land, orphanhood, years spent in dreary dun-
geons in Pentridge or on hulks, had managed to engender 'flashness', but Nicolson was convinced it was there.
He furthermore ordered that the home of Ellen Kelly,
inhabited by an orphaned brood and widowed mother,
and being such a dangerous place, not be entered by
a constable acting alone. Perhaps the Superintendent
knew the calibre of his men only too well, for there were
growing girls amongst those orphans.[7]

If the police at Greta were not quite as successful as
the Captain hoped, his brethren elsewhere were
proving their mettle in a more satisfactory manner. After
his release in August 1876 young Jim Kelly had not
stayed about the Eleven Mile for long. He went off to
New South Wales and with a friend named William
Campbell, who also called himself Manly, he was suspected of stealing horses in the Tumut area. Jim had
changed his own name to Wilson, and as such he
appeared at the Wagga Wagga Quarter Sessions on
29 June 1877 charged, with Manly, of stealing two saddles, two bridles and two horses from the residents of
Wagga Wagga itself. Both were sentenced to three
years' imprisonment, so in July young Jim found himself
in Berrima Gaol where he remained for nine months until

his transfer to Darlinghurst in April 1878. It had been a brief period of freedom for James, who was now given the opportunity to complete the apprenticeship in boot-making he had commenced, aged thirteen, at the expense of the people of Victoria. In New South Wales the Kellys of Greta did not enjoy the same fame as they did in Melbourne, so the fact that the mother colony harboured such a hardened criminal as young James, known to the authorities as Wilson, went temporarily unnoticed.[8]

Back in the days of the gold-rushes a family named Hart was on its way to the Ovens only to discover that, by settling near Wangaratta, it was possible to make a living by selling the produce of their few cows and hens to the miners as they passed. With the years Richard Hart and Bridget, his wife, reared a family, one of whom was baptized Stephen. Another child was given the sweetness of Esther, but the family called her Ettie, and in 1877 she had grown to grace of form and visage. The man Edward Kelly often saw her in those happy days and his heart was moved. But they were days in which Ned was still footloose after the years of his gainful employment, and between the two there stood many shadows with only the promise or the hope that in better times to come Esther, then aged only sixteen, could look to a future with the dark one of the hills as companion.[9] As for young Stephen, the shadows had already lengthened for the promise of the child who had started under teacher Patrick McLoughlin at Wangaratta Catholic school in 1864 had not been fulfilled, and by the mid-1870s he had become one of the Greta mob so it was understandable that the police were on the watch. Like the rest of the mob, if not indeed the majority of those youths who wandered from place to place in the northeast, Stephen was not exactly careful as to whose horse he rode. But illegal use was a good, sound charge to fall back upon if it were clear that stealing could not be proved, and hence Stephen went off to Beechworth from the Wangaratta Police Court in July 1877 to serve twelve months' hard labour on three charges. Steve was only a slip of a boy, standing a mere five feet six inches, with a fresh complexion, brown hair and hazel eyes; his trade was said to be that of labourer, so it was to the advantage of the state to put his skills in that regard to better use than hitherto had apparently been the case.[10]

On Sundays the clan gathered at Ellen's place to play their rough bush sports of jumping, running and horse-riding. Even Ellen joined in the latter, as she too had become part of the new country since the landing at Port Phillip over thirty years before. She could take a hurdle with the best of them, but it was Ned who excelled them all, whether on foot or on horse. He could give any of them a start and beat them over a hundred yards. He could stand and ride on a horse's back at a pace and take a fence kneeling, he could bend down and pick up a handkerchief from the ground at full gallop and through it all he could laugh because life was young, and in the district he was respected, especially when the tale was told of his long ride to Beechworth with a child whom he found with a badly broken leg, being tended by a distracted, lonely, mother in a hut, back in the ranges. In the evenings the shanty rang to laughter, to song and verse and perhaps they even rejoiced at Bannerman's 165 runs and Australia's win over the Englishmen at Melbourne in March 1877, and hoped with the *Mansfield Guardian* to beat them in the 'old country' soon. When the fires burnt low, the quiet tones of the Rosary were heard in which Ned took his turn, for the old faith still lived despite the departures from its tenets, although, unlike the squatter, James Whitty, they were unable to offer a stained glass window to the new church of St John of the Cross consecrated by Archbishop Goold in February 1875. Some there were amongst them, like Ned and Joe Byrne, who hoped that in the end a balance would come to the scales of eternity, in recognition that those whom the law judged notorious and beyond its mercy were still the beloved children of a Creator who had sworn a covenant even with the little ones of Greta.[11]

But if there were an occasional Sunday of happiness when they rode down to the Eleven Mile, back on the King, Ned and his stepfather had not fared well at prospecting, and the visit of Nicolson to Greta began to show fruits. Ned found himself the centre of suspicion even if it were no more than over an incident as simple as running in a wild bull from the ranges and giving it to a publican, to be then accused of theft. The owner denied that he had ever accused Ned of stealing but the squatters of the district, who had picked the eyes out of the good land on the King and on the Boggy Creek and who were given to impounding the stock of the poor, began to turn on Ned. He resented bitterly the fact that, with impunity, two large landowners Whitty and Burns could impound sixty horses in a day 'all belonging to poor farmers'. The owners were then forced to leave their ploughs or harvesters, go to Oxley and find or borrow the money to redeem their stock. What enraged Ned even more was the fact that the local policeman, Michael Farrell, was a horse stealer and indeed stole one from George King. The upshot was that Ned rashly decided that there was one law for both the rich and the poor,

so he and George went into the horse-stealing business
in the grand manner. It was an easy matter to take horses
from paddocks, almost as easy as it was for the squatters
to take them from the roads. The difference lay in that,
whereas the squatters turned over strayed stock to the
embrace of the law, Ned and George sold them and they
roamed right up into New South Wales to do it.[12] That
others, who were innocent buyers of the stolen stock,
would be implicated in these events was not as clear
at the time to Ned as it might well have been, perhaps
because he harboured the foolish delusion that if the
wealthy, the powerful and the officers of the law could
deprive the poor of their livelihood, it was reasonable
enough for them to retaliate. In that broader canvas of
the northeast, where the squatters and the selectors
were confronting each other over the question as to who
were to be the masters in the land, it was inevitable that
some would go from its face like the grasses before the
harsh winds of drought. Who they were to be was as
yet not quite clear in September 1877, but in the mean-
time Ned betook himself to Benalla for an afternoon's
relaxation.

Whatever else the police thought of Ned, they did not
think he was a drunkard, and the only time the word
had been used previously in his regard was when Flood
had accused him of pretending to be drunk at Greta
in early 1874. But on 17 September Ned was unquestion-
ably drunk and he was arrested for riding across the
footpath in Benalla. Whether this was one of the ways
the police had decided to employ to take the flashness
out of Ned is uncertain, but he vehemently maintained
that his drink had been spiked by the publican at the
behest of the police. After a night in the lock-up four
policemen were detailed off to take Ned into court, but

young Constable Alexander Fitzpatrick deemed it advisable to take more specific precautions, so he decided to handcuff their prisoner. Ned resented such proceedings, given the minor nature of the charge, and he fled into a bootmaker's shop where his resistance proved too much for the four policemen, although Fitzpatrick held him by the throat, the others ripped off his trousers and Constable Lonigan violated his own and Ned's remnant of dignity by tearing at his genitals. After swearing that he would have it out with Lonigan, Ned surrendered to a local Justice of the Peace who put the cuffs on him. Here was the big chance Nicolson and Standish awaited, for it covered assault of the police and resisting arrest, and if three years were the fruits of the felonious receipt of a horse, how many could Ned look forward to for this fracas? The significant difference was that instead of a perjured thief in the person of Murdock, the event in Benalla was witnessed by a just man called William McInnes J.P. Ned was fined 1s on the drink charge, £2 for resisting, £2 more for assault and was obliged to pay 5s to Fitzpatrick, because his uniform was torn. Admittedly nothing was given to Ned for the assault on his own person, but then he was a member of 'the criminal class' and it was already much that he could ride away free from Benalla.[13]

Matters did not go quite so well for the younger fry of the Greta mob who, being members of that same class, were liable to prosecution at any moment, but equally, being young and carefree, were not as circumspect as they ought to have been were they determined to enjoy their freedom. On 27 September 1877 Dan and his cousins, John and Thomas Lloyd, went on the spree at nearby Winton. What transpired cannot be ascertained with certainty given that the shopkeeper, who initiated

the charges, was later gaoled for perjury on account
of the evidence he gave. At all events the result was that
Ned's old adversary of Ah Fook days, as well as one
of his assaultants in the Benalla bootmaker's, Sergeant
Whelan, got the lads up on a charge of unlawful entry
into Davis Goodman's shop, stealing therefrom, and
assaulting the person of Maurice Solomon. As it was a
shop it was difficult to prove that citizens, even of the
ilk of these young hoodlums, were transgressing the law
when they entered it during business hours. Furthermore, as nothing had been stolen, the theft charge
remained unproven and the assault charge against
Solomon was withdrawn. Nothing daunted, Whelan
rang out another of wilful damage of property to the
value of £10, so the magistrate, being satisfied on this
count, ordered three months gaol for each of them and
payment of £2 10s for the damages. Not entirely satisfied,
the sergeant charged Tom Lloyd with assault upon Mrs
Goodman, his intent being rape. When Tom was
brought up on this charge he was given three months
for common assault, but its very nature was such as to
give the upright serious pause for thought as to the menace that roamed unchecked in their midst: thieves,
youths prone to violence and bent even upon that
unspeakably foul crime of rape. The local paper was
pleased to declaim that they were part of a regular gang
of young ruffians brought up from infancy to lives of
roguery and vagabondism and hence no one need be
surprised at this latest proof of their iniquity. It mattered
not that it was basically a fabrication resting on the word
of a perjurer, and Ned's outrage and his attempt to have
the charge against Dan upset on technical grounds
impressed only Constable Thom, who reported to his
superintendent that Ned was at home on 1 November

getting together evidence to prosecute the Goodmans for perjury.[14] Dan and the others went off to Beechworth and shortly afterwards Ned decided that a change of circumstances would benefit him, and perhaps help to cool down the atmosphere about Greta. He rode off to New South Wales, up through its western plains and on those tracks of the Riverina, and through the long distances of County Bland, called after the same convict doctor who gave his name to the mount near his birth-place at Wallan. Ned Kelly was free for a time.

The year 1877 had been a tedious one for Captain Standish. Nothing much had come of his attempts to curb the unruly elements on the Eleven Mile, although the news that three young ringleaders of the Greta mob were to spend Christmas in Beechworth prison was assuredly a source of comfort to him. But there were other things, too, in which he could take solace. Not for the Captain to concern himself with paltry sums like minor fines and wages of a couple of pounds a week, for he was a man who gamed for higher stakes. On 8 December the weather in Melbourne was sultry and not at all to his liking, so he settled in to a game of loo at his club. The night wore on and at 5.30 a.m. Captain Standish decided to call quits. He went to his bed the richer by £558 while the citizens of Melbourne slept on, trusting that peace and good order were in competent hands.[15]

How that night was passed in Greta is not recorded, but Dan and Jim were in prison, Ned was gone, George King no longer heard of, while Ellen, fruitful of womb to the last, was once more with child. To those of both worlds it could have been said that more was given to those amongst them who already had sufficient.

Tea and Scones

It was Monday 15 April 1878, the beginning of Holy Week,
when Constable Alexander Fitzpatrick rode out of the
township of Benalla. Alexander's mind was not
especially turned to the Passion of the Person whom his
own religion of Presbyterianism recognized as
Redeemer. Rather more pressing were matters bearing
upon his own predicament as a young man whose
passions had been given free rein, and a time of reckon-
ing was fast approaching. The Constable was just
twenty-two years of age and his birthplace was Mount
Egerton, near Ballarat, Victoria. His early calling had
been that of a boundary rider, but shortly after his
twenty-first birthday he had decided to join the Victoria
Police. After three months training accompanied by
good conduct at the Richmond depot in Melbourne, he
was ready to become a fully fledged enforcer of law and
order in the colony, and his superiors sent him to Benalla.[1] Although Ned regarded him as having a face
which revealed the puniness of his heart, there was

something about Alexander which appealed to the
fairer sex, and his winning ways with a girl had already
resulted in fruitful, if passing, unions. Before he joined
the force he had wooed Jessie McKay of Meredith, not
far from his own home at Mount Egerton. He was more
than relieved to obtain the steady employment of a
police constable, as Jessie had persuaded him to pay
maintenance for their child for two years. He was equally
pleased to leave the district as he had no intention of
forming a permanent alliance with Miss McKay.[2]

Once down at the Richmond depot Alexander felt that
he could now turn his attentions to a young lady with
whom he was already familiar, and indeed to whom he
was engaged, named Annie Savage, who lived at
Frankston. Annie, however, did not prove quite as amenable to the young Constable's charms as had Jessie, so
he turned to the forceful argument that what would be
acceptable and indeed truly pleasurable in the state
of holy wedlock would prove not a whit less enriching
before that blessed event. As with Jessie, so with Annie,
it was an enrichment indeed, and in December 1877
when Alexander came down from Benalla, to which he
had been transferred in July, she became pregnant. In
many respects Alexander was a man given to observing
the genteel niceties of the suburbs and he had obtained
the consent of Annie's parents to take her as his wife,
which they had gladly done in writing. It is indeed probable that the formal written consent was especially
comforting to the Savage family as the profession followed by the father was that of solicitor. It was a source
of some surprise to them all when, on this momentous
December visit, Alexander put off the happy day until
Easter. By February Annie had another cogent reason
for a wedding, as she was by then aware of the perma-

nent reminder of her beloved's December visit, so she wrote again and again stressing the urgency of the situation.[3] But how could the innocents of Frankston begin to fathom the charms of the northeast and the effects they were having upon the intended groom? There was all manner of opportunity for a dashing young constable in that country, and in his own especially engaging way Alexander had made friends and acquaintances far and wide, amongst them the young lads and lassies of the Eleven Mile. Jessie and Annie impinged on Alexander's mind on that mild and fine afternoon of 15 April 1878, but Kate Kelly was even more central to its basic workings.

To Alexander's superiors the thought that alone and unaided the young Constable would have even contemplated penetrating Ellen Kelly's lair was unthinkable. Had they known it to be so they would have assumed that the purpose of his visit was on official matters and indeed there were good and sound reasons for the law to take cognizance of the inhabitants, or erstwhile inhabitants, of that particular shanty. A warrant had been issued on 15 March 1878 for the arrest of Ned for horse stealing and the police of the northeast had been on the lookout for him ever since without results, which was not surprising given that he had left the colony in December. On 5 April another warrant had been put out for Dan, again on horse stealing, and although Fitzpatrick had not seen it, much less carried it on his person, he had heard of it.[4] But such matters were trifles compared with the fact that he was on his way to Greta to take charge there in the absence of the new incumbent, Senior Constable Strahan. In any case he had seen Dan three days previously and had not been minded to arrest him then, so why be bothered now, even in the unlikely

event that their paths would cross?[5] As he rode along
he came to Lindsay's pub at Winton and refreshed himself with lemonade and brandy. Thus fortified he proceeded on his way and came to Ellen's place in time
for afternoon tea. Mrs Kelly had a freshly baked batch
of scones, while Kate sat on a sofa darning socks, and
the new baby, Alice, slept peacefully. It was the kind
of domesticity to which Alexander had looked to with
Annie, but then Annie was far away by the sea at Frankston whereas Kate was alive and well in Greta and what
better place to partake of tea and scones.[6]

The time passed pleasantly enough and after an hour
or so Alexander decided to investigate the source of the
sound of wood being chopped behind the house. It was
Brickey Williamson armed, allegedly, with both axe and
revolver and, after an interchange as to his right to chop
wood on that land, Fitzpatrick came down to the house
again and met Bill Skillion and shortly afterwards Dan.
For reasons best known to himself, the official instincts
of a constable asserted themselves, and he decided
the time was ripe to arrest the lad. Nothing loath, Dan
requested a breathing space to take a meal before
departing for Greta lock-up as he had been out riding
all day, so he and Alexander went back inside where
Ellen began to remonstrate with the Constable for his
breach of hospitality, and asserted that her son would
not be taken out from her presence that night. Actions
followed words and Alexander was struck with a fire
shovel which wounded him in the wrist. Deciding that
he was well out of it all and that perhaps he had been
indiscreet in visiting the Eleven Mile, the policeman took
horse and came to Lindsay's where his wound was
dressed and his spirits solaced with liquor. Sergeant
Whelan had to be faced in Benalla and some sort of

story had to be concocted to explain the empty station
at Greta, and the reason why Alexander had been so
rash as to visit unaccompanied the noted den on the
Eleven Mile. Perhaps too he thought that if a sufficiently
strong story could be brewed it could go well with his
superiors who were assuredly soon going to be asking
anxious questions as to his philandering with Miss Savage, if indeed not also with Miss KcKay and, if others
are to be given any credence in these events at all, with
Miss Kate Kelly.

Now a shovel wound to the credulous, and especially
those to whom the word of a constable is in itself a symbol
of veracity, is sufficiently like other wounds as to bear
elaboration. It was a slightly inebriated Constable who
poured out his tale of murderous assault to the horrified
Sergeant Whelan on his arrival at 11 p.m. at Benalla.
It seems that, as Dan was eating, a crazed figure
appeared at the door who began to blaze away with
a revolver. Now this particular madman was an unusually poor marksman for at a distance of some five feet,
in a small room filled with women and children, men
and girls to the number of ten, he missed his target
entirely on two occasions. Taking keener aim he hit the
mark on the third, for the bullet sped its five feet, struck
Alexander's wrist, travelled under the skin and lodged
itself there. The maniac was closely related to most of
the people present, but he appeared unmindful of the
danger he posed to them all. His name was Ned Kelly
and, upon the Constable regaining consciousness, his
wound was tended by the now solicitous Ned who
helped remove the offending bullet with a penknife. Ned
then told Fitzpatrick that he would not have fired at him
had he recognized that it was his old friend Fitzpatrick
of happier days. Mutual arrangements were then made

for Alexander to repair to Benalla, and then tell a cock-and-bull story that would prove satisfactory to the police. Indeed he proved in the event only too ready to tell his story, which in essence claimed that Ned had tried to murder him, aided and abetted by his mother and brother, Dan. Furthermore the Eleven Mile on that afternoon was a veritable armoury, bristling with weapons of all varieties, for Brickey Williamson and Bill Skillion had also produced revolvers and helped Ned in this attempt to take the life of the temporary custodian of the law by the Greta swamps.[7]

What feelings of relief welled in the breast of Sergeant Whelan when he heard this yarn can only be conjecture based on the firmly established determination of the police to conduct a campaign which would result in the final stamping out of the menace posed to society by the people of the Eleven Mile. Into this widely cast and well woven net they had all fallen and the truly splendid part was that it had cost so little to achieve. Assuredly Alexander was wounded and the local medical practitioner, Dr John Nicholson, had to be called, but the outlook was rosy indeed. The doctor came and was not surprised to smell the brandy fumes emanating from a young man who had been exposed to such grievous danger. He examined the wrist and found two wounds one and a half inches apart, one of which, in his opinion, may have been caused by a bullet. It apparently did not surprise him that it was merely a skin wound with no injury to the tendons and very little loss of blood. It was enough that he give assent to the proposition that it was possible a bullet had done this injury.[8] All the rest would follow from Alexander Fitzpatrick's mouth, which was one sworn professionally to speak the truth before and of the law in all its majesty. Sergeant Whelan had no doubt that such would prove the case, but meanwhile Standish and Nicolson had to know of this latest and most enormous transgression by the clan which had violated the peaceful hills of the northeast. Warrants had to be sworn out and for so many: Ned, Dan, Ellen, Brickey, Bill – they were all there. Ned had done it, but they had aided him so they were all fully implicated.[9] What of Kate? Had she no part in this? Others thought she did, and notably Ellen, who had resented the way Alexander had handled her daughter of nearly fifteen years, threatening her at revolver point as he made his advances, but who would believe that story? Were they not all shanty Irish with no reputation to preserve or treasure? What man of just and decent feelings would incline his ear to the stories concocted by the inhabitants of the Eleven Mile sluttery who were slatterns all, while Constable Alexander Fitzpatrick was a youth of established moral rectitude? What did it matter that he was the sole witness to these events whose word would be relied upon, for he was the one to whom injury allegedly had been done and the law would take full account of that?

Holy Week of 1878 was not a happy one for Ellen Kelly. She had seen much coming and going since Monday evening. Dan had left for the ranges, but Brickey and Bill had stayed on as they thought they had nothing to fear, while Ellen herself had nowhere to go in any case, with the baby and the other children to look after. By the evening of Tuesday it seemed that all was well, as no uniform had been seen in the locality. Nonetheless all was not well, nor indeed was Sergeant Whelan entirely satisfied with the course of events. After the doctor left he decided that there was no real need to expedite the capture of the gang of would-be murderers a few miles away. There was still much to be thought of and talked about with Alexander, who needed a well-earnt rest before embarking on any further dangerous missions. Furthermore one of his superior officers, in fact the second in charge of the whole force, Superintendent Charles Hope Nicolson, was by chance in residence a few miles away at Wangaratta, and Whelan could rely upon him for weighty advice in this delicate affair. It would not be wise to rouse him from his bed in the middle of the night, despite the fact that such a delay might allow the criminals to put miles between themselves and the law. No, far better to let him sleep, and even have his breakfast, before disturbing him with such momentous news.[10]

Meanwhile Whelan could at least get out the warrants which, with the help of Mr. F. McDonnell J.P., was done. Care had to be taken to clarify the charge against the arch criminal, Edward Kelly, who 'did wound with intent to murder the informant, Alexander Fitzpatrick, a police constable whilst in the execution of his duty by shooting him with a revolver'. Dan, Ellen, Brickey and Bill were all accessories to the act and 'did aid and abet Edward Kelly' in it.[11] Had those at the Eleven Mile known what was afoot they may have decided to seek refuge in some safer clime, but all unawares they went about their business calmly on that pleasant autumn day, and even Brickey went on with the wood chopping that had so interested the industrious young Constable the previous day, though whether he still carried arms as before is unclear.

After breakfast Sergeant Arthur Loftus Maule Steele presented his superior with the auspicious telegram. Sergeant Steele was a former member of the Irish constabulary, a practitioner of the faith held by his Queen, and a smart and attentive gentleman whose progress through the ranks had not been rapid, but upon whom Charles Hope could rely without reserve. Present too at those deliberations was Inspector Brooke Smith, whose charge was the whole of that infected area and who had had the temerity to suggest in the recent past that all was well in his inspectorate. These were worried men in that council, for had not the very Premier himself, one Graham Berry, sacked a wide range of leading public servants a few months previously on a day called 'Black Wednesday' making of Victoria 'a byword and a jest' to some and causing other prudent ones to ask 'What will they think of us at home?' It had even been suggested that perhaps the police force itself, as an organized body, could be dispersed and its work made the responsibility of local municipalities. What then would become of their moderate comfort and self-esteem? Clearly here was a chance to prove to Victoria that all was not well in the body of the colony and that an efficient, centralized, courageous, devoted and well-led police force was an absolute necessity to ensure the restoration of that body to full health. Thus they deliberated, and indeed it was well to do so cautiously, for were they not dealing with a man set on murder and others of the same ilk? Nicolson was the one who had put forward the plan to take the flashness out of them all, while Brooke Smith was in charge of the district, so they were clearly the men to lead such a dangerous mission. By noon it was decided: the two superior officers would hold the fort in Wangaratta, while Sergeant Steele could test his mettle as the leader of the expedition to the Eleven Mile. There were five of them to be arrested, armed criminals of the worst type with revolvers at their hips and, as for the woman, a shovel in her hand. Sergeant Steele set out with Constable Brown to effect this triumph of law enforcement.[12]

Meanwhile life went on much in its normal vein at the Eleven Mile. Brickey continued to split timber, Bill Skillion attended to the needs of his small holding, while Ellen had enough to occupy both hands and mind with the child left orphaned by Annie's death, her own children and the baby. Unusual occupations, perhaps, for people who had actually assisted at an attempted murder, and at that of a constable, but then these were people to whom, it seemed, criminality had become a way of life and that they would mingle the nefarious with the normal was a source of no surprise to Sergeant Steele, familiar as he was with the deviousness of the criminal classes. Accompanied however with no other reinforcements than Brown, Steele was cautious in his approach and spent some hours observing these domestic and rural scenes from a nearby hill. At about nine in the evening they arrested Brickey who asserted that he had not seen Fitzpatrick at all, much less assisted at his close shave with death. For reasons Steele never cared to explain he did not then arrest Ellen although she was at home and he observed her to be there. Instead he took Brickey into Greta where he was lodged in the lock-up. Steele was able to call upon Strahan to assist himself and Brown, and after midnight of the same day, it now being the Wednesday of Holy Week with the weather crisp and fine, the three policemen set out for the Eleven Mile.

No difficulty was placed in their path by Bill Skillion who was prevailed upon to leave his wife and children, protesting meanwhile his innocence, but the problem of the child at Ellen's breast gave Steele pause for thought, yet only momentarily, for clearly the humane

course to adopt was to take both infant and mother into
custody. Strahan took the opportunity to address some
questions to Ellen as to Fitzpatrick's visit, which she
denied had ever taken place and she further asserted
that she had not seen Ned for four months, which Kate
insisted was true to her knowledge also. Notwithstanding these denials, the other children were left in the tender care of Jimmy Quinn, qualified at least on the
grounds of kinship, and off into the night this second
cavalcade set out. When giving his evidence later
before the court the Senior Sergeant did not reveal
whether the cocks in the fowl-yard crowed as they
passed by. Thus they came to Greta and, having lodged
there in its narrow places, a dray was procured in the
morning, by means of which mother and wailing infant,
together with the bemused Brickey and Bill, were conveyed to Benalla to await committal for the offence of
'aiding and abetting Ned Kelly with intent to murder
Constable Fitzpatrick'. In the watch-house of that township Ellen and baby Alice were lodged in company with
one of those called in older and wiser societies an innocent of God, but in that place he was referred to as a
lunatic.[13] In such company they passed the concluding
days of Holy Week and fine days they were of mid-
autumn so that, had such fancies taken her, Ellen could
have cooed to her infant that on Easter morn the sun
danced over Benalla as creation rejoiced with Creator
in victory over death. Whether the architecture of that
particular prison allowed the inmates to watch the rising
sun is of interest of that kind which men are wont to term
academic.

In that same week the alleged cause of all these sor-
rowful events was carefree and moderately happy, far
to the north in distant places to which no news came

of the mother he had so lightly discarded to the mercy
of his Californian step-father. Ambling quietly from
place to place, Ned had come into a vast country, stretching mile upon mile with its rivers, plains and uplands.
Across the Murrumbidgee and then the Lachlan he had
wandered, until he passed by Saddleback Peak and
came into the valleys watered by the Macquarie and
the Talbragar. There were towns there with men and
women who took quiet pride in their taming of the west,
and the prosperity they had won from the land, and even
in Wellington itself no one thought any longer of the
heartbreak of those missionaries who had fought each
other and government to ensure the welfare of those to
whom that placid valley had been home for aeon upon
aeon, and who were now gone from the land. But in
Orange and Dubbo daily commerce went on apace and
gave no heed to the fact that Ned, already known to the
minor barons of the press of north-eastern Victoria as
'notorious', was in their midst. In the autumn of 1878 a
small boy named James Pennycooke was camped with
his father between Orange and Bathhurst, when a man
who identified himself as Ned Kelly rode up to their camp
with three others. Ned asked for food, but discovering
the meagre nature of their supplies he rode off into the
night with his companions.[14]

Who those companions were was never an easy
matter for the New South Wales police to ascertain, but
it was clear that a gang of men had been engaged in
horse and cattle stealing in the district around Dubbo
during late 1877 and throughout 1878. One of them was
said to be a convicted cattle stealer, Thomas Law, who
had escaped from Parramatta Gaol in 1872. By May 1878
the police had become very concerned about the depredations of the gang which had grown up around Law,

who was known by various names including Midnight and Starlight and, as a bewildering Pimpernel, had ravaged the countryside with nonchalant effrontery.[15] In early September the 'Law' gang was suspected of stealing horses and cattle in the Dubbo district, and it was concluded that some arrests had to be made in order to placate local resentment. Although the New South Wales police did not connect Ned with the gang they did assert that, on two separate occasions, he was in the Wagga Wagga area and on the Murrumbidgee in 1878. It was known also that the family had relatives at Goulburn and Wagga Wagga and that a certain William Kelly was an associate of Law. On 18 September William was arrested in a cellar of the Wonbobbie Inn, near Warren, by Constable William Souter of that township.[16] The police heard that another gang member was hiding out at the same inn so, on Friday 20 September, Senior Sergeant Wallings left his wife and eight children in Dubbo and, accompanied by Constable John Walsh of the same town, set out to effect the arrest. They took with them Constable Souter and arrived before the inn as dawn broke over the Macquarie marshes. The three policemen saw a man catching a horse in a nearby paddock and, upon Wallings calling out for him to stand and identify himself, he fled. Souter and Wallings pursued him. Shots were exchanged and Wallings fell, shot at a distance of ten paces. The father of the Dubbo children lay dead while the murderer made his escape into the hills.[17]

An immediate magisterial enquiry was held which came to the conclusion that the murderer was unknown and that there was no evidence to identify him. A reward of £200 was offered for his capture and he was described as being between five foot six and five foot eight, twenty-

seven to thirty years old, of medium build, with dark hair
and brown whiskers and moustache – a description
which scarcely fitted Law and certainly bore no resemblance to Edward Kelly even were he present at these
transactions.[18] Nonetheless by the end of September the
police had concluded that Law, whoever he may have
been, had shot Wallings and when Sub-Inspector Duffy
of Bourke, together with Constables Hatton and Grey,
were informed that their quarry was holed up at a pub
at Enngonia on the Warrego, about twenty miles south
of the Queensland border, they set out in pursuit. On
3 October they attempted to take the offender but in the
subsequent gun battle he escaped while Mrs Shearer,
owner of the inn, was shot dead by a police bullet. Two
days later this man, or perhaps another man, was come
upon at the Maranoa Station on the border and
wounded 'unintentionally by the police while shooting
the horse on which he was endeavouring to escape'.
They took him to a hut on the Irara Creek where he died
on 6 October refusing to the end to tell them his name.
On 12 October, and hence six days after his death, the
grave was opened and although Constable Walsh,
brought there for the purpose, admitted that he had only
seen Wallings' murderer for two minutes, he was able
to recognize the corpse 'by the cast of his features, and
the whiskers in particular'. A week later it was found at
an inquest held at Irara Creek that 'George Wilson,
alias Thomas Law alias Harry Wilson alias Midnight
being the murderer of Senior Sergeant Wallings was
killed by a shot fired by either Constable Hatton or
Grey'.[19] The Premier of New South Wales Henry Parkes
was sufficiently concerned to call later for a full report
on the matter but the document which was finally set
before him did not clarify it at all except to prove that

the police did not know who killed Wallings or who it was that died at Irara Creek.[20] The one fruitful feature of it all was that when Thomas Browne, alias Rolf Boldrewood, sat on the Bench at Dubbo in 1881 and heard the incredible tale of Law, he used him as the basis for his fictitious character Starlight who 'refused to tell his real name to the police when he was dying'.[21] He did not seem to understand that Starlight, were he indeed Law or Midnight, Gibson or Reynolds or any of the other real life characters who rode those hills and plains in 1878, scarcely had any substance left that could be ascertained by the mere pinning of a name to it.

In the circumstances it is not strange that Ned could lay claim to knowledge of the murderer of Wallings although there is no proof that he himself was in any way implicated in that dreadful event. Ten days after the inquest held at Irara Creek, Ned stood talking to Constable McIntyre while awaiting the return of two other police officers to their camp at Stringybark Creek. Before them lay the body of Constable Lonigan and, while death stalked in those ranges, it was not a time for idle chatter. Ned asked McIntyre what had become of the man whom the police had pursued for the shooting of Sergeant Wallings. He called him 'the Sydney man'. McIntyre replied that the police had shot him. Ned said that such being the case they had shot the wrong man, and implied that the police were out to do the same thing in his regard.[22] Neither in respect of the events relating to Fitzpatrick which led to Ned's being at Stringybark Creek, nor in relation to the death of the man at the hut on the Irara, could it be said that Ned was wrong. But by then the matters of right or wrong had all been transcended by another abstraction even less definable by men. They called it fate.

A Killer 8

When God rumbled in the thunder of Mount Sinai, the command was simple and stark. Thou shalt not kill stood there for all men and for all time, and it passed down the ages until it came to the mind of Edward Kelly, who shared the heritage passed on by Moses. In its passing lesser men had taken it up and weighed it meanly, so that the ancient imperative of absolute prohibition had been weakened, twisted and rendered sterile. It was forgotten that the great command spoke to the killer who had to live on, lessened by the measure of that which he had taken from another. Like Cain, the killer walked henceforth in the desert of his own deprivation where no word of sophist or theologian brought comfort, while the bursting forth of new life in any form never restored the taken one. But in the high spring of 1878 such concerns were not present in the mind of Ned as he rode down those long miles from the north. He knew that a warrant was out for his arrest, which scarcely troubled him as it was not a novel event. But the news had come

to him that his mother was to stand trial and that was
another matter entirely as for the first time she was in
jeopardy because of the behaviour of her tribe. It was
a troubled Ned who came to the Turn Back Jemmy Hotel
about eight miles from Jerilderie in early October and,
having rested there and sold a mare, he went on across
the river and came home again to Victoria.[1]

Indeed it was time for Ned to come home for, since
his departure in the previous year, all had not been well.
Both death and births had augmented the meed of sorrow at the Eleven Mile, George King was no longer
heard of, which was not necessarily a source of great
deprivation and, before all else, there was the Fitzpatrick affair. Beyond these confines other matters also
had arisen affecting the lives of people, and for which
Ned had to bear some responsibility. Hitherto the
tangled skeins of his life, begun a mere twenty-three
years before, had woven only his own destiny and no
thread in it was sufficiently strong as to shape irrevocably his own future or to entangle the life of another.
In those previous years Ned had not become a committed thief, an unrepentant layabout, an unmitigated liar,
drunkard, lecher or man of violence. Nevertheless he
had been unable to acquire that stability and incentive
which for some men is concomitant with the acquisition
of permanent employment or alliance with a girl with
matrimony in view. Certainly there had been the association with Ettie Hart, but the absence in New South
Wales and the threat of imprisonment posed by the
expected warrant had tended to weaken the bond from
Ned's side, although there was no indication that anyone had replaced her in his affections. Yet there was
much of the vagabond in his existence, of which the
meagre swag with its few items of personal apparel was

a reminder. With Ellen about to appear in court there was no home to which to return, and while Jim was serving time in Darlinghurst, it was Dan to whom Ned turned to get the full account of the Fitzpatrick affair. He found him on Bullock Creek in the Wombat Ranges near Mansfield.

The camp at the Bullock was situated in country that only one thing, apart from its natural grandeur, would entice men to settle there and that thing was gold. Huge messmate and white gums stood like sentinels filtering the light of the sun to the ground, while the silence of the place was broken only with bird cries by day and the gentle moaning of the dark trees at night. When rain fell, it came down black and bleak and the creeks in the gullies ran and leapt with its profusion. In the earlier years prospectors had been through and taken the readily available gold, but they had moved on quickly leaving only the ruins of makeshift huts to mark their passing. Yet some traces of the gold remained, and Dan had no difficulty in finding enough to buy provisions and maintain some form of comfort. He had taken up residence in a renovated and heavily fortified, former prospector's hut, which stood on a twenty-acre clearing affording space for horses to run, and strangers to be observed as they came up to the camp. Dan had been joined since mid-year by Joe and Steve, both now released from Beechworth, and Tom Lloyd also formed part of the workforce as well as a useful go-between for financial transactions.[2]

There was much to discuss upon Ned's arrival and the whole sorry episode of 15 April had to be explained in detail. Upon one thing in particular Ned was insistent, and that was, as a form of defence, any reference to his younger sister's honour in the affair had to be avoided.

But time was pressing as the trial was to take place in
a matter of days and all that could be done was to rely
on the commonsense of the jury in the matter.
Nonetheless the course of events so far had not been
such as to give reason for confidence for, despite the
fact that Dr Nicholson had refused to swear that Fitzpatrick's wound was caused by a bullet when the case
had come up for a first hearing in May, the bench of
magistrates had been sufficiently impressed with the
gravity of the charge of aiding and abetting to murder
that the prisoners had been committed for trial at Beechworth at the October General Sessions. That the proceeding necessitated Brickey and Bill spending six
months in gaol while awaiting trial seemed of no concern to anyone, especially when Superintendent
Chomley was gracious enough to accede to the request
that Mrs Kelly be allowed bail, given Alice's presence
in the Beechworth Gaol, which was deemed a most unfit
place for her confinement.[3] Ned heard of the frequent
visits to the Eleven Mile by the police under the direction
of Inspector Brooke Smith, the petty harassment of the
women and children, the threats issued against his own
person which implied that were he ever confronted by
a member of the force he would not be asked to surrender
but shot on sight. It all made his blood boil and he wondered whether any man could have patiently suffered
such insults for as long as he, but boiling blood was no
substitute for concrete action so he and Dan decided
that they would give themselves up to the police were
their mother set free. The offer was relayed to Sergeant
Whelan through a police magistrate, Alfred Wyatt, but
the communication was either discarded as contemptu-
ous by Whelan or, if taken further by him, it was not acted
upon.[4]

The other news that Ned heard concerned the fate of a group of unfortunates who had been sufficiently gullible or greedy as to involve themselves in the horse trading deals he and George King had organized in August 1877. They had taken eleven horses stolen from Whitty's property at Moyhu to a farm owned by Andrew Peterson, near Howlong in New South Wales. There Ned, an expert in such matters, had altered the horses' brands and later sold them. The buyers, Samuel Kennedy, William Cooke and German immigrant brothers called William and Gustave Baumgarten, were in good faith and paid full value for the horses. William Baumgarten then sold three of his horses to a certain John Stutters, so what had been an act of felony on the part of Ned and George had implications for five others, and when Sergeant Steele began to take an interest in the matter, it boded ill indeed for them all. Ned was gone to gamble and ramble on northern plains, George had disappeared from human ken, but the others were at hand and they found themselves arraigned on various charges of horse stealing. Cooke was sentenced to six years for one horse, Kennedy went for four years, while William Baumgarten also received six years. Stutters and Gustave were fortunate enough to be given the benefit of the doubt and remained free.[5]

It was all very well for Ned to lament the innocence of these people and to proclaim ironically that they were as guilty as the Queen of England. The fact remained that they were imprisoned because of his act in the first instance, and no amount of bluster would result in their freedom. It was certainly true that the local Stock Society had, by its rewards, made it attractive for the police and members of the public to uphold the rights of property. In subsequent court proceedings the credibility of witnesses was frequently suspect, the police were at pains to secure convictions and judges moralized about such holy matters as the inviolable right of the wealthy to accrue greater wealth, while they sentenced men to long terms of imprisonment for petty theft of stock to which dubious ownership was frequently claimed. It was true also that stock theft was an expression of the widespread conflict between those who held little or no land and that 'rapacious class' of 'shepherd kings' who held so much.[6] But none of these factors was likely to be of any moment in the tribunal Ellen, Brickey and Bill had to enter on 9 October.

Judge Redmond Barry had come to feel at home in the Beechworth Court House. In October especially, it was an exceedingly fine locality to visit with the crisp air of morning and evening and soft days with just a hint of the heat to come. It was regrettable, perhaps, that some of these felons had to while away so long in prison awaiting his coming, but he was not responsible for the organizing of the courts nor, indeed, could he be expected to show much sympathy for those foolhardy enough to put themselves in jeopardy in the first instance. On this particular visit he felt no sympathy whatsoever, for he had observed that he was to be confronted with assorted representatives of the notorious Greta clan, in the persons of the very matriarch herself, and two of the menfolk. It was tedious that the police had hitherto been unsuccessful in hunting down that villainous archfiend, Ned, who was responsible for the barbarous, in fact murderous, assault upon a young constable. In good time, doubtless, Ned's day would come and Redmond Barry was not one to urge on indelicately the course of justice. The last of the wattle had faded its gold and given place to its greener tips on the trees

Barry could see from the windows of the courthouse, while beyond, the mountains stretched to the horizon reminding men of majesty and order. Below him Ellen looked frail, worn and pinched by her fate. Her hair was still black and the set of her chin, with an occasional steeling of her grey eyes, indicated that her spirit was far from broken, but today would tell its tale.[7] Beside this woman, Brickey and her son-in-law seemed inconsequential. There were two other men present in court on that day who had come across the roads from Mansfield to assist at this proceeding. One was a sergeant of police named Michael Kennedy, the other Constable Thomas McIntyre.[8]

The Constable Alexander Fitzpatrick who stood before Judge Barry to give his evidence regarding the affair at the Eleven Mile in the previous April was a much changed man. An impressive weight of responsibility had fallen on his youthful shoulders for, on 10 July, Anna Savage had become wife to Alexander at Mornington, Victoria, according to the Presbyterian rites, and since then the union had been rendered further blessed by the advent of a son called Victor Gregory in September. It has to be acknowledged that Alexander did not enter lightly and without aforethought into such a state. It seems that Mrs Savage had become so alarmed at his apparent unwillingness to accept his responsibilities that on 1 July she wrote to Captain Standish to ask him to use his every effort to make amends, 'for his desertion and heartless silence are unpardonable'. She thought his behaviour could only be explained on the grounds that he had 'become acquainted with some one else', but that no way was open to her of gaining satisfaction, for her 'child would sooner die than go into court'. In the event the good Captain, who understood the reluctance of respectable people to go into the courts, was in a more secure position than Mrs Savage to exercise authority over the Constable. He demanded an immediate interview with him in Melbourne and when word arrived to that effect, there was some good-natured banter at Beechworth amongst the police who rightly assumed that the summons was 'something about girls'. Inspector Brooke Smith told Alexander to follow any advice Standish gave him 'cheerfully' and that advice was peremptory and final with its simple statement that either he marry or be sacked. It has to be assumed that the union entered into a few days later was done so 'cheerfully'.[9]

The jury and judge listened as Fitzpatrick repeated his evidence, which was not upset even in respect of Bill Skillion when local farmers swore that he was in their company throughout the afternoon and evening of 15 April. The jury retired to deliberate and no one wondered that they numbered in their ranks a former sergeant of police, William Chadwick, who had been discharged in 1875 after serving several years at Eldorado.[10] Upon their return they found the three prisoners guilty, but Judge Barry decided that he would deliberate at length before proceeding to a sentence. In the end, perhaps, he was mindful of the fact that Ellen had spent two months in Beechworth prison with her baby awaiting bail, so he only gave her three years' hard labour. He noticed that Brickey and Bill had already done six months so he gave them six years' hard labour, while expressing the conviction that their imprisonment would lead to the dismemberment of that lawless group which converged on that hapless neighbourhood about the Eleven Mile.[11] Not content with this prophecy the judge was minded to turn to the little woman in the dock and tell her that had her son Edward been in that place with her he would have received a sentence of twenty-one years, so heinous was his behaviour. The editor of the *Ovens and Murray Advertiser* could not have but concurred with this righteous sentiment of the learned gentleman for he had publicly recorded his opinion that Ned had to be regarded as 'some noxious and dangerous beast', who had to 'be got out of the way lest he do further mischief'.[12] At all events the woman in question was quickly disposed of for, after two weeks in Beechworth, she was taken down the road and placed in the Melbourne Gaol where she eked out her time until, with remissions, she was regarded as a fit and proper person to return to society on 7 February 1881.[13] By then, much had changed at the Eleven Mile where many voices were forever stilled.

Spring had bloomed to fulness by late October 1878 and in the towns and villages of the northeast the lads of good repute had games to play, crops to watch ripen, fencing to repair after the winter and mild evenings to while away in the numerous bars where song, drink and dancing soothed their spirits. The footballs had been put away and cricket practice had started, while over at Benalla things were already in earnest with a victory by Beechworth over the locals by one slender run on Saturday 19 October.[14] Noticed only by a few, another game was also in earnest in those parts. This time the quarry was a man and, although the prize was a meagre £100, it was not to be lightly discounted by members of a force which paid 8s 6d a day to a sergeant second class, and 7s 6d to constables who had joined the force before July 1870, while those unfortunate enough to join after that date had to make do on 6s 6d.[15]

For his apprehension Ned Kelly was worth £100, and

not overmuch attention need be paid to the manner of
its doing, nor indeed to the state of the said Kelly after
his capture, but when a sergeant or a constable could
augment his income of £150 or less for a year to £250
it was an enterprise to be undertaken in a serious vein.

During the months since April there had been a good
deal of coming and going on the part of the police of
the north-eastern district in search of Ned. Inspector
Brooke Smith had put himself up at O'Brien's Hotel in
Greta at what Standish regarded as exorbitant expense
to the government.[16] From the safety and warmth of
that establishment he made his sporadic forays to the
shanty through the pass where with noise, bombast and
futile vandalism he had managed to render further miserable the inmates of that home, inhabited now by
defenceless women. Ned had these visits described to
him vividly.

After the arrest of my mother there was none of our family left
but five sisters. The police would come to the house, Inspector
Brooke Smith in particular who has since been discharged
for his cowardly conduct towards my family. They used to
search the place and destroy all the provisions by emptying
them out on the floor. He would say to my sisters, 'See all the
Police I have out today. I will have as many out tomorrow. We
will blow your brothers into pieces as small as the paper that
is in our guns.' Some told my sisters that they would not ask
their brothers to stand as they knew they intended to fight.
They would shoot them first and then tell them to stand afterwards.[17]

Others had taken the matter more seriously than
Brooke Smith, and Constable Flood, now stationed at
Benalla, and Detective Michael Ward were especially
assiduous in their devoted pursuit of their game. In late
May the two joined forces, and Ward did his best to

induce some of the locals to put Ned away and thus
share in the reward.[18] All their actions and movements
had no effect whatsoever, so that in the end Ward concluded that what could not be found did not in fact exist,
at least in those parts. He thus gave it as his considered
opinion that the quarry was not even in the colony, much
less in those wild and rugged regions between the King
and the Broken Rivers, and that, of course, was an
opinion with which Ned would happily have agreed
from his safe distance by the Talbragar beyond the Murrumbidgee.

All of this speculation was laid to rest when word came
that Ned was verily in their midst in early October with
his offer of surrender, so a concerted effort to find the
truly retrievable was mounted. Not surprisingly it was
thought that Ned had gone back to the world he had
known as Power's cub, up in those fastnesses where the
King takes its rise, and hence in late October, after the
safe disposal of Ellen and her two murderous accomp-
lices, two parties of police set out in a kind of pincer
movement with the intention of taking Ned, and Dan too,
in those places between Greta and Hedi. One set out
from the north at Greta while the other departed from
the south at Mansfield. The one that had its origins at
Greta is of interest only in that it was led by Senior Constable Strahan. Before his departure he met Pat Quinn
who offered to lead him and his party to the hideout of
the Kelly brothers provided he was assured that Strahan
would not shoot them. 'If I come across them I'll shoot
them like dogs,' replied Strahan and Ned's confidence
in immunity from being slaughtered by well-meaning
policemen was not strengthened when he heard of those
ominous words.[19]

On Friday 25 October 1878 at about 5 a.m. a party

of four horsemen was observed by the few residents of
Mansfield who happened to be awake at that hour. They
were dressed as prospectors and appeared law-
abiding and purposeful as they proceeded out of the
town. Dawn was breaking and the dew was falling from
the leaves but to the north-east, to which they headed,
the ranges lay unbroken and soon they were in places
of scarcely penetrable bush. To these men that country
was still alien, even after years in which duty had forced
them to roam it, because they were all born and reared
in Ireland. The youngest was part of the expedition
because he was a good cook and, given the uncertain
nature of the prospecting venture and the lack of clarity
as to when it might terminate, it was as well to ensure
some degree of material comfort. The others were fit,
strong looking men clearly accustomed to the bush and
able to handle their horses with mastery. All four were
in their thirties and any casual observer would have considered the chances of success of such a party high
indeed. A more percipient observer would perhaps
have wondered why it was necessary to carry a Spencer
rifle, as well as a double-barrelled breech loading gun,
on such a venture as gold prospecting and, had he been
able to see the revolvers they all carried, he would have
concluded that the old free and easy days of mining
were gone. The party proceeded further back into the
ranges while the spring morning broke into loveliness.
The cook, Thomas Newman McIntyre, vied with another
to kill a tiger snake and being himself successful turned
and said, 'First blood, Lonigan'.

The leader, Michael Kennedy, decided to pitch camp
by Stringybark Creek, some thirteen miles from Mansfield as the crow flies, which they reached at about 2 p.m.
Kennedy took the Spencer rifle and went off alone until

4 p.m. They settled down near a deserted prospector's hut and the evening came on fine with a cold night and little laughter to solace these men. Two of them, Kennedy and Lonigan, were married and some dark presentiment had moved in Lonigan, for he had returned twice on his departure from home to hold his wife and look in at the four children asleep in their beds. Kennedy was an open-hearted, confident man who looked only to the present. His parting with Bridget, his wife and mother of five including a baby, had been secure and loving for it was an expedition much like any other and he set out without hesitation and no turning back. Kennedy was especially pleased to have his friend and trusty fellow worker, Michael Scanlan, with him on this occasion for here was a smart, tough, soldier-like man who flinched at nothing and whose hazel eyes told little of the emotions that governed his heart. In the morning it was Scanlan to whom the leader turned and intimated that they would go off looking while the others would hold the camp. Picking up their arms the two set out and Kennedy turned to the cook and said, 'Mac, don't be uneasy if we are not home tonight.'[20]

At about noon Lonigan was lying down reading the *Vagabond Papers* and McIntyre decided to go hunting for lunch. He saw a flock of parrots and a quick burst from both barrels sufficed to provide a meal and to make those ranges echo and re-echo with the sound. It was more than enough to confirm the worst fears of the party of young men prospecting a mile away. Ned and Dan had already examined the team of fellow prospectors the previous evening and, while not recognizing any of them, had rapidly concluded that these men had come into those hills in search of their fellow men, and by the quantity and quality of their arms it was apparent that

they bore no good will to their quarry. Ned knew
Strahan's party was out and the possibility of their sur-
viving an encounter with two groups of well-armed
police was slender indeed. At the Kelly camp there were
five young men who in most respects were a fit match
for any opponents in almost all forms of physical combat.
But they had not come out into these hills to kill or be
killed and their weaponry consisted of two old pieces.
To Strahan's threat of shooting him like a dog, Lonigan
had added his mite for it had come to Ned that, before
he left Violet Town, the policeman had said that were
it the case that Kelly had to be shot then he was the very
man to do it. Ned remembered well the occasion in Benalla when a whole contingent of police, or so it seemed
to Ned, had unsuccessfully attempted to handcuff him
and he was reasonably sure that Lonigan, who had
played a mean role in Benalla, would not have let the
lesson of the encounter escape him. The only sensible
thing remaining to be done was to surrender or flee. The
former had its problems for who would be sure of not
being shot in the act of surrender if Strahan's words were
to be believed, while flight without good horses, ammunition and firearms was a risky business. On the other
hand with the police camp so well supplied in all of these
commodities it was clear that, provided the police surrendered, a well-provisioned flight was possible.

The shadows about the Stringybark had already
begun to lengthen when the four stole up to the camp
situated about thirty yards from the little creek. Tom
Lloyd remained behind at Dan's hut in the clearing.
Only Ned and Dan were armed but Joe and Steve came
because there were four policemen and if it came to
physical combat the sides would be numerically equal.
At Ned's call McIntyre threw up his arms. Lonigan ran,

dropped behind a log, raised his head to take aim at
Ned and was shot through the right eye. Crying 'Oh
Christ, I am shot', he fell dead, but his killer scarcely
looked at him whom he had slain for the living were still
quick about him. When Ned was told it was Lonigan,
it is not evident that he repented of the slaying, for it
was clear that never again would the policemen take
his fellow man by his private parts with purpose set of
sending him to that Kingdom to which the spirit of
Lonigan had already gone. Meanwhile a grotesque
and piteous figure, clothed in apparel that enveloped
his boyish frame so that he appeared as some animated
scarecrow, ran about shaking with hysteria. It was Dan,
who looked at his brother and knew that another road
had opened to them, but where it led except to an end
like Lonigan's only his forlorn yapping could indicate.

Ned spoke at length with McIntyre whom he entreated
to call upon Kennedy and Scanlan to surrender at their
return. He blamed the Fitzpatrick incident for the whole
sorry affair and McIntyre was unable or unwilling to sustain a contrary argument. McIntyre showed no curiosity
in how it came to be that Ned was so certain that the
New South Wales police were mistaken in shooting that
man whom they took to be the murderer of Sergeant
Wallings, but he smoked tobacco and drank tea at Joe
Byrne's invitation and gradually relaxed, so that when
the horses were heard approaching the camp he was
ready to do his best to warn his companions. McIntyre
spoke and Scanlan went for his rifle, fired at Ned and
was shot dead. Kennedy thought McIntyre was joking,
laughed, saw how matters stood and started firing as
he jumped from his horse. Ned followed Kennedy and
in the end shot him through the chest. He died with his
mind full of the woman and their children. McIntyre had

escaped on Kennedy's horse to spend the night in a
wombat hole. For Edward Kelly there was no hole to
retreat to, except that one of his inner spirit where all
bluster was dampened and where in its hollowness
there was only the sound of that ancient curse to echo.
Henceforth he knew and carried within himself the
knowledge that he was a killer.

Wombat Hole   9

When night fell at the Stringybark on 26 October three men lay dead, while another four shared the knowledge that to them alone the great crime was accountable. That they were men emerging from boyhood, native sons who had never shared in the prosperity which the land of their birth had offered abundantly to others, and members of a clan or a mob which had been subject to harassment, was inconsequential. For them there was no turning back, because nothing could now wash away the stain of blood, even if the dark rain fell in torrents in the Wombat and the mountains were darkened for day upon day. These four had become as one in the compounding of a communal killing, even though one mind had planned the step which led to the slaughterhouse by the creek. In the recesses of that soul stood guilt, for what did it matter that provocation, self-defence, lack of premeditation or other justification could spring to the lighter part of the brain, and hence to the lips? Such things, and such reasonings, were for

men, and Ned would use them with men, but when he
looked into that other place of his being he could only
summon up the supplication learnt long ago in childhood and now realizable as never before. 'Lord Jesus
have mercy,' he breathed, and breath itself was answer,
for he still had a life to which expiation lay open at every
twist of the crooked run ahead.

The four spent the night by the bodies which they plundered of all valuables, for what worth were they to the
dead even if the widow Kennedy was to grieve that her
husband's watch, as a metallic reminder of both life and
the manner of death, was taken from her? Horses, camp
utensils, ammunition and arms – they took all and in the
first light were off, leaving Tom Lloyd to share the secret
of those deeds. Dan shook still with the palsy of dread
and much cursing was heard despite Ned's attempt to
still such futility. Only activity could quell such stirrings
and to run was all that was left. With Tom Lloyd as scout
they went to Greta on the Sunday where they changed,
ate and told Maggie and Kate of the deeds done the
day before, and in the night they went off into the ranges
between the Eleven Mile and the King. They were seen
as they passed near to Beechworth and word of their
passing was spread abroad. It was clear that further
flight was imperative so through those mountains and
their passes they rode until they came to the mother river
as they sought refuge in those distant places known to
Ned in New South Wales. But the river denied them passage, swollen as it was with the heavy rains and the
waters of melted snow from the high places where it
sprang, so they turned their backs to the north and came
down the tortured miles in search of refuge, solace,
warmth and food. The horses, with their riders, were
exhausted and men and beasts were soaked and

miserable. As they passed under the bridge at Wangaratta their paces quickened because the Warby ranges
were at hand with their hills that ran down to Greta and
the creek country. A week had passed since Stringybark
and the dead were buried, but the dead have a way
of riding still, as those horsemen knew in heart and fibre.[1]

Constable McIntyre had been a school teacher in New
South Wales before he joined the Victoria Police, and
then he had served two years as warden in a police
prison.[2] His temperament and training had scarcely fitted him to the task undertaken in the Wombat but then,
chosen for his culinary expertise, nothing else rightly
could have been expected of him. The fortuitous nature
of his escape on Kennedy's horse from the scene of the
killings while the Sergeant did battle with Ned and Dan
so impressed itself on his mind that when he eventually
slipped exhausted from the horse, he holed up in a wombat hole, and, facing the west, looked at the last redness
of the setting sun and thanked God for deliverance while
imploring His continued mercy. In his diary, as he sat
in that hole, he also wrote words which established that
Lonigan had attempted to draw his revolver, and therefore had not been shot down in cold blood. But McIntyre
was already deranged and the long night in his hole,
as he heard again and again the gunshots of memory
and smelt the acrid powder that had singed his nostrils,
further drove him into the recesses of his mind so that
henceforth he was to live with the tall mountain trees
and the bloodied bodies of his companions. The
McIntyre that crept from that hole on Sunday morning
was a piteous creature, and having stumbled the
thirteen miles into Mansfield, the tale he told of murder
upon his arrival in the afternoon filled that whole little
town with horror, while Mrs Kennedy held her children

and mourned for the man she knew would never now return.[3]

The person in charge of the forces of law in Mansfield was a sub-inspector named Henry Pewtress. Of English birth he had spent twenty-six years as a policeman, but his posting to the remote fastnesses of his Mansfield charge was as recent as August of that same year, 1878. He was quick to admit that he knew 'nothing whatever of bush life' and that his leading an expedition to track down the four horsemen in that vast space of mountains was to stress the falseness of his position. Unaware that he could use the telegraph on a Sunday, he decided to send Constable Thomas Meehan to Benalla to pass the word of what had occurred. Thomas was unarmed because all of Mansfield had been deprived of weaponry, including a fowling piece belonging to the local Anglican minister, in order to arm the prospecting party led by Kennedy. Understandably nervous, the policeman saw visions of armed men at all points of the road and eventually he dismounted, removed his boots, and proceeded on foot to Benalla, arriving on the Monday and incurring the lasting displeasure of Pewtress for his foolishness and his eventual dismissal from the force for drunkenness.[4] As a result of these proceedings Captain Standish was apprised on Monday of the ominous outcome at Stringybark Creek but in a garbled form, according to which the police were shot while 'preparing their breakfast'. In communicating the news to the Premier, Berry, Standish admitted that the police were called upon to surrender and that 'Lonigan placed his hand behind for his revolver when he was shot dead'. He asked that a reward of £200 be offered 'for such information as will lead to the apprehension of each offender, that is £800 in all'.[5] The Captain decided to send Superintendent Nicolson to take charge of the hunt which, commencing on Monday 28 October 1878, was on in earnest.

On the Sunday evening a melancholy party, led by Pewtress and including McIntyre and the resident medical practitioner, Dr Samuel Reynolds, had left Mansfield in the late and wet evening for Stringybark Creek. An even more melancholy party returned on the following morning with two bodies strapped to the back of a horse and the mortal remains of Constables Lonigan and Scanlan were deposited in the local hospital's morgue. While the little town mourned, Wild Wright and his deaf brother, Dummy, drank deep in a local pub and the elder brother was heard to say that he proposed to go out and join Ned. Both brothers were arrested on a charge of abusive language, which possibly caused some puzzlement to Dummy, but it had the effect of quelling the disturbing elements in Mansfield and prevented their outrages offending the ears of various clerical personages present in the town. The Anglican bishop of Melbourne, Dr Moorhouse, had come on visitation to his flock and he grieved in his large heart for those wayward ones who had survived at Stringybark Creek, as well as for the dead. The body of Sergeant Kennedy was not found until the Thursday. It lay where he fell, covered with his cloak and with the ravages of death already upon it. It was brought in to Mansfield and Dr Reynolds was called to look upon it as he had done with the bodies of Lonigan and Scanlan. But his inquest was rapid and, unlike those other bodies inflicted with senseless violation after death by unknown persons to whom no guilt ever accrued, Kennedy's bore one large wound only caused by 'a charge of heavy shot' to the chest fired at close range 'which passed completely through the body

and out at the back'. Dr Moorhouse was flanked by two
Catholic priests whose names, as it happened, were
Kennedy and Scanlan, and all sectarian divisions
ceased while Mansfield buried its dead. In his sermon
on the Sunday morning his audience was hushed as the
Bishop said that the killers were 'waiting in the mountains, as outlaws, for their execution' and that they were
the dead rather than those who were buried. In haste
to remember those men who had gone prospecting for
the living, a fine monument was erected in 1880 at the
crossroads of the township to remind posterity of the high
motives of the dead. Posterity chose to ignore its import
and bestowed upon it a name that even in the halls of
heaven had to cause chagrin to those three men of the
law, for it was henceforth called by many the Kelly monument.[6]

If it took the police some time to identify Joe and Steve
as the other miscreants present at Stringybark Creek
based on the garbled and erroneous descriptions given
by McIntyre, it took them even longer to settle down into
anything like a methodical, planned pursuit of the four.
Although Standish had decided that Nicolson, his
Assistant Commissioner, was the appropriate man to
lead the hunt he distrusted him and, safely ensconced
in Melbourne, he gave him neither appropriate assistance nor encouragement. Nicolson unfortunately had
to rely upon two manifestly incompetent adjutants in the
persons of Brooke Smith and Pewtress. John Sadleir, who
had been moved to Benalla from Mansfield in July 1878
as superintendent, was the only ranking officer in whom
Nicolson could place any faith, but from the beginning
their judgements diverged in that the Assistant Commissioner thought, with most of the residents of Mansfield, that the four were still in and about the Wombat,

while Sadleir was convinced that they would have attempted to cross into New South Wales. But Sadleir was not the man to argue with his superior because both men, and their chief in Melbourne, knew that 'no officer felt secure in his position under the Berry regime'. The head of government had given it as his public opinion that 'the police service could be carried on altogether without officers,' so it was no time for sensible men to fall out, with unemployment breathing at their necks.[7]

In the stately chambers where men sat in a body called the Legislative Assembly of Victoria the name of Kelly was officially mentioned for the first time on 29 October. These men were the representatives of the people and as such they were outraged at the threat to the life and liberty of the citizenry manifest in the doings at Stringybark Creek. Graham Berry, whose career began as an apprentice draper aged eleven some forty-five years before at Chelsea, England, had grown to moderate prosperity in Victoria and was now at the height of his powers. He was an accomplished politician who blended his gifts with tempered radicalism so that he had become the darling of all those who wanted the power of wealth and landed property reined in, provided it were done with sanity and the blessing of constituted authority. But 1878 had been an uneasy year for Berry because it had been made evident to him that, across the way in another place called a Legislative Council, there were men entrenched in the conviction that they represented not the whole people, but that portion whose wealth, education and settled interests in the colony entitled them to their paternal care. Since 8 January, Berry had warred with those men, and they had won, so that he had it in mind to take ship to London and implore the masters of them all, who reigned in

Downing Street, to take up their pens. But surely here was an opportunity to join both chambers in unison, for were not those young hoodlums of the northeast the declared enemies of them all, who would, if allowed to go unchecked, shake the fine edifice of civilization called Victoria to its very core? People in high places had used the word revolutionary and attached it to Berry's name. In the opinion of the Premier it was time for all to realize that there were genuine revolutionaries in the land, unlettered and uncouth scallywags whom the state would turn against and crush with a mighty blow.[8]

But to achieve that aim required means. Berry assured his assembly that they were at hand, for had he not offered a reward of £200 for the heads of the miscreants and it mattered nought whether they were brought in dead or alive? Furthermore he had contacted that embodiment of police efficiency, Captain Standish, and told him to spare no expense, especially in relation to the acquisition of arms to use against the four. Mr J. H. Graves, who sat there as representative for Delatite, was aware that his own constituents were endangered, so he was searching in his questions and on the following day he told of the terror that had gripped the citizens of Mansfield, and was not placated when Mr Langridge, who hailed from Collingwood, said that the police would accomplish their task in a few days and hence there was no need for panic. But Berry was master of it all for he had talked again with Standish, and agreed both to increase the reward to £500 per head and to introduce a bill based on the example of New South Wales that would declare them outlaws in the land, to be shot down on sight by anyone who cared enough for the common-weal of the citizens, and who was not unmindful of the considerable financial return accruing to such an act.

He knew just the man to expedite the bill: his Attorney-
General, Bryan O'Loghlen, Irish, Catholic and the son
of a baronet to boot. A few years later Sir Bryan would
decline to prosecute the directors of the Mercantile Bank,
the closure of which had brought much suffering on the
provident poor of Melbourne, but in this case the lads
in the bush had no one to plead that perhaps they still
deserved to be treated as human persons, rather than
game to be gunned down with impunity. The bill was
drawn up and by the afternoon of Thursday 31 October
it had passed through both houses. In the upper
chamber Mr Henry Cuthbert, member for the South-
western Province, mindful perhaps of his 1,100 acres of
verdant land in the Western district and his 169,000 on
the Lachlan, and the threats posed to his quiet possession of opulence by the landless ones, spoke out in
defence of the doings of his peers. He reminded his
hearers of the urgency of this just measure and, though
he conceded that it was normal to establish the guilt
of the accused, it was painfully obvious that in this case
the Kelly brothers had done that effectively enough for
themselves. He concluded by admitting that it could be
said that to have such a penal enactment as this written
into the statute books was 'a blot on our legislature'. But
he comforted those politicians on their benches by promising them that it was only a temporary measure.

   There was however a period of grace, for the criminals
were given until 12 November to turn themselves over
to the police at Mansfield. But the day passed so the
wheels of the law and the printing press turned rapidly
and smoothly. The luminaries of that land were there
by name and signature on the proclamation when it was
sent out to the post offices and police stations of the bush
on 15 November. Chief Justice Sir William F. Stawell

declared it, Sir George Ferguson Bowen, Governor,
signed it, assisted by Bryan O'Loghlen, Attorney-
General. Beneath it they added majesty and deity by
asking God to save the Queen and throughout, the message was woe betide the Kellys. Had Ned and Dan been
aware of the contents and deep meaning of that Act,
they could not but have wondered why it was necessary
to proclaim that henceforth they were legally incapable
of transferring property. Each of them had one thing now
to transfer – a body. Hence it was that Edward and
Daniel Kelly of Greta in the colony of Victoria passed
beyond the ken and protection of the law and became,
as it were, the equivalent of the ferocious beasts of other
lands, for Australia possessed none of that variety,
except for those who stood upright in the manner of men.

Joe and Steve were still unknown quantities and in
New South Wales, where their description in the Victorian *Police Gazette* was accepted as a guide to recognizing them, innocent people were put in jeopardy,
because McIntyre was unable to be accurate in telling
of those others whom he had seen only in a haze. But
in Melbourne the legal draftsmen found no difficulty in
associating two unknowns with Ned and Dan, so they
too passed beyond the pale.[9] Meanwhile the *Ovens and
Murray Advertiser* remained constant in its convictions
on the perfidy of little Greta and all its human product.
The four were like tigers who, 'having once tasted blood
. . . will stay at nothing'. The upright of the district were
summoned to arouse themselves and to scour the
country without respite 'until these foul murderers are
brought to justice'. When the Act was proclaimed making them outlaws, the editor rejoiced because its provisions placed 'Ned Kelly and his comrades altogether
outside the pale of humanity'. They were henceforth

'animals to be got rid of by any means, fair or foul . . .' and the very letter of the Act in achieving the extermination of such vermin ought to be followed. Over at Mansfield the Act was also received with gratitude although it was admitted that some thought its measures were too severe. It was judged wise to print its details in full lest some unwitting person might transgress them 'innocently'.[10]

The response from the public was not as dramatic as the newspapers had dared to hope. By the end of the year a mere twelve civilians had offered their services to the police to help capture the four, including a certain James Halligan from Bourke across the rivers. Their numbers were swelled by Constable Simon Johnston of the Macarthur police station who volunteered for the northeast, while a former Constable, Hugh Bracken, left his position as a warden at the Beechworth Asylum and joined in the hunt. To these were added the seventy-odd men drawn in from elsewhere in the force, but mainly from Melbourne, so doubling the strength of the police in the northeast. Many of them were more accustomed to the easier life of a city or suburban beat, where neither steed nor weaponry was a necessity, but in those early days enthusiasm was high, for it was a widespread conviction that Christmas would see men united with their families and the scourge of the countryside forever quelled.

One man however was possessed of higher wisdom: Captain Standish knew that a difficult task confronted him and his men. He began to busy himself with many matters, mostly in the form of hurried telegrams to Nicolson, Sadleir and others, to the New South Wales and Queensland police warning them that the four were across the Murray and then again not across the Murray;

he saw reinforcements off on the train, warned the banks
to be on the lookout for a raid, ordered black trackers
from Coranderrk, called upon McIntyre in hospital in
Melbourne, and visited Brickey Williamson in Pentridge. Poor Brickey had decided that any course was
justified, provided it helped relieve him from his present
undeserved misery, so he talked on at length about the
things he thought Ned might do in the way of escape.
He even obliged by doing a sketch of the locality
between the Greta home and the Black Range with a
'big log' drawn in to indicate where Maggie Skillion
would be likely to hide food for the four. It was all heady
stuff for the Captain. Only one thing prevented his actual
departure for the field of combat: he had to attend to
a matter which he anticipated with joy on Monday 4 November. The morrow was a most important day in the Captain's social and financial calendar, for it was the first
Tuesday in November so the Chief of Police went to the
Melbourne Cup together with 37,000 others to see
Calamia win. He then departed for the northeast.[11]

Who indeed could say that the Captain had not earnt
his day's respite, for in the northeast things were not at
all well with much coming and going, much sound and
fury, much cursing and folly, much following old tracks
that led nowhere, and even the panic-stricken act of
police firing upon police, which induced a fevered Standish to order the devising of a signal or password to prevent such a regrettable eventuality re-occurring. One
amongst them all kept his head, sleeping late, ignoring
messages, eating well and gradually slipping into a
state of torpor and terror which became his fixed mental
attitude hereafter. Ned knew him well and called him
a 'misplaced poodle' who was as capable of command-
ing his men as Standish was of 'mustering mosquitoes

and boiling them down for their fat on the back blocks
of the Lachlan'. He was Superintendent Brooke Smith
who posted men outside his door to prevent his body
being snatched by the outlaws. But those gentlemen,
had other, more worthwhile, objects in mind.[12]

When the four returned exhausted from their flight to
the Murray, the wheat crops were standing up with fill-
ing heads in the paddocks and it was time for normal
men to look into the question of the machinery standing
idle in the sheds since last summer, and the fitness of
the horse teams to draw it. The evenings had lengthened, and the sun of early November had begun to show
its bite in the noon hours, while that whole valley that
spread out below the Warbys was one of peace with
its tall stands of timber, its river flats, its selectors' shanties and the odd squatter's residence of more substantial
proportions. Down there were the small towns – Greta,
Mohyu, Oxley, Whorouly, Winton and others. In other
days they were places to ride into and rein up at the
hotel with the flashness of a smart gallop or dust-filled
halt to catch the eye of the local maidens. They were
places too into which a youth or man went to transact
small matters of business, such as the repair of a saddle
or the shoeing of a horse, a haircut or the acquisition
of a few needed provisions. But those days were gone
for the four, who could never again ride with impunity
into the dwellings of men without fear clutching at the
heart in anticipation of the sound of the bullet that would
signal death itself. It was as well to be exhausted in those
days, because there were many hours to sleep, which
engendered avoidance of those moments in which the
future had to be thought upon as the past had to be
forgotten. The one immediate problem was finding
someone in whom trust would be implicit, total and prac-

tical because even outlaws must eat. From his earliest childhood Ned knew that in one of his family the loyalty of Red coursed strongly. To his sister Maggie he turned, and she proved worthy of his trust.

Over at Mansfield Superintendent Pewtress had contributed his final faithful service in the hunt for he had waited throughout the day of 12 November for the four to turn themselves in. No horseman rode into the town on such a business as giving his body up to the Queen's protection, so Pewtress departed to take no further part in the proceedings. Captain Standish became more than ever convinced that his weighty charge, as master of his men, was perhaps to prove more onerous than he had initially thought. There were so many possibilities to ponder. A Pentridge prisoner, Michael Woodyard, who professed to know the Kellys well over a period of eight years, had proved useful in that he had helped to identify Joe, and even to describe his eyes as full and remarkable in their greyish blueness and to sound the ominous note that they were 'bullet eyes'. He also said that once across the Murray the Kelly boys would set out for the back blocks up beyond the Darling, for that was a country they knew thoroughly. It was all very confusing for Standish with Sadleir advising him to get the Crown Lands Department to 'put pressure on a few selectors near Greta and Wombat who notoriously harbour the Kellys'. Sadleir hoped that such pressure, implying as it would a threat to the selectors' precarious hold on their pitiful acres, would induce them to turn the brothers in. Then had come the information that the police would find their quarry if they were to come down in force on the Woolshed in the vicinity of the Byrne home. Admittedly it was all clouded by the fact that the word had come through the slurred lips and hazy brain

of a drunken wood splitter, but it was time to be decisive
so Standish decided to lead a charge himself on that
tiny place called Sebastopol. They awakened the whole
locality with clattering hooves, causing Mrs Byrne to
drive them all away with derision from her humble
abode but nonetheless evoking memories of great
deeds across the seas in Crimea. In the process the Captain made a fool of himself, of his men and of the whole
affair which *Melbourne Punch* thought was 'daily
assuming amazing positions of singular incredibility'.
The journal indulged in the light-hearted nonsense of
printing a letter allegedly written by Ned to the editor,
in which the outlaw said that although he had his 'men
patrolling the various ranges' they were unable to 'come
across even one Bobby', and another in which Ned commanded Standish, Brooke Smith, Nicolson, and Pewtress
to surrender themselves at his residence at Greta before
the 16 November.[13]

On his return to Melbourne to which he was pleased
to repair, Standish was comforted to feel that he had
managed to acquire the services of a valuable secret
agent while he was engaged in the pressing business
of charging Sebastopol. It seems that Constable Strahan
had fallen in with a 'light-looking, high-shouldered
man' with the toughness of a bullocky's whip in his
slender frame and the look of one whose mind was on
things that others flew from, even in thought. He was
Aaron Sherritt, and he had a good and plausible reason
to be about the Byrne home where Strahan met him, for
he was engaged to a daughter of Mrs Byrne, and hence
he was close to the family, as he was to the four with
whom he had often ridden. Strahan thought he would
be useful to the police, but Aaron would only take the
word of Standish that it was a thing blessed to authority

for him to sell both himself and his mates. The Captain gave his word for the integrity of such an act. Some memory of childhood, some bond forged in those very hills as they rode together, some remnant of decency stirred in Aaron as he said he would do it with no precise sum of silver named. He asked that Joe's life be saved, and Standish gave him an assurance that such would be the case. Charles Hope Nicolson was appalled that such a transaction could be conducted within the hearing of several others, including young constables, and he remonstrated with his superior, but Standish felt secure because he was dealing with a set of mere hill ruffians, one of whom was as likely as not to desert his fellows. Nonetheless the Captain was not so gullible as to take all men and all things at their face value, and when he was shown the text of a letter purporting to have been written by Ned and Dan he closely examined it and sent back a telegram to Mansfield to state that he thought it 'very improbable' that it was written by the brothers. It was indeed a fearsome, if not loathsome missive, for it threatened to do to death a certain Edward Monk in a truly gruesome way as a reward for his activity in assisting the police to find the bodies of the poor dead policemen. The police of Mansfield were then moved to look elsewhere for the author of this document, and they came upon an old arsonist and villain of low repute named Walter Lynch, who in due course was sentenced to two years for his penmanship. But the damage was done because the letter had been printed in full in the *Federal Standard* and some men, and women too, went in fear of those brothers who would threaten to gouge the eyes from an innocent human being.[14]

Brickey, who was no judge of the timbre of a woman whatever other insights he may have claimed, laboured under the delusion that 'Mrs Skillion would put them away if she was properly worked'. Maggie however continued to be the main support of the four. She regularly baked and cooked for them and managed to deliver her precious cargo every couple of days, to the bovine annoyance of the local constabulary who watched and followed her constantly, to no avail. The hills, bush and gullies of the Warbys and Black Range were no obstacle to a woman to whom a good horse was as wings to a bird, but to the police such places were well nigh impenetrable and Maggie could afford to play games with them at will. Standish himself had to suffer the chagrin of reading useless letters from William Donnelly, a friend of the Kellys and Wrights whom he had planted as a spy under Maggie's own roof. Standish persuaded the ex-cattle thief to pass on any useful information but all William's information proved futile. The irritation of people being at large, who were allegedly prepared to offer assistance to the outlaws, was irksome in the extreme so Standish advised Nicolson not to hesitate to use the powers given under the new Act to lock up the Quinns, Lloyds and other 'associates', as it would be a great advantage to do so 'if it were even only for a few weeks'. This kind of incrimination by association, with the concomitant possibility of incarceration, was not lost on Ned who had become known to the police as 'Captain'. If the police were determined to make it hard for his friends to assist him it was necessary for the outlaw leader to devise a way of rewarding people for their favours. It was not without reason that Standish began to insist that the banks be watched.[15]

With the wind, the dust and the increasing heat of a mid-November Melbourne, it was all becoming tedious to the Captain. A mere walk down Collins Street was sufficient to irritate him as he knew that others beside himself were reading *Punch* and there was even the possibility that mild banter was entered into behind his back at the Melbourne Club. What calibre indeed did his force possess, he asked himself, when he had to suffer the humiliation of telegraphing to his fellow senior policemen in New South Wales on 15 November the information that Joe Byrne was the third member of the four while it was likely that the fourth was Billy King, to be told that in New South Wales they knew about Joe and were equally clear that Aaron was the other outlaw? A day later a country editor was able to publish the news that it was neither Billy nor Aaron, but Stephen Hart who made up the party, so that it had taken three weeks even to identify the full complement of Kelly's murderous crew. Was it any wonder that in New South Wales they were laughing, priding themselves on their police and their proficiency as shown by the case of Sergeant Walling's murderer, and predicting that if the Victorian outlaws crossed the border they would be smartly eliminated?[16]

As if mere anonymity were not enough, the four had allegedly begun to appear everywhere, whether as drunken, yelling shearers at 2 a.m. in Mansfield or as fleeing robbers near Murchison, while their leader was being impersonated by the inebriated, or the infatuated, or the devious, at divers spots in the northeast. Further to all this the new rifles the Captain had dispatched to his men proved unworkable, the black trackers were in his estimation of 'no use', Donnelly had rendered himself totally ineffective by going around informing others that he was informer and then resigning; furthermore Wild Wright was rampaging around the Wombat daring the police to arrest him, and even

a representative of Victoria's lunatic fringe had joined
in the farce with a letter to say that he had been informed
by a spirit that the four had slain themselves, and their
bodies were to be found a mile and a half south of
Stringybark Creek. In a more serious vein the story was
beginning to circulate that a girl and not a would-be
murderer was the centre of the whole affair. Kate was
described as 'very good looking' and it was remarked
'all the family are not deficient in that way'. But one of
Standish's correspondents almost drove him to apo-
plexy. A certain G. E. Buckmaster had been a mounted
constable from 1858 to 1870 when he resigned. He had
the temerity to write to the newspapers blaming the
police, and in particular, Hall, for the subsequent
behaviour of the Kellys and he also cast grave doubts
upon the competency of Standish himself, to say nothing
of Pewtress. Buckmaster now had the temerity to offer
his services to the Victoria Police to track down the
outlaws, and Standish had to explain to the government
that he was a drunkard and a blackguard. To one piece
of information, however, he did respond with alacrity.
A rumour circulated that a Seymour bank was about to
be held up, so he sent up three foot constables to parade
the streets of the town in plain clothes. Nothing untoward
occurred, and then the Melbourne papers of 5 and 6 December announced that the outlaws had crossed into the
mother colony so the Captain inserted a confident note
in his memo book and settled down to his normal routine
at his Club. His premature complacency was reinforced
on the following day when the four were heard of at Bre-
warrina near Bourke. Meanwhile the gentlemen in question were actually moving down through those ranges
called the Strathbogies.[17]

Happy Christmas 10

In January 1838 George Faithfull, son of William, after thinking long on the matter, decided to go forth from the districts about Bungonia with his herd and his brother's flock and settle in that promised land to the south. He came down the route marked by Mitchell until he saw those plains named after Oxley, which still looked green and lush in late summer. Such was surely a place for his beasts to fatten, so he turned off there and sent his overseer ahead with his brother's flocks. They were to be taken as far as the river, broken into by all the creeks which flowed on those plains to the further south, and indeed they arrived there safely. But the men of that country had watched those vast flocks and herds coming down from the north for month after month; their elders had pondered on what was to become of their sacred places, of the game which to them was food, of the women who seemed not averse to commune with these paler ones and of the young men who found much delight and merriment in the strong drink that turned their minds to foolishness. The old ones took counsel amongst themselves, and when this new mob of men and sheep arrived at the river on 11 April they threw their dark bodies with their meagre weapons upon them. Fifteen convict shepherds, precursors in bondage of their attackers, dropped their arms and fled, but for seven of them it was not done with sufficient speed and by night they lay dead. To Governor George Gipps, grappling with asthma in the Sydney humidity and staying up late into the night to send his despatches to London, it was all a horror. Men came and begged him to make war against these savages, but George recoiled in righteous anger because on the one side he saw unbridled greed and on the other, poor, defenceless creatures who shared the lot of humanity with him. Neither the greedy nor George need have worried, for the black man was to retreat so that forty years later he was only a memory in those parts. Benalla flourished as a little town on the place where men had died, Euroa grew up to the south on its pleasant creeks, and a few miles north of that town a fine homestead stood on the banks of a stream called after the Faithfulls. To that place, four men on splendid horses rode up in the early afternoon of 9 December 1878 and what followed was a happy enough affair for all, but especially for the horsemen and their leader.[1]

At the station homestead Ned was quickly in command. In short order, the men present were all safely locked up in an outbuilding and Ned made himself known to the lady in charge of the home, Mrs Fitzgerald, who ever afterwards remembered his courtesy and manliness as she fed him and his fellows. Her husband went to join his friends in their place of temporary detainment while those other dozen men who worked the broad acres for Younghusbands were gathered up as they came in from their labours. In the course of the afternoon, a hawker named James Gloster arrived to whom the leader introduced himself with the words, 'I am Ned Kelly, son of Red Kelly, and a finer man never set his feet in two shoes.' This introduction was followed with threats to the life and person of Mr Gloster were he so minded as to prove troublesome. The hawker and his youthful assistant joined the others, amongst whom there was an ex-constable, turned groom, by name George Stephens. In the night-watches Ned stayed awake and to his attentive audience went over and over Stringybark Creek which by now had become a nagging pain at his heart, denied again and again that it was a tale of murder, while asserting that his absence from Greta on the night of Fitzpatrick's visit cleared him of any responsibility for the scratched arm of that young man. In the morning a jocular group came up to the station in a spring cart. William Casement, who farmed near Euroa, had taken three of his Melbourne guests who worked in the government printery for a morning jaunt shooting kangaroos, which sport was deemed suitable to allay the jangled nerves of these men of the city. Their sport was short-lived, and a joking case of mistaken identity in which the Kellys were believed by the hunters to be police, and impudent police at that, resulted in further bombast from Ned and the quick incarceration of the passengers of the spring cart.

The morning passed pleasantly while two items of serious business were attended to with precision. The railway line, with its accompanying telegraph poles, ran a couple of hundred yards from the house; wire-snippers were produced, the line cut and some poles chopped down. A gang of four railway fettlers passed by, stopped at the sight of this destruction to government property and were cordially invited to join the now swollen numbers in the makeshift prison. While unwillingly detained, Mr Gloster had several items of wearing apparel appropriated by Ned and his men, who decked themselves out in new gear in the form of hats, boots, breeches, shirts and ties to which they added a touch of perfume, as was the way of the young blades of the bush. Lunch was then served, with Ned as ever careful that they were not brought low by poisoning, after which Joe selected a stationhand to assist him in guarding his fellow prisoners while Ned requisitioned both the hawker's van and the spring cart for an afternoon drive into Euroa. They crossed the ford on the creek in front of the house, with Dan in the Casement cart and Ned, accompanied by the hawker's boy, bringing up the rear. Through the brown paddocks, down the road a couple of miles and by 4 p.m. they were in the town. Steve, who was not well known locally, had visited the place over the previous few days. He rode ahead to partake of a pleasant lunch at the North Eastern Hotel and await the arrival of his 'Captain'.

The main business being transacted in Euroa on the sleepy December afternoon was that of burying the dead in the body of the child of a local citizen, and the renewal of the licences of the local hostelries by Alfred Wyatt. The magistrate sat in the courthouse listening to the pleas of the district publicans as they presented their cases for the continued good favour of the law in respect of their premises. His mind however was not on such mundane matters and, to the surprise and gratification of all concerned, he transacted the business within a quarter of an hour and all went happily away. Mr Wyatt was pondering on the meaning of the cut telegraph wires which he had observed as his train passed by Faithfull's Creek an hour or so previously. In another part of the town a quiet procession set out along the Sydney road to the cemetery a mile from the town. The parents sat in grief, while the pine box rattled in the hearse conveying a young Australian to his resting place at the foot of the Strathbogies where the gums sighed to the gentle breeze. Meanwhile, across at the National Bank, just over from the railway station, a matter of an entirely different nature was in hand.

Mr Robert Scott was somewhat surprised when a young man insisted that, despite the fact that the bank was no longer open for business, he should cash the cheque which was presented before him as manager. He was even further surprised when the same young man intimated that, as he was Ned Kelly in person, his purpose there was to relieve the bank of its wealth, which in due course he did to the tune of over £2,000 as well as the mortgage deeds of the district's selectors. Some bluster and banter were engaged in, small whiskies drunk, Mrs Scott insisted on changing her dress, a nursemaid fainted and was brought around and in short enough order a fascinating cavalcade set out from the bank and proceeded north through the town. Dan was given pride of place in the hawker's contraption which held, besides him, two bank clerks and a female servant. Mrs Scott, decked now in finery becoming to a bank manager's wife out for an afternoon drive, followed in the family buggy with her mother and her seven children. The spring cart bore Ned, Scott and a further female servant, while Steve rode slowly in the rear. This parade passed the cemetery with the dignity befitting the solemnity of the occasion and, with one minor mishap when the horse drawing Ned's cart fell and had to be rested for a brief time, they all arrived back at the homestead in time for the evening meal.

The actual feeding of this numerous tribe of forty-one

composed of outlaws, free women and children, and
bondsmen in the outhouse, did not tax Mrs Fitzgerald
nor her ample pantry. The evening turned to dusk while
Ned spoke of the letter he had penned to Mr Cameron
M.L.A., commanded the men not to leave the station for
three hours after his departure with the threat that the
overseer would pay dearly for disobedience, and then
joined Dan, Steve and Joe in a spirited display of fancy
horsemanship. By eight o'clock the ranges beckoned so
they were away across the main road and up by Mount
Wombat, through the Blue Range and then down into
the valley and home. All that had passed at Faithfull's
Creek had been done in the high manner of outlaws
who stretched the law to their own purpose without viol-
ating the dignity of human beings. They had refused
to accept a collection made by the men in the night, Ned
had given a watch to Gloster's boy but they had taken
Gloster's goods and he was a hawker not given to for-
giveness, while Joe had removed Scott's watch, perhaps
to remind him that three hours meant that by any time-
piece. In the minds of almost all who had participated
in the festivities surrounding the robbing of the Euroa
bank, the leader himself left an impression of gentility,
firmness and purposefulness which contrasted with the
horror stories that circulated after Stringybark Creek.
That particular horror Ned himself carried into the high
places beyond the ken of men.[2]

The members of Her Majesty's constabulary in the
northeast were somewhat taken aback at the Euroa
affair. While the *Melbourne Punch* had a heyday, with
a cartoon depicting Ned as Premier of the colony in
place of Graham Berry, who was about to depart on his
mission to Downing Street in an attempt to have the constitution changed, the police licked their wounds. On

the actual day of the raid the main representative of the
law in Euroa happened to have been absent on more
pressing affairs elsewhere, while his temporary assistant, Peter Percival, was in bed with a cold and sore
throat. To make matters worse the two superior officers,
Nicolson as the man in charge of operations, and his
lieutenant, Sadleir, had been rused away from the area
by false information passed on by John Quinn that the
four were to make another attempt to cross the river into
New South Wales. Accordingly they had decided to set
out to Albury to organize their capture and by chance
they met an agitated Mr Wyatt M.P. as they were about
to take the train at Benalla for Albury. It was the very
evening of the Euroa hold-up, but the two policemen
had remained impassive as Wyatt produced a piece of
cut telegraph wire from Faithfull's Creek, and they proceeded on their way. At Euroa itself all had remained
quiet until, the curfew over, the word was spread that
the bank had been robbed and no one appeared to
know quite what to do. Clearly the four bush boys, who
had so coolly perpetrated the deed, had to be chased
but by whom and with what? Volunteers had abounded
for such a task, though when the actual moment for pursuit came, they disappeared quietly to flaunt their bravery at kitchen tables and in hotel bars.[3]

Captain Standish was at a public dinner at the Melbourne Town Hall on that night of 10 December and on
his return to his Club he was informed of the day's proceedings at Euroa. He rushed forthwith to the telegraph
office and spent the whole night making the wires hum
with instructions. Nicolson returned from Albury and
helped organize a search party on the following morning, with no fruitful results except lost and confusing
tracks. General disorganization followed until Standish

himself arrived at Benalla on the 12th to find that the
robbers had been seen in four separate places, distant
at least one hundred miles from each other. Disbeliever
as he was in the quality of ubiquity, the Captain was
inclined to reject these reports and to ponder long on
why it was that such ill-success plagued him and his
men. He was especially irritated with the inhabitants of
the northeast itself, as to him they consisted of friends,
relations and associates of the Kellys; very many were
openly avowing their sympathy with the offenders, while
all but a handful of the rest were arrant cowards and
thus gave no useful information. It was an indictment
of a large segment of Victoria's population, and the facts
that such people seemed perversely to have chosen to
dwell in such an inaccessible part of the country, that
hundreds of them allegedly assisted and supplied the
outlaws, that they remained impervious to the dire provision of the section of the Felons Apprehension Act by
which the law could fall heavily upon them, drove the
chief policeman into a veritable flurry of exculpatory
prose addressed to the highest authority in the land.
One piece of good news he had, however, to convey to
that worthy: Ned's associate of the boggy days of 1870,
Ben Gould the former hawker, had been seen in and
about Euroa in the days preceding the hold-up. Furthermore he had, it seems, engaged in the very great curiosity of ordering German sausages and corned beef
which he was observed neither to consume nor sell. To
an astute mind, all of the implications of such behaviour
were clear. Ben had been spying out the land for the
boys while they themselves were living up in the hills
replete on a diet of sausages and beef. Standish acted
swiftly and had Ben arrested.[4]

Captain Standish was a keen observer of one thing
in particular: sport in all its varied manifestations. It was

summer and an Australian team had just returned victorious from a tour of England, to be praised by no lesser
a luminary than Dr Moorhouse. His words on captaincy
were important to Standish for it appeared to the bishop
that a good captain, obeyed without question, was
indubitably of the essence for a successful outcome to
a cricket match. Now Standish was prepared to admit
that the strength of the other side in the particular game
being played in and about the northeast made it difficult
for Nicolson. Nonetheless he had been bowling away
now from some weeks without, so to speak, a chance
given, much less a wicket taken. A firm hand, a steady
eye and steely nerves were needed and, in Standish's
opinion, Nicolson was clearly 'utterly prostrated by
bodily fatigue and mental anxiety' while his eyes were
very bad. As prompt as he had been to nab Ben Gould,
the Chief Commissioner was equally incisive in respect
of Nicolson who was despatched to Melbourne while
Standish avowed to Berry that there was no officer in
the force 'in whom I have more thorough confidence'.
Nonetheless he was pleased to inform Berry that Nicolson's replacement would be Hare who 'will be of the
greatest use to me, as no one in the Force is better fitted
for this work than he is'. Hare sat down in the Benalla
police station to read the assembled and assorted docu-
mentation left behind by Nicolson while Standish, with
fitful forays directed to bring the detested sympathizers
to heel, spent his time in the more comfortable pursuit
of reading novels. While so doing he pondered on his
conviction that, try as he might, it was going to prove
a very long day in the field for his side. His subordinates,
who did not share his perceptions, wondered why he
'showed a great want of interest in any work in the Kelly
pursuit'.[5]

Partly due to this want of interest, but more importantly

as a result of their familiarity with the northeast in its
wild spaces of mountain, valley, river and plain, the four
outlaws were able to settle down in moderate comfort
for the Christmas season. The fact that they were now
financially independent, consequent upon their visit to
Euroa, helped to make them further welcome amongst
that group of close relatives and supporters who were
prepared to supply them with shelter, food and other
necessities. All of this was understood and appreciated
by the youngsters, Steve and Dan, but to Joe, and to Ned
in particular, it was mere bodily comfort which solved
nothing. They remained vermin to be gunned down without compunction and others were implicated with them.
Ellen Kelly was pining away in a Melbourne prison
where the baptism of her baby was some form of contact
with a world beyond walls. Mrs Byrne lived in her frugal
widowhood, and wondered if Joe would be destroyed
in the welter that had of necessity to ensue as a result
of the dark deed done in the Wombat. Ettie Hart knew
now that she would never stand at an altar beside the
wild, strong boy from Greta, and in the home at Wangaratta her parents anguished over the impetuosity that
had led Steve to wander onto a path of blood. There
had still been the faint hope in a mother's breast that
it could not be her Steve they spoke of as an accomplice
at Stringbark Creek, for he had never been a boy of violence and she could not comprehend how he had given
himself over to killing his fellow men. But that hope had
been stilled when the word of Euroa came, for Fanny
Shaw, his classmate of happy days in the little school
at Wangaratta, was a maid at the bank and had recognized and spoken to Steve, so now all was lost.

Ned knew that it was all very well for Frank Harty and
Isaiah Wright to proclaim their undying loyalty and their

conviction that he was the finest man in the land, because words cost nothing, but the constant, unswerving and unquestioning devotion of his sister Maggie, and his cousin Tom Lloyd, needed no proclamation to ensure its continuation, while no reward would ever tempt them to betrayal. But there was that wider world in which men and women of integrity read of Ned and his companions, looked long at the engravings which depicted them as cold-blooded murderers at Stringybark Creek and saw him portrayed with the eyes of a venomous snake, and Dan with the cruel features of a rat.[6] Mrs Scott had been pleasantly taken aback when she saw Ned at Euroa and she remarked on his good looks and bearing, while her husband thought he was 'a splendid specimen of the human kind, tall, active, athletic, and rather handsome'. But an evil image had been created and somehow it had to be set right. Ned did not know why Donald Cameron, M.L.A. for West Bourke and journalist by profession, had stood up in the Legislative Assembly on 13 November and asked the Premier to enquire into the statements made about Benalla 'which seemed to point to the conduct of certain members of the police force as having led up to the Mansfield murders'. All he knew was that the question had been asked and in Ned there boiled all his hatred of Flood and Fitzpatrick.

What could he say of Flood, for the woman he had seduced had been long since stilled in her grave and of her Ned would never speak? But Fitzpatrick was another thing, so he had written to Cameron and set it all out, asserting again that he was far off in New South Wales when the young trooper visited his mother's home. He deplored that his own character could not have been painted in blacker hues even had he 'robbed, plundered, ravished and murdered' all those who ever crossed his path. Despite it all, he could still assert that by God's grace his conscience was 'as clear as the snow in Peru' and he was astonished that articles of human dross such as Fitzpatrick could lead the members of the Legislative Assembly astray for, as long as an outlaw like himself remained free, it would be a case for the police of 'double pay and country girls'. In the end he ran out of paper and concluded with a 'sweet good-bye' and the reminder that those arteries of the commercial interests of the colony called railroads were vulnerable to attack. The letter was posted at Glenrowan on 14 December and, after its delivery to a startled and probably embarrassed Cameron, it was passed to the government. But if Ned sincerely hoped that his pen, dipped whether for effect or of necessity in red ink, would prove stronger than deeds he was mistaken. Although Graham Berry thought the letter was both 'clever and straightforward', Standish dismissed it as a 'tissue of falsehoods' and his view prevailed. One journal spoke of 'a tale of bitter wrong to one of the Kelly's female relatives by a constable' but Fitzpatrick was safely married and all honour done to the lawyer's daughter from Frankston. As for the people of the Greta creeks and the upper King, Standish had plans – for the menfolk at least. After all, when even the head of the government had begun to regard as useless the spending of further money on arms and other equipment, when it was perfectly clear that no identifiable progress in tracking down the outlaws was being made, it was time to take some action. Nonetheless Christmas was almost upon them, so while the four celebrated it with a Christmas dinner and a gathering of the clan at Greta, Captain Standish did equally well a few miles away at Benalla

and a temporary and wholly fitting period of truce
reigned in the northeast between the respective comba-
tants.[7] From the feasting at Greta the mother whom they
loved, with a love bordering almost on worship, was
absent; it is not recorded what form the feasting took
in prison.[8]

It had been an especially poor season in the
northeast, with much rust in the crops, rendered even
worse by the fact that it was the third in succession and
as a consequence the harvest was both meagre and late.
But there was enough for seed for the following year
and the small selectors were conscious that it at least
had to be stripped to ensure some minimal form of existence in the future. For some farmers and selectors it was
to prove an especially frustrating harvest because on
2 January 1879 Standish swooped. The provocation was,
of course, extreme, for how could he bear with continued
equanimity the opprobrium, constant sniping and ridicule poured on his head and on his force since the happy
events of Euroa? The press had enjoyed a veritable bon-
anza in which Ned was praised for his generalship, Joe
for his coolness in holding twenty-two prisoners without
mishap, Steve for his dexterity at riding around disguised as a woman, and the police scorned for their
seemingly total ineptitude. The guards, engine drivers
and stokers on the trains had been armed, attachments
of the Garrison Artillery had been stationed in the main
towns to protect the citizenry, bank managers and their
staff were engaged in pistol drill, arms in greater quantities were being freighted into the northeast, and the
whole fabric of civilization there was beginning to be
warped with militarism, alarms, rumours and laughter.
The reward itself had been increased to the immense
sum of £4,000 and even the Chinese were offered an

inducement to share in it, on the probable grounds that they would make more by turning Joe in than by supplying him with the opium to which he was alleged to be addicted. There were constant reports of sightings of the outlaws, impersonation of them by reckless youths, and stories about how they were living on the fat of the bank, but somehow they remained elusive to handcuff, gun or even official surveillance, despite the widespread conviction that they moved about as freely as if they were indeed as innocent of blemish as the snow of the high Andes. To Standish it was clear that those damnable people who remained impervious to threat or bribe, who faced financial ruin and spurned a fortune for betrayal, who housed, comforted and fed the four vagabonds, were responsible for his discomfort. Who could blame the poor, harassed policeman if his action was reckless, ruthless, ill-advised and discriminatory? Hare and Ward thought it was a splendid idea of Standish to bag as many as could be conveniently detained while only Sadleir, who knew the people of that country well, saw only ill coming of it. At any rate bagged they were, to the tune of thirty arrests with twenty-three detentions. They were not charged with harbouring the outlaws but with giving them 'information tending to facilitate the commission by them of further crimes'. It was a singularly inept charge requiring precise proof, but it mattered not what the charge was as long as terror was struck into the hearts of these miscreants. Unfortunately for Standish they were a breed for whom mere detention at the pleasure of the Queen across the water held no terror.[9]

The men taken with such abruptness from their homes and harvests were designated for that single honour by the old guard of the north-eastern police force, including Flood and Mullane. It took some days to line twenty detainees up in the Beechworth Gaol where they were charged before a magistrate, with an unwilling Sadleir appearing for the police, while three more appeared at Wangaratta. It was not difficult to select some of them, as their names and associations, combined with constant form over previous years, made them as obvious for inclusion as the old hands of an Australian XI. Wild Wright, Jimmy Quinn, Tom Lloyd senior, Frank Harty, Pat Quinn and two more Lloyds were all there, as well as Steve Hart's brother, John. The others were all dubbed as active sympathizers, which scarcely anybody doubted to be the truth and to whom another thousand could probably easily have been added. But no prison could have held them and it was deemed advisable to quarter twelve strong and bold members of the Artillery in the gaol so as to ensure that those who there represented the Kelly following were held in good order for their court appearances. Lest a veritable siege be mounted to release them, it was considered necessary to spend £700 in iron plating the doors and otherwise setting in order the building, for no one could tell to what lengths those people might go to see the release of their loved ones.

The case was put that the proceedings were in direct violation of the law and after a week's consideration, it was decided that neither mental nor verbal gymnastics could prove sufficient to convince even the most pliable magistrate, as Mr Foster J.P. of Beechworth was proving himself to be, that eight of the men could continue to be held, and accordingly they were released. The other detainees came up for remand after remand, with not a shred of evidence being submitted as to their guilt, and the clear injustice of the proceedings was so painful to the upright that even the editor of the *Ovens and Murray Advertiser* began to lament that so many were being disaffected that widespread doubt was now being cast on the veracity of Constable Fitzpatrick's story, which was increasingly identified as the matrix of all the evil. The paper berated the 'Berry mob as ten times worse than a thousand Kelly gangs' while the police force was judged rotten to its core, and a laughing stock to the whole country. Mr Zincke, for the defence, caused further embarrassment when he reminded the court that these men's crops were rotting and their families suffering, that one had a wife in confinement and that the long-flaunted British freedom of the individual would be rendered pitiable in the sight of other less worthy peoples, such as the Italians or the Russians, were the proceedings in Beechworth widely known. Captain Standish, however, was not a whit abashed by all this, and perhaps he was even comforted when he heard that one villain had reaped her just deserts in the whole affair. When the amiable and bounteous Mrs Fitzgerald of Faithfull's Creek station was observed to have a large number of sixpences in her possession, the deduction was not that she was saving them for the innards of future Christmas puddings and the consequent delight of the innocent, but that she was guilty of receiving coinage stolen from the Euroa bank. The case against her was not sustained but she was summarily dismissed from her position.

Meanwhile her four, erstwhile young guests had spent their Christmas vacation in and about Greta and the summer was wearing on. They had decided to take a trip up beyond the big river and they had more than sixpences in mind.[10] Before their departure, Ned is said to have penned a letter to Bryan O'Loghlen in which he repudiated the story of McIntyre that they had killed in cold blood at Stringybark Creek and proclaimed that they had been forced by circumstances to become 'outlaws and outcasts'. He charged the law with a 'manifest injustice' in imprisoning the innocent people against whom there was no proof, and declared that the police were incompetent cowards. Indeed he himself had accompanied one party on a search for Ned Kelly! His conclusion was, 'Beware, for we are now desperate men.'[11]

When the Aborigine passed beyond the reedy place to which he had come for ages, the men who supplanted him called it Jerilderie and it thus retained some remnant of former loveliness.[1] The invaders of that vast, plain country marked it little, as first cattle and then sheep moved further to the north and west. Beside the Billabong Creek in the late 1850s a small community grew up with two stores and then a public house, followed by the other conveniences men call civilization. The land, with its places sacred to the old ones, came to know another holiness with the rise and fall of the auctioneer's hammer and the reedy place was given its village and suburban boundaries. New names now held the ground – names like Powell, Brett, Taylor and Brown – and by the 1860s the burial places and the rock ovens were deserted, except by the wild dog who had come down in ancient times and stayed faithful on the outskirts of a world he knew not.

Jerilderie in February 1879 was replete with wealth

and enterprise. Its five hotels, and a store for each of them, its courthouse where Mass was said because it boasted no church, its school, lock-up, barracks, blacksmith's shop, three bootmakers and a post office bore testimony to the progress of its three hundred inhabitants. Back in 1875 the august fathers of the Bank of New South Wales had cast their eyes approvingly on Jerilderie, and Mr John W. Tarleton had been despatched to conduct the business of the bank in premises forming part of the Royal Mail Hotel. Peace, decency and an enormous solitude reigned in the town on Saturday, the eighth day of February 1879, while on those plains that flung to the north, where the land stretched to the dead heart of the continent, the sun shimmered and danced to a macabre mirage. Meanwhile the tall timbers and the country of the south lay quiet also, except for two pairs of horsemen carefully and leisurely picking their way to the township.

The horsemen came in pairs because their quartet had already struck a blending of fear and astonishment in the hearts of the citizens in the far-flung towns and homesteads of the lands beyond the Murray. In Jerilderie the local scribe, Samuel Gill, and Senior Constable Devine of the New South Wales police force, were full of foreboding after the news of Euroa, and Gill had drawn attention to how defenceless the place was in several articles in his *Jerilderie Herald and Urana Gazette*, but had been laughed to scorn by the yeomen of the district who felt certain they could deal adequately with any loutish incursion from across the border.[2]

The fact that Steve Hart had visited the town vending horses, was familiar with the locality and was well known to Devine, gave some citizens pause for thought. It was further said that the leader himself had been seen and

spoken with on the roads of the blacksoil plains, and
Ned was remembered at the Turn Back Jemmy Hotel
where his quiet reserve had been noticed and spoken
of later.[3] With the hindsight afforded by Euroa and its
doings, a bank was a liability in a township where the
only link with the white man's protectorate was the frail
wire that hummed in the still air of February.
Nonetheless no one noticed the horsemen as they converged in a united group at Pine Rise, five miles east
of Jerilderie, at four o'clock that afternoon.[4]

The weeks since Euroa had passed in an outpouring
of Ned's spirit. To exclaim and proclaim before the con-
verted or the cowed, whether around the fire at home
in Greta or at the homestead on Faithfull's Creek was
one thing. It was another to tell the world that tale of
misunderstanding, persecution and innocence which
Ned took to be the truth about himself and his family.
The business about the sharing up of the spoils of Euroa
was a matter Ned readily understood, but stood apart
from, as the girls, his close intimates and a wider circle
of the Greta people took and quickly spent their share.
To Ned all that was a necessity, but it was mere dross
in comparison with the sustenance of his spirit which
could only be achieved by addressing a wider audience
and convincing the just of his worthiness to stand
amongst them. Above all he needed to absolve himself
of the charge laid against Cain; hence Stringybark
Creek and its cause needed unfolding. Ned was uncon-
cerned about men's attitude to horse stealing and bank
robbery for he knew he was not alone in his regard for
the necessity of bread. But the eyes of Kennedy lay open
in the long hot nights of memory since October of the
year before, and Ned took up the pen as the only weapon
left to quell that restless spectre in his being.

Ned wrote in his own hand without aid. After eight thousand words, the small sheets of notepaper had become a large bundle which he carefully tied together with string, and then carried about his person until the chosen moment arose for his testimony to achieve more permanent form. He jealously guarded his bundle on that ride from the back ranges near Greta to the Murray between Mulwala and Tocumwal, and in the crossing of the river it had meant more to Ned than horse or gun. Now, as he reined in above Jerilderie it weighed heavily against his breast and, whatever else was to happen in the township beyond, it was imperative that the document be given over to the public. All that passionate urge for self-expression which had lain dormant in Ned since boyhood, except for its passing and violent manifestations with fist and horse, was there in the broken but upright sentences of his bundle. In it too was the flaming intensity of his hatred of police brutality and venality, especially of the Irish police who served 'under a flag and nation that has destroyed, massacred, and murdered their forefathers'. To him an Irishman in the uniform of the Queen had become 'a traitor to his country, ancestors, and religion' because he had 'left the ash corner, deserted the shamrock, the emblem of true wit and beauty . . .' The hours around the fireplace at Wallan, at Avenel, out at dark Glenmore and in the Greta hut were there too, for song and folklore and history all blended in his passion, while a thousand years of thraldom's venom spat forth in those ardent sentences. In that writing, all Ned's identification with the poor and persecuted rang forth, and towards the end he sounded a high note of hope for he thought of his loved ones and beloved place, 'the widows and orphans and poor of Greta district where I spent and will again spend many a happy day fearless, free and bold'.[5] Hope, however, on Pine Rise lay dormant, because other matters pressed which required prudence and foresight.

Towards sunset the horsemen and their mounts were refreshed after the long ride from the river. On the outskirts of Jerilderie, and about two miles to the east of the centre of the township, stood a rough hotel on the south bank of the Billabong Creek. It was called after the commonest sight on that track between Deniliquin and Wagga Wagga, and thus the Woolpack Inn was the resort of teamsters, drovers and men whose purpose was obscure except in movement. The presence of the four horsemen aroused no surprise or comment, either in the mind of William Davidson the owner of the inn, or in that of Mary the Larrikin whose real name was Jordan, but whose heart was light and jolly. Nor is it recorded whether the sight of the manhood of Ned or Joe aroused other feelings in Mary's heart, but she long remembered the meal she served, and treasured afterwards the florin Ned gave her in gratitude for her refusal to serve Joe the whisky his turbulent spirit demanded. The meal passed in pleasantries, while the questions asked by Ned as to the strength of the police force in the town went answered but unheeded, and Mary sang a Kelly song for the merriment of the company and assured the lads that the Kellys would not harm them.

Meanwhile, at their police station two miles away, the resident upholders of the law, Devine and Richards, had concluded their business for the day by depositing a fractious drunk in the lock-up with the hope that heat and thirst would restore him to his senses. Senior Constable Devine then returned to the bosom of his family, while Richards took to his single quarters in the barracks at the back. At 11.30 p.m. a black horse was quietly ridden to the verandah of the station. Astride the horse Ned called to Devine to arouse himself and be quick to come and quell an impending riot at the Woolpack Inn. In short order Devine, who recognized Steve, and Richards were consigned to their own lock-up; Mrs Devine then fed supper to the four, and was reassured by Ned that no harm would befall her and the two children or anyone else, providing all behaved sensibly. Jerilderie slept peacefully, unaware that the order therein prevailing had passed into hands beyond the law.

Father Richard Kiely arrived before 11 a.m. on Sunday to find all in readiness for the Mass he was to offer at the courthouse. On Ned's instruction Dan helped Mrs Devine prepare the symbols in that place where the sacred and the profane intermingled for a brief hour for the benefit of God's remnant in Jerilderie. Mrs Devine was instructed to leave a note for the priest explaining that the family were all to be away for the day, and thus he ought to have his breakfast at the Royal Mail Hotel.[6] The priest departed fortified by his acceptance of bush hospitality, the four across the road at the station strode about in the uniforms of a system they despised, but were happy to use, and Devine and Richards passed the hours in morose monosyllables with their gleeful, but now sober, fellow prisoner. In the afternoon Harry Richards was persuaded to beat the streets of the town in the company of Joe and Steve, who passed as police sent down to help hunt the outlaws, but Devine remained in his lock-up because Ned had decided that there was too much spirit in the man to let him loose in public. After his good day's work Joe returned to seek solace in the company of Mary the Larrikin. Later, he found himself explaining his behaviour to an outraged Ned, who could forgive impetuosity based on Joe's need for female companionship, but rejected the stupidity that endangered the morrow by incautious conviviality at the Woolpack.

Andrew Nixon was a youth of seventeen working his apprenticeship as a blacksmith for Samuel Rea in a large tin shed next to the post office in Powell Street. Across from the tin shed the Royal Mail Hotel could be seen, and in front of that section of it occupied by the Bank of New South Wales stood a row of empty hogsheads awaiting transport to Deniliquin for refilling, later to assuage the not inconsiderable thirst of the citizens of Jerilderie. Andrew came to work early on Monday morning and was not surprised to find two strange police officers wanting their horses shod. Dan and Joe explained that they were off to the border before evening to help catch the outlaws, although Andrew wondered at Joe's absentmindedness when, upon returning from a shopping expedition, he left his bread and steaks behind on a shelf in the blacksmith's shop. The two horses, a grey and a brown mare, were shod and Joe requested that the bill be sent to the New South Wales Police, which came to be regarded later as a particular piece of insolence in the upper echelons of that force.[7]

It being a hot morning with the dust in Jerilderie Street rising, the licensee of the Royal Mail Hotel, Charles Cox, already had a steady clientele by eleven. When Constable Richards entered the bar and introduced his fellow policeman with 'Cox, this is Ned Kelly', he replied with the politeness of one whose options were limited: 'How do you do, Ned?' he said. What followed in the bank across the passage was quickly done. The teller, Edwin Living stuttered badly and the sight of Joe's revolver did nothing to calm his nerves, but gave him a halting tale to tell for life. Young James Mackie was

a junior clerk and made of sterner stuff, but his pluck
in going for a gun was met with cool contempt by Joe,
whose head and hand were steady despite the night
at the Woolpack Inn. John Tarleton was flushed from the
bath he was enjoying after a long ride in from the bush.
Once dried and dressed, he witnessed the robbing of
his bank, while the bar parlour gradually filled up with
callers either at the bank or the hotel. They included
William Elliott, the young schoolteacher who also acted
as church secretary. He dismissed his pupils at 12.30 and
called at the bank to pay in some money to the church
account before going on for lunch at McDougall's Albion
Hotel. His business proved simpler than originally intended for, having been commanded to jump the counter
by Joe, he was ordered to hold a bag by Ned who proceeded to fill it with the plunder. Hence Elliott stayed
about to observe all the subsequent transactions and
then live on for over fifty years to talk and write about
them.

James E. Rankin and H. D. Harkin were men of moment
in the township. Magistrates and merchants both, they
were not the kind to tolerate any incursion threatening
the ordered and business-like proceedings of their community. Upon being advised by Samuel Gill that something fishy was going on at the bank, they conspired
to investigate and set aright the matter, were such to
prove the case. Mr Rankin was even heard to proclaim
'We'll stop this' as he stepped across to the bank. Harkin
and Gill fled when confronted with Ned's revolver but
Rankin was a bonny Scot whose twenty stone rendered
him less agile. He tripped over a heavy footscraper in
his flight whereupon Ned nabbed him, so he joined the
other guests in the parlour. Gill stopped in town long
enough to consume a great deal of brandy and to leave

a message for his wife as to his providential release.
Then, fortified, he proceeded six miles on foot to the Carrah homestead where he alerted the inhabitants to the
doings in Jerilderie, embroidering his tale with the information that Rankin had fallen to a bullet in his body
rather than an obstruction to his foot, and that the four
were shooting people right and left.[8]

At the back of the hotel a jockey called Henry Tiffen
had been put to work by Ned on a project which involved
the burning of the deeds of properties, bills of sale and
mortgages which had been found in the safe. To Ned
all such instruments were the means by which banks
blighted the lives of the poor, but he listened to the plea
of Living, the teller, not to destroy his insurance policy.
Ned's ignorance of the transactions of the business
world was massive, and he was unaware that destroying
the documents availed little, as most of them were in
duplicate elsewhere. Nonetheless it revealed his need
to strike out at a world whose fruits he could only dimly
perceive, as he had been reared on the miserable acres
of Avenel and Greta. Yet if Ned was ignorant, the mag-
nanimity of his character came through in Jerilderie
where he spent a good part of the afternoon reining in
the meanness of Steve's petty spirit, which revealed itself
in his readiness to pilfer whatever he fancied, after the
manner of a pirate or a vulture.

All in all, little Steve had a lean day in Jerilderie. His
discomfort began early when he found he could not control the shaking of his revolver, and people were in
danger of being shot because he was afraid to shoot.
To bolster his nerves he ordered a brandy and soda from
Charlie Cox, which Dan quickly had changed to rasp-
berry and lemonade. Later he took a fancy to a hunting
saddle owned by the bank teller, but Living's stammered

plea that he was too poor to manage a replacement caused Ned to order its return. Stabled at the Albion Hotel was a blood mare, the much-loved property of McDougall's daughter. She was distressed when the mare was taken by the lads, and upon representation being made to Ned as to her distress he yielded it up. Steve upbraided him for his unwarranted decency, whereupon Ned rounded on him and called him 'a bloody thing' – an expression which so wounded Steve that he told Constable Richards he'd prefer to be shot than called a 'thing', thereby indicating that some faint remnant of integrity remained to his personality.[9] Finally, an incident with God's sole representative in Jerilderie left poor Steve bereft of any spoils by which he could fill that particular void in his heart which showed so clearly in his countenance.

The Rev. J. B. Gribble was one in whom burnt a spirit that demanded he be a lover of justice and a hater of iniquity. He began his days in the cloth of a Congregational minister and in this persuasion he came to Jerilderie in 1878. There he lived on the outskirts of the town, in the old homestead which had served as the first dwelling of the white man in that reedy place by the Billabong. On that Monday, which saw the forces of iniquity reigning in his town and terrorizing his flock, Mr Gribble went about his own and God's business at his home until late in the afternoon. He then decided to take the air and walk down Jerilderie Street. On hearing of the presence of the four and the theft of the McDougall mare, he interceded successfully for her return and then, while returning to his home, came across the chagrined Steve, who relieved him of his watch even though Gribble had pleaded that no one would take a poor parson's watch. Steve replied that he cared not a whit for such of God's

servants as poor parsons, and kept the watch. Not to
be deterred Gribble went to Ned, then drinking his stirrup cup in the Albion Hotel, and shouting for the group
of happy sympathizers there forgathered. 'Mr Kelly, a
few moments please,' said Gribble from the doorstep
of that place of debasement. Ned turned and came to
him. 'Yes, Mr Gribble, what is it?' he enquired cour-
teously. Upon hearing the cause of the visitation, Ned
accosted Steve and commanded the return of the watch,
which Mr Gribble took, and was seen no more in Jerilderie that day. It is said that the parson looked on Ned
with a great welling of love in his heart and, in later
years when he had become a beloved father to the remnants of those tribes who had lived long in that land,
he remembered the one who had treated him with gentility in the dust of Jerilderie. Steve he neither forgot nor
forgave, and it is recorded that he told young Willie Rankin to shoot him down 'like a dog' if he saw him again.[10]
And thus, in the heart of God's man, there remained a
wilderness that excluded Steve from its embrace, but
perhaps was peopled in time by those to whom a wilderness was home.

During the course of the afternoon Ned alternated
between cold efficiency and blustering flamboyance.
The plan worked to its finest details, from the locking
up of the policemen to the destruction of the telegraphic
equipment at the diminutive post office adjacent to the
blacksmith's shop. Young Andrew Nixon watched as
Ned knocked the insulators off the window sill with his
revolver butt, and heard him warn the bystanders to
keep back lest the weapon discharge, and he shared
Ned's and others' amusement at the futile attempt made
by Charlie Naw to cut down a telegraph pole at Ned's
order. Those acts and the destruction of the bank records

were the only deeds of violence done by the leader, whose control of men and events was apparent to all. Some, however, noticed the sharp nervousness of Steve and the leaf-like trembling of his slender frame, the non-chalance of Joe whose mind was elsewhere, if not back with Mary the Larrikin, and the docility and inflexible obedience of Dan to the order of his brother. Like a detachment of guerillas from a beleaguered army, to whom survival depended utterly on unity, the four had coalesced into one and, when Joe said to the bank teller, 'I am Kelly', it was as if that act of transference of person-ality, by which their weakness was subsumed in Ned's strength, had become a physical reality.

Perhaps Tarleton, perhaps the canny Scot Rankin, or even the old Polish chemist Gartman, knew in their being that Ned had already begun to touch the edge of the borderland between sadness and madness. Certainly all three upheld the dignity of men in Jerilderie on that hot summer's day, and even Ned was nonplussed when Gartman, who had fought in several revolutions, said in guttural tones but with no hint of a quaver, 'So you are Ned Kelly are you? Just what I was going to say: come and let us have a drink.' They knew, as the younger Elliott also knew, that all Ned's blustering threats about shooting Rankin, Richards, young Mackie and Living, of burning down Mrs Devine's home, of returning to deal death to any who betrayed him were mere verbiage, except insofar as they gave form and meaning to the last line of the bundle Ned still carried against his heart. 'I am a widow's son outlawed and my orders must be obeyed.'[11]

In the humble street of Jerilderie, Ned spoke to a little boy whose name he asked and who replied 'I am Jackie Monash', and their meeting was a kindly one in which

the rough colonial past met the commonwealth of the
morrow and man and boy shared in the making of them
both. But other matters then pressed so Ned sent Joe,
Dan and Steve to prepare for their departure while he
staged a grand performance before a captive and
partly tipsy audience in the bar room of the Royal Mail
Hotel. Thirty or so in number, they listened to his sorry
tale of persecution in which reality jousted with hatred,
love with vengeance, nobility with debasement and
awful finality with ineradicable futility. Ned knew that
he was crossing the borders into a land from which no
return was possible, and in desperation he tried to make
men understand what drove him there, and remember
for posterity at least the things that had curtailed and
encompassed his freedom. Flood was there in mind and
tongue as was Fitzpatrick, that 'low, drunken blackguard' who had threatened Kate at revolver point to
yield to his low advances and whose perjured evidence
had sent the hunters to the dreadful, gum-ringed arena
of Stringybark Creek where he lived who killed first, but
only for a time, and even then with wind moaning
through that wilderness of his heart.[12]

One thing alone remained to be done in Jerilderie,
and that was to give permanent form to Ned's scribbled
bundle. But Gill, the printer, had gone to warn the folk
of Carrah and Ned sought him out in vain. He had
decided on printing the bundle in Jerilderie and was
willing to pay handsomely for the task, but whether from
his own pocket or from the £2,140 taken from the bank
is unclear. Ned was at a loss as to how to proceed, and
eventually was forced to leave his manuscript in Living's
care, to whom he said 'This is a bit of my life.' Living
assured him that it would be passed over to Gill on his
return, but it was a vain and empty assurance with which

he never complied and Ned's bundle disappeared from
sight, and the testament he trusted would proclaim to
all his probity became, to some, a literary curiosity and
to others, the lesser charter of a stillborn republic.[13]

Evening was drawing in when the four horsemen, after
the usual spectacular display of riding by Ned and Steve
and the release of the drunk from the lock-up, rode singly
out of Jerilderie, setting their faces to the south and hence
towards Greta and home. Ned had come to do two things
– rob and publish. He succeeded in the endeavour of
lesser import, and the fruits of his plunder were soon
scattered far and wide amongst that circle who depended more and more on the leader. He succeeded in
another way that, even in his day or moment of fleeting
existence, became apparent. A gang rode into Jerilderie, a gang of four outlaws with a price on their heads
and blood on their hands. When they rode out a myth
was already born – it was the myth of an invincible collective that coalesced in the person of Ned himself. Some
celebrated the myth in the doggerel of the bush ballad,
others acted it in the person of the suburban larrikin,
perhaps Mary Jordan and those of hot hearts dreamt
of it on rough or lavendered pillows, others again feared
and hated it and determined, in the manner of Superintendent Hare, to efface that foul breed and its memory
from the surface of the land. Others again were broken
by it and the policeman named Devine was amongst
them. He never recovered from the dreadful indignity
of incarceration in his own lock-up, and the taunts of
cowardice and ineptitude unjustly levelled by many at
him, as well as at the townsmen of Jerilderie, rankled
deeply.[14] He departed quietly in 1880 and while on the
road to the south he met a man named John Dykes, newly
called to serve in Jerilderie as its Presbyterian minister.

To him Devine sold his one hold on Jerilderie – seven
acres of land which became in time the paddock of the
manse.[15] The town itself returned to slumber in the sun,
and talked on and on of those three days of thraldom
in which it had helped fill the void of wilderness in Ned's
heart. Meanwhile in the skies the eagles hovered grace-
fully, while the legend below took flight.[16]

Shadows in the Ranges 12

To men who walk in freedom the night need bring no
fear. It is a time for tranquillity and repose, for a cessation
of the exertions of the daytime, for the gathering of the
loved ones and ultimately for the recreation of body and
spirit called sleep. To men who walk beyond the law
none of this is possible. In the light there is relative security from surprise, from the carefully laid trap and from
ambush. The eyes of friends and strangers can be
watched for the signs of betrayal, the quickly startled
birds rising from trees give warning of an alien presence, while the rising of distant dust or the breaking of
fallen wood alerts the senses. When the shadows of evening fall another aspect comes over all things and menace stalks with their lengthening. Who will now stand
sentinel for the outlaw because to do so is to risk life
itself, and only blood or a consummate love brings mor-
tals to that pass? In those hours he can only turn to those
of his kind, but even there lurks danger for who will not
be tempted to sell others to save himself? Hence it is that

night is a time of true darkness in which a man so placed lives in the inner core of his own being and knows fully what it is to be alone. Release comes with the dawn, but as day follows day he longs to break from a routine that saps his spirit. In the end, like the cornered fox or the hare, he turns from hunted to aggressor and, when death comes, it is embraced, for it has called him to stand and be counted as a man again.

The four who rode back across the river from Jerilderie bore the badge of outlawry lightly on their youthful shoulders. They were going home to the hills and mountains of their childhood and youth, to those few who loved them and to the many who would resist the temptation to sell them. Furthermore they brought with them a guarantee that the bounty of Euroa would be replenished, and hence that those who helped them materially would suffer no pecuniary loss in the doing. It was a happy group that came to Greta to share out the spoils, to tell the stories of their confounding of the hapless police of Jerilderie, of Living who had trembled, of Tarleton in his bath, of the parson whose words 'Good-day to you Ned Kelly' were so graceful, and of the larrikin lass who had consoled Joe in that other colony. To Ned there was expectation and hope, for his bundle, he believed, would find permanent and impressive form in print, and soon he would be able to read the vindication of his lifetime, blighted by the guilt of others. And so they came home rich and singing to a land where few sang, and fewer still were rich because it had been a bad season for the poor selectors of those parts. Some of them had even been on a deputation to the Commissioner for Crown Lands to beg that, after three consecutive bad years, their rents might be allowed to stand over for three months. It was a source of no surprise to them that the banks would extend no money, and the money lenders only at exhorbitant interest, but they felt that the government, which had seemed bent on the path of justice for the poor, would listen. But those men in their Melbourne offices turned stony faces to the pleaders and, while Ned's story of his calamities was silenced, their tongues remained forked to the selectors who came home empty handed.[1]

While the weather held good it was an easy time for the four. They could move from place to place, visit the Pig and Whistle near Moyhu, camp a night near Greta, another at the Woolshed, back at Glenmore, or wherever their fancy or the reports on the movements of the police, dictated. Indeed, if a later statement is to be given credit, Ned even spent three weeks in Melbourne where he had some good, tailored clothes made and where he enjoyed himself immensely. To know the exact whereabouts of the police parties was not only an advantage but a source of huge fun, for even from close quarters those worthies could be observed by day and avoided by night. A favoured spot for a camp, where the four spent several weeks upon their return, was on the Fifteen Mile Creek at the edge of the timber line where the scrub ran down the back of Glenrowan to the beginnings of the plain country. It was right in the heart of their stronghold where the Nolans, McAuliffes, Millers and Bowderns all held selections. Greta was only a half hour's ride away through the gap, and the Warby range to their back ensured that encirclement was impossible. A fence line made of piled-up logs and stumps ran down to John Bowdern's. There it was possible to partake of a drink, to dance and sing to the accompaniment of a concertina, and to pass the time in pleasant conversation. Despite the fact that a police camp was located only a couple of hundred yards from Bowderns, the four often came down that fence line on an evening without hindrance from their hunters though they were careful not to assume that they were let to do so, as if the chase for them were a mere triviality impinging upon an otherwise peaceful if unproductive existence. Such an idyllic state of affairs did not, however, long prevail.[2]

The news of Jerilderie had a truly startling effect upon Standish. On the one hand he could take comfort in the fact that depredations of such a daring nature committed on New South Welsh soil were scarcely his responsibility and that, if the Victoria Police were made to look foolish consequent upon Euroa, their brethren across the border had been made to look even more inept. Nonetheless it was undeniable that such a scourge had its origins in the Captain's domain, and were those damned fellows to return, and it appeared likely that they would, then more decisive action than the desultory reading of novels was required. He had been emboldened by the news that the Jerilderie raid had so moved the head of government in the mother colony, Henry Parkes, that he had offered to donate £4,000 of his taxpayers' and bankers' money as a reward for the capture or extermination of the outlaws. It was a sum which Bryan O'Loghlen, as Acting Premier of Victoria, could scarcely resist matching, as a consequence of which the four, by mid-February, were worth a cool £2,000 apiece, or in total a staggering £8,000, which the *Ovens and Murray Advertiser* confidently asserted was larger than any reward yet offered for the apprehension of criminals since the beginning of the world.[3] It was clearly time for Standish to be more decisive, but the more the effort the less the return except in exhausted men and horses, bills for equipment, forage and arms and general frustration.

True he had interested himself in procuring a formidable group of thirty-two spies and informers who were graced with the title of secret service agents, including old Pat Quinn who went under the pseudonym of P. Foote. Collectively they had come up with nothing despite the £150 spent on their employ.[4] The main difficulty was that the outlaws were far too elusive, leaving less trace than the whirly-whirlies that passed over the stubbled paddocks. They appeared so much part of the northeast that it embraced and hid them from sight. Standish concluded that these native sons of the land were to be caught only by native sons even more ancient in their lineage and more expert in their reading of the signs of men's passage. He bethought himself of the blackman whom he had hitherto scorned as a worthless ally.

The question that had to be decided was where to look for the appropriate black men. A mere fifty years' residence in Victoria had sufficed to enable the whiteman well nigh to obliterate the very presence of a race that had been there from antiquity, let alone any aboriginal skills that such a race had collected. But in the far north of the continent, with its vaster and less hospitable spaces, such had not been the case to anything like the same extent. Apprised of the famed skills of the Queensland black trackers, Standish telegrammed his counterpart in Brisbane to despatch a party of them, under suitable management, by sea to Sydney and thence by rail to Albury. The wires of civilized men carried message after message on this singularly interesting topic over the next few days, while agreements as to rates of pay, divisions of authority, future sharing up of the reward and such practical matters were attended to and agreed upon.

The gentleman in charge of the northern expedition was a youthful-looking Mr Stanhope O'Connor, a retired lieutenant who rejoiced in being a nephew of Sir Hercules Robinson, the retiring Governor of New South Wales. He was to be paid £30 per month while the black men, despite their necessary expertise, were to receive £3, but some compensation was there in the resplendent uniforms in which they were decked. Their blue tunics and caps were trimmed in red, and their breasts and waists were belted and hung with sockets for cartridges. It was conceded that they were far superior a class to their southern counterparts, but relief was expressed that although it was their custom to consume the remains of their fallen enemies in Queensland, no such behaviour would be tolerated in Victoria where they would be 'denied the perquisite of eating the bodies of the vanquished bushrangers'.

The speed of communications was such that by the 11th of March six black men were in the field, and hence it was that Ned, who had scorned the intrusions into his beloved northeast of the tentacles of civilization called the telegraph and the railway, had much more formidable opponents to contend with. These new ones were not as those who had taught him a little of their wondrous skills as a boy at Avenel. They had not come in communion as fellow Australians with the simple purpose of tracking game for the campfire. They had come to hunt Ned and those who went with Ned, and their coming cast fear and pitched deep resentment into his soul, for he now knew that he was in very truth an outcast and a fugitive in the land that had given birth both to hunted and to hunters. One of them, called Sambo, longed for the far places and the familiar faces of his people in the north. He fell ill, pined away and died, to be buried

in another's tribal grounds, and it was fitting that he was
put to rest as a pauper for he had come owning nothing
and his spirit left the northeast as it had come.[5]

While these transactions were afoot the group of
detainees were still whiling away their time in Beechworth alternately hoping, brawling, blaming others and
fretting. Not for them the excitement of Jerilderie, the
exhilarating meetings with the outlaws in the bush
around Greta; not even the humdrum chores of a later
and lean harvest, and for one Robert Miller, sick and
old, a struggler on a few acres taken in the middle of
his harvest, whose only crime was that he had married
into the clan, it spelt ruin. They were detained at Her
Majesty's pleasure on remand after remand, while the
officers of that personage were engaged in manufactur-
ing evidence designed to give permanence to their
detention. The proceedings in the court had begun to
border on the ludicrous, with much bandying of legal
opinion between Wyatt on his bench, the advocates for
the prisoners and even between bench and dock. Wyatt
was solicitous for the welfare of the men before him, and
reminded James Quinn that the only thing that stood
between Jimmy and the drop was Wyatt's hand on the
rope which he proposed to grasp firmly, and keep him
in prison for his own good. Isaiah Wright was an old
favourite of Wyatt's, and the whole courtroom, as well
as those who read of it later, was startled when the
magistrate said, 'I would give you fair play if I could,'
because hitherto it had been the innocent impression
of many citizens that, as in cricket so in court, fair play
had been the basic rule of the English game. Mr Bowman
took up this point and asserted that the gracious court
of Beechworth was being degraded as it had become
the stage of 'one of the greatest crimes against English

justice ever known'. None of this moved Standish, who had already gambled heavily against the odds and was determined to trust his luck to the end. But it all became sickening to Wyatt who retained more than a remnant of decency in his being, and he was happy to relinquish his magisterial post to another called Foster, who for a time at least was prepared to go along with the travesty perpetrated by Standish and Ward.[6]

The thing that worried some less committed observers of all these proceedings was not merely the overflow of sympathy from the men illegally detained in Beechworth onto the outlaws at large in the district: it was a much more fundamental question which, with the straight-forward precision of the unsophisticated bushman, Wild Wright summarized for the benefit of the court. In Wright's opinion the true heart of the matter lay else-where – in the person of a mother imprisoned in Melbourne. Wright stood in the court and said, 'You will not get the Kellys until Parliament meets and Mrs Kelly is released and Fitzpatrick put in her place.' This statement put the whole problem back in the arena of Greta itself, the widow and her daughters, the young Constable whose word had started it all, and the judge who had, with great and benign complacence, accepted that word and despatched those criminals to prison. What happened to those in that courtroom who had done nothing more, in the company of hundreds of others, than sympathize with a family whom they believed had been deeply wronged, was immaterial. They knew that in the ultimate analysis any evil done in their regard would be as the brush of a plover's wing to the anvil blow which had shattered irrevocably the family called Kelly. Nothing now could unsmirch female honour, nothing could erase the felon's mark, nothing could recall the dead who lay at rest in Mansfield while the widows mourned. But surely something could still be done to make the young man of fevered loins and lying tongue confront the responsibility that was his. Even in that parliament to which a guileless Wright had looked for redress, the behaviour of Fitzpatrick in respect of Kate had been mentioned. But it was fatuous of those who knew the truth to expect relief from that quarter, where much larger matters of state engaged the minds of those who sat there. Indeed it soon proved the case that the men of Beechworth found freedom for, on the 22nd of April, to the chagrin of Standish, Mr Foster released them and like wild birds they sought immediately a refuge back in their valleys and mountains. Meanwhile, Constable Fitzpatrick was both enjoying himself and broadening his outlook on the ways of men, and women too, in the city of Sydney[7].

With the waning of summer the outlaws were beginning to find that life was not all a merry round of songmaking and convivial meal-taking. The arrival of the trackers had reduced them to moving about on foot, because commonsense dictated that while a man on the ground could more easily obscure his tracks, such was not easy for a horse. With this constant source of irritation it had come to Ned's mind that some form of flight might in the end be inevitable, and what came to him came also to Standish. The captain was in a better position to act on his intuition than Ned, and hence he decided to send young Fitzpatrick to Sydney in order to watch the trains from the south on their arrival, and the steamers for parts distant on their departure. It was well known that the Constable was in an unrivalled position to recognize Ned and Dan, and hence the choice was obvious. It was even more obvious that his safe removal from the colony was advisable in order to ensure that his evidence would remain integral, for was it not the case that perjurers could be bought by both contestants in an argument? Furthermore Alexander was a decided source of irritation to the higher powers of the force. Apart from the fact that Miss Jessie McKay of Meredith still deemed it necessary to remind the police that she too had a hold on Alexander by virtue of his undenied paternity of her child, there was the Constable's added and unfortunate characteristic by which he seemed recklessly to run up bills, causing irate and exasperated creditors to claim payment from the police force. Indeed Assistant Commissioner Nicolson, supposedly recuperating in Melbourne, was so vexed by it all as to exclaim that the settlement of Fitzpatrick's affairs was all becoming too much for him. Sydney was the obvious solution, so Alexander was despatched to survey the platforms and docks of that gracious city wedded to its harbours and bays.[8]

As was his custom, Alexander was almost immediately in strife in Sydney. He found it both difficult and tedious to get to the railway station on time, despite his acquisition of an alarm clock to aid him in that purpose. He was staying at the Railway Hotel and, doubtless feeling lonely in a strange city, he fell in with a group of characters, thieves, prostitutes and sundry others of like ilk who used him to their own good purposes to the extent that the New South Welsh Commissioner recommended his immediate withdrawal, lest it be found necessary to prosecute him for lying, false pretences and consorting with criminals. When these matters were communicated to Standish he heartily concurred with the verdict. He even gave his own opinion of Alexander with the words, 'He is, I fear, a useless and worthless young man,' which

coincided exactly with the opinion held of the same
gentleman by Ned, his mother and all those with whom
he had been in contact in the northeast, to leave aside
that of the Miss Jessie McKays of the world. But it has
to be conceded that Alexander rendered one service
to his profession while in Sydney. It had come to the ears
of those in authority at Darlinghurst prison that the
young man residing in that establishment under the
name of James Wilson was in fact a brother of the notorious Kellys. Though there was no urgency, given that
James still had a year of his three to run, it was necessary
to establish the truth of the matter beyond doubt. Armed
with a photograph of the young James from six years
before when he was a slip of a lad of thirteen, Fitzpatrick
visited the prison and inspected the man who had grown
from five foot four inches to six foot in the intervening
period. It was indeed James Kelly, so the records were
set straight and Alexander departed, justified as to his
usefulness in this matter. Back at Benalla he received
an unusually warm reception from Standish, who stirred
himself sufficiently to deliver a severe reprimand and
warned him that any further misdemeanour would warrant his removal from the force. His main reasons for
retaining his services were in gratitude for his valour
at Greta in the previous year and 'the probability of his
being required to give evidence in some future enquiry'.
For that probability to be translated into reality, it was
necessary to lay hands on the four, of whom nothing bordering on the factual had been heard since their return
from Jerilderie.[9]

If Alexander had found himself lonely in Sydney, the
same could not be said of Superintendent Hare in the
northeast of Victoria. In a very short time he had struck
up a friendship of remarkable warmth with that member

of the criminal classes of those parts known as Aaron
Sherritt. The thing that most impressed itself upon Hare's
imagination was Aaron's physique, and he was convinced that it was sufficiently remarkable, both as to
appearance and gait and indeed in all ways, that the
very citizens of Collins Street would have stopped in their
tracks to view him had he perchance strolled in their
midst. Aaron took Hare hither and yon searching for the
four, and the Superintendent never ceased to marvel
at the hardiness of the fellow for Aaron could spend
nights together lying coatless on the ground when the
creeks were iced and the trees bowed with frost. The two
of them spent much time watching Mrs Byrne's home for
a chance visit from her son and his companions and,
though it all proved fruitless because the four stayed
back in the mountains, it afforded Hare the opportunity
to learn a good deal about Ned from that remarkable
specimen of humanity, Aaron. As for endurance, Ned
was the far superior in Aaron's opinion. Were it to come
to a physical encounter it was clear to Aaron that, though
he could vanquish Joe, Steve or Dan, 'Ned Kelly would
beat me into fits.' To Aaron, Ned was 'an extraordinary
man' who, being 'superhuman', was thereby 'invulner-
able' and nothing could be done about him.[10] Hence
it was that out on the faces of those strong mountains
a legend was taking form of a boy, grown now to
manhood, who allegedly transcended the laws that cir-
cumscribe mere bone and muscle, whose spirit was
unfettered and would forever remain free. The person
of the legend had nonetheless to sleep and dream, to
rest awhile and be refreshed, to hear some word of
comfort if not of love, because the bonds that chained
spirit to flesh were strong and could not awhile be
broken.

Despite the fact that some word had clearly come to the four that Joe's companion of childhood and youth, companion too in petty criminality, Aaron, was now enmeshed in some form of association with Hare and Ward, they could not bring themselves to throw him over. On the twentieth day of the watch set up by Hare to catch them at Mrs Byrne's, the widow, scurrying from rock to rock like a small wallaby, had come upon the police camp after seeing a discarded sardine tin glinting in the sun. A figure lay on the ground with a hat over his face, which only partly disguised the fact that the recumbent one was none other than her prospective son-in-law, Aaron Sherritt. Here he was in the midst of the enemy, while all the time the old lady had trusted him to be the first to bring her word of threatening presence. But Hare was quick to disguise Aaron and send him off to another place to show himself, and get up an alibi. That evening he came back to Hare in mortal fear, but he composed himself, and taking up his flute he went down to the house of the women to charm them with his grace and his tunes. But it was all up between himself and them, for never again would they trust him and he ceased thereafter to pay court to Miss Byrne.[11]

Another to keep the bond between the lads and Aaron was his young sister, Anne Jane, who had grown to love and admire Ned and Joe since her childhood. She could ride over rocks and gullies with the swiftness of a mountain stream, she wore her hat band under her nose like the boys of the Greta mob, she was already wooed by Patsy Byrne, Joe's younger brother while Ned and Joe loved her as if she were their sister. On two occasions in April the outlaws came to Sebastopol and to the homes of the Sherritts and Byrnes, where they were met by a man who called himself, in correspondence with the police, 'John Smith'. This worthy one was especially appalled at the relaxed composure of Ned and Joe who roamed about 'fearless, free and bold' within three miles of the police station at Beechworth. On one occasion, a Sunday, they actually held a party with Ned, Joe, Kate Byrne, Julia Sherritt and Anne Jane Sherritt present, and enjoyed much merriment, and were not at all perturbed that the lives of four of them were in fearful jeopardy. On another occasion, a few weeks later, he met Ned and Joe again with Anne Jane at Mrs Byrne's. His disdain was unbounded when this wild creature, 'as wild as the Kelly gang', laughed and took a revolver and fired it off saying to Mr 'Smith' that she was 'going along with Kelly to bushranging'.[12] To him all this was incomprehensible. Three constables lay dead, the Kellys went their merry way as if nothing untoward had transpired, while the police were helpless to prevent them pursuing their scandalous path. It was all too much, and simply proved to his satisfaction that members of the constabulary who could while away the hours drinking vast quantities of booze, eating tinned foods and telling one another yarns in caves, were a mere pack of cowards who would never catch the Kellys.

The one thing that Hare thought he could do in this predicament was to split the unity of the gang. To him that transferral of personality, by which Joe had been encompassed within the very orbit of Ned's being, was unfathomable. He had no way of knowing that the dark, older one and the quiet, light-hearted Joe now moved and spoke in a oneness that no bribes or offers of indemnity would shake. How could he plumb the mentality of men who had grown to distrust the police, so that even their most innocent of actions were overlaid with evil? To Ned and Joe, all those enforcers of the law called

Flood, Hall, Mullane, Fitzpatrick, Ward, Brooke Smith and the dead Lonigan were the embodiment of deceit, cruelty and wretchedness – they were men who could take advantage of the innocent, use them to their own ends and then bring down the force of law upon them by perjury and threat. Both the outlaws knew that for them every last shed of innocence had been torn away amongst the tall trees of Stringybark Creek, but there were also the others whom the law had pursued with relentless voracity. Ellen Kelly, Brickey and Bill, the girls and the children, were ever present in their thoughts and, for Ned, there was the memory of a father who had tried for years to go straight and had been laid low in the end by a carcass. Who then could have any dealings with the superiors of this hated cabal who had come up from Melbourne to finish them off, bringing also black men to haunt and harass them in their dreams? What confidence could be placed in Hare, when his trusted lieutenant Detective Ward was notorious throughout the Beechworth area for his dalliance with the girls of the district, frequenting the racecourse with them at night and generally making himself odious to those classes whom he professed to protect, but in fact despoiled?[13] Nonetheless, Hare thought that Joe could be brought to see that in betrayal lay manliness and security, and he made it known discreetly that such would prove the case when Joe helped to bring his leader to the bullet or the gallows.

In these circumstances it is not surprising that Joe sat down on 26 June 1879 to write a 'few stolen lines' to dear Aaron. He wanted his friend to know that he was still in the land of the living, without fear of capture. He and 'Neddie' had decided to ask Aaron to join them because they were convinced that he was on their side, even

though the Lloyds and Quinns took the opposite view
and wanted him shot. This was something that Joe refused to contemplate, even if for no other reason than
the suffering it would entail for Aaron's mother and his
sisters, Julia and the much-loved Anne Jane. He told
Aaron that he had been able to sleep at his own mother's
home for three nights in late May, and had left some
money for him that he hoped had been passed on by
his brother Patsy Byrne. The letter further revealed that
there was a deep cleavage in the four over the behaviour
of Steve Hart, who was clearly regarded as untrust-
worthy, and hence likely to be shot if he disobeyed
orders. Furthermore it was emphatically the case that
Constable Mullane was regarded as such a 'bloody
snob' and so extremely offensive that his life was in
jeopardy. Aaron, however, could be assured of a 'jolly'
life, even were it to prove a short one, by joining Joe and
Ned, bringing his brother Jack with him and engaging
in the merry pastime of robbing a bank. Their meeting
place was to be on the side of Puzzle Range or under
the rocky prominence called London and, if in the mean-
time Aaron came across their tracks, he was to keep his
'puss' closed. Amidst all this bombast and bluster, mixed
with a rough but pleasing felicity of expression and shot
through with sheer loneliness for contact, Joe, who
signed himself as one forced into outlawry, wrote one
sentence final in its import. 'I was advised to turn treator
[sic] but I said that I would die at Ned's side first.' And
so out of the mountains came this message that showed
so emphatically that neither outlawry, nor the fear of
death, nor betrayal with the chance of life, weighed with
Joe, for he at least had determined where his death was
to be.

Captain of the Northeast

The impact of the exploits of four young Victorian scallywags on the world of the northeast was immense. It was none the less so in other parts of Australia. From Brisbane to Hobart, from Mallacoota to Albany, from Adelaide to Darwin, the names of the four were household words, and children had begun to play games modelled on events at Euroa and Jerilderie. But it was through song and verse that the prosaic became the poetic and the humdrum was translated into the heroic. Across the face of the land, into the shanties of the outback, through to the stations of the high country, and down into the pubs and alleyways of the cities, the story of the Kellys had come in ballads. The yearning of man from his origins in antiquity to throw off the yoke of authority, to reject the imposed form of a narrow society, to set his own limits to his life and the manner of its ending, became the stuff of legend. It was a thrust to freedom chiselled by a few, and through the ages those who had chosen that path and paid the price were often en-

shrined in the folk memory of the peoples from which
they had come. With the four it was thus, but though
his companions were there as minor actors on the stage
created by the songmakers, it was Ned who stood in the
centre. Within weeks of Stringybark Creek the tale was
told in song and Ned was both brave and bold, while
Joe's barmaid on the plains out of Jerilderie was able
to sing of the Kelly gang, with whom it was so grand
to be, and go on a spree, and this note was struck before
the grass had grown over the graves of those gunned
down at Mansfield. The vestiges of the Jerilderie letter,
with its pathos in Ned's longing for the valley below
Glenrowan, was there in 'Farewell to My Home in Greta',
and Kate, rather than the staunch and beloved Maggie,
was chosen to warn 'Edward darling' to shun home and
flee to safety beyond the great peak of Bogong. Thus
it was that Ned was transformed into the man whose
word was law, who ruled supreme, and who would
rather die as a Donohoe the brave than be captured
and taken into slavery. It was all enough to turn the
strongest head, but the cold frosts and biting rain, the
dark camps at night and the long watches of the day,
the threat from foe and even friend made that world of
the ballads remote and fanciful. The songmakers lived
in freedom while the burdens of their songs were beyond
it all, teetering on the brink of those other chasms that
their beloved mountains could only prefigure.

Whether Captain Standish heard the ballads is
uncertain, but it is clear that by the middle of June he
was sick to the teeth of the whole affair and that sickness
became worse when his attention was drawn to the alle-
gorical tale called 'The Book of Keli' in which he and
his whole force were mercilessly lampooned in the
pages of the *Mansfield Guardian*. At times he even

became fanciful, and had the notion of actually getting out in the field himself. Clearly he could not cut the sporting figure of the police chief in person, so he ordered a false moustache and beard to be sent up from Melbourne. There is no evidence that he ever performed in such a pantomine, but it had its theatrical effect in that the poor, harassed man at last decided that on this particular stage he had no role, except as bookmaker, and indeed a generous one at that, for he had offered odds of twenty-to-one that the outlaws would not be captured on one particular search, and it has to be assumed that he collected. Clearly he could use this and other talents to much better effect back in Melbourne where, from his office and his club, he would be able to manage affairs in a manner to which long use had made him adept. In any case it had all become dreadfully tedious living in the same hotel as that awful bore O'Connor, whose benighted black trackers were proving as useless as the Captain had prophesized, and who had himself taken to badgering Standish, while all he wanted to do was lead a peaceful life in Benalla. O'Connor had added a final insult to all this by marrying Nicolson's sister and why this particular, and even normal enough act on the part of a policeman, should have so offended Standish is unclear, but by 14 June he was on his way back to Melbourne, in time to meet his political superior, Berry, on the latter's return from London.

It was not evident to all the citizens of the southern metropolis that Berry's ambassadorial visit to London was almost as fruitless as that of Standish to the northeast. But the fact was that, though he was accompanied on his mission by the learned and devoted Professor Pearson, the men of Downing Street had been neither impressed with his argument nor his accent. He had the misfortune of never having recovered from his humble origins so that Hicks Beach, Colonial Secretary, became Icks Beach, which pleased that trusty baronet not a whit. As to the proposition that the steady men of Westminster should so favour the process of democracy as to support Berry in using a lower house to reform an upper house, it was a thing, if not unheard of, then at the very least emphatically not to be supported in those halls. In any case when that great organ of British propriety, *The Times*, could draw attention in its column to the inability of Berry's government to bring a pack of Irish scoundrels called Kelly to heel, then it was better to let such ineptitude do its own mischief and hence leave Berry to his fate. But, to his supporters in Melbourne his return had to be suitably celebrated and on the evening of 17 June he rode into his city. Standish holed up at the Melbourne Club and wrote to Sadleir back at Benalla, 'Berry makes his triumphant entry into Melbourne tonight by torchlight. I am not going to carry a torch myself.'[1]

If torches were the order of the day in Melbourne it was ammunition that was needed by the lads in the northeast. As escape by sea from the colony seemed impossible while such vigilance was maintained at possible ports, a decision had to be made whether to continue to lead a life on the run, or to break out and make a stand. The presence of such a large contingent of police, to the number of 176, together with the forces of the artillery and the constant watch over the banks, made either a hold-up or a stand a dangerous and even foolhardy matter without the necessary arms. At Stringybark Creek and at Jerilderie it had proved easy to obtain weapons, but ammunition was another matter, especially as a good deal had been used in keeping fingers and eyes quick and accurate with practice. In June Maggie, Tom Lloyd and Mick Nolan went to Melbourne where they stopped at the Robert Burns Hotel in Lonsdale Street. The three visited Sandridge on two occasions, which was an innocuous enough pastime, but the detectives detailed to keep surveillance over them had one ominous report. Mick Nolan went to Rosiers, the gunsmith in Elizabeth Street, and there he bought 200 Martini-Henry rifle cartridges, 200 Webley revolver cartridges and ordered a further 200 Spencer revolver cartridges. His explanation for the acquisition of such an impressive amount of ammunition was that he was leaving for New Zealand, where he had a brother, but to what purpose he proposed to address his purchases was never stated. The evening *Herald* of 14 June gave due prominence to the arrival in the city of the trio, so they quickly disappeared with warrants being sworn for Tom and Mick's arrest. Two detectives boarded the train taking Maggie and Tom back home, but found no trace of the bullets and Mick was nowhere, although it could safely be assumed that his cargo never reached New Zealand but that it found its way to the northeast. That at any rate was the considered deduction of Standish.[2]

As the decision had been taken to hold out in their heartland, it was necessary to find a valid reason for making such a decision worthwhile. Ned's words in the Jerilderie letter that he would do something to awaken Victoria, its police and the British army itself, unless justice was done to his family and friends, had fallen on deaf ears. But it was easy to extend the group to whom, in his eyes, justice had been denied, to that far wider circle of people in the northeast who felt that in some way the struggle of the four was the struggle of them all. That such were there was obvious to the blind, for how else could it be explained that a king's ransom went unclaimed while four young men roamed freely, far and wide, through an area inhabited by 40,000 people: many of them clearly shared that same sense of resentment towards and rejection from 'acceptable' society. For the past decade they had waited and listened through a series of bad seasons while politicians promised reform, demagogues shouted about land laws and taxes fell heavily on those who had little or nothing, while the landed ones, who were often absentees spending their wealth in 'Paris and London', were treated lightly. Laws that made the 'poor man poorer and the rich richer', that enabled the land to be turned into a vast sheep walk while the dream of yeomanry went sour, caused some hotheads, even in newspaper editorials, to talk of force being used to redress these wrongs.[3]

For a while it had seemed that all might be well because in May 1877 Berry and his men had again come to power, and the realization of hopes seemed possible. It all came to nothing quickly and the leader, who had promised so much, had been forced to go off cap in hand to London to try and convince the mighty that the lowly also had a place in a new society. Added to all this, one segment of society transformed ancient wrongs, both imagined and real, into immediate ones in this new land. The Irish of the northeast were attached by light strings to their Church and by none at all to the Crown. What did it all mean to them when the seats of power were already occupied and the rungs of society held by others' boots? It meant that somehow, sometime, action was necessary and with a leader from among themselves all things seemed possible. He was there in their very midst and so it happened that on a Sunday

in the winter of 1879, at Greta in the northeast, a group
of men, amongst them Ned, met and talked of a republic
that would unite that great vastness, give purpose to
their lives and promise to the generations to come, and
cut them all free from the ties that bound them to an alien,
unloved and unintelligible Crown whose most visible
instruments, the police, were hated. They recorded their
deliberations in childrens' school books; they knew that
physical force had to be the basis of their resistance to
authority and they went to their homes with hot and hasty
thoughts in their minds and silence on their lips. Ned
knew that this was a step which spelt finality whatever
its outcome and once it was decided to so act, he pulled
back into the womb of humanity and went down to the
home of the Byrnes and there in that humble place he
held a babe in his arms; held long and longingly for
perhaps the presentiment was there in him that such
communion as this would not come his way in life again.[4]

The one police officer who was a constant factor of
stability and commonsense in the northeast was John
Sadleir, stationed as superintendent at Benalla from
July 1878. He took a keen and intelligent interest in the
whole proceeding of the hunt, but had to assume a position of attentive inferiority while his superiors quar-
relled amongst themselves and thereby demoralized
the others. The manner in which Standish and Hare
ignored the possible benefits that the black trackers
could bring to the work of the white police appalled him,
as did the fruitless and unco-ordinated search parties
mounted by Hare. He was henceforth relieved when, in
June, Standish left and further comforted when in July,
after a fall from his horse, Hare went to join Standish
in Melbourne where the Captain could enjoy his 'infatu-
ation' for the handsome Hare, which Sadleir regarded

as 'a mild form of insanity'. The return of Nicolson gave Sadleir heart in that the new commander called off the search parties and refused to act unless specific, recent and genuine information was received as to the whereabouts of the outlaws. In this manner Nicolson hoped that the decreased level of activity of the police would lull Ned into a false sense of security, prompt some rash act and result in capture.[5] But all through the winter and thereafter, well into 1880, not one genuine, substantiated sighting of the four was made, although it at least saved the police from making fools of themselves by chasing off after every alleged appearance of their quarry. One particular report that must have caused some confusion and amusement was that of a party of nine armed men at Mooroopna, near Shepparton in November 1879. Upon investigation they turned out to be cricketers, doubtless getting in some useful practice! From Melbourne, Standish observed the lull in police affairs in the northeast, and, being concerned about the general level of lawless behaviour in the city, he began a gradual diminution in the numbers of constables employed in the hunt, so that from 176 in February 1879 the total had dropped to 127 in August.[6]

Nicolson was determined not to rush about wildly in the manner of Hare, accompanied or otherwise by Aaron Sherritt who was in any case engaged in firstly courting Kate Kelly to no good purpose, and latterly a local girl named Ellen Barry with more success.[7] In addition he did not put the same confidence in Aaron as Hare had done, so he had to rely heavily upon two other agents with whom he had a greater affinity. Both were professional men – the one a teacher and the other a medical practitioner. The teacher was James Wallace, a man of some capacity, intelligence and energy who had been a schoolboy companion of both Aaron and Joe Byrne. Like Aaron, however, his information was of doubtful validity for he was clearly a double agent who worked assiduously to the confusion of the police and the comfort of the outlaws, whom he provided with supplies, including brandy, and whose tracks he did his utmost to obscure. The doctor was a decidedly more reliable proposition. In his profession he could move freely amongst a wide group of people, many of whom were prepared to share their knowledge as well as their symptoms with him. He adopted a suitable pen name in his communications with the police, calling himself 'Diseased Stock', and thus he could write of his information in the manner of a veterinary surgeon referring to the well-being or otherwise of the district's cattle. Despite his intimacy with the people of his neighbourhood, and the evident trust placed in him by them, the fortress of silence that had been thrown up around the four was such that only tantalizing glimpses were afforded to the observer of that other world where the young outlaws moved with comparative ease, were fed, clothed and given shelter, and wherein they plotted that final act which would excite the attention of the world. All that the police could do was to wait and to write to one another about the supposed doings of Ned whom they continued to call, appropriately, Captain, given the proven capacity of the leader to conduct a successful campaign, while Joe was known as Moonlight, Dan as Sneak and Steve as Revenge, because Ned was said to have called him that at Jerilderie.[8]

Despite the constant threat posed by the presence of the black trackers, and the knowledge that police spies were active, the four seem to have led a normal enough existence in their fortress. At times there were close

shaves, but Ned still found it possible to go to Melbourne
for a few days, to dance with a policeman at a fair and
to visit his relatives and intimate friends with comparative ease. The four outlaws had a day out at the Whorouly races in 1879 and managed to evade the attention
of three policemen appointed to apprehend them, while,
at the Mohyu races in the following year, Ned took
pleasure in watching Maggie come home second in the
Hack Race behind one of the Lloyd girls. As the least
likely place to hide seemed to be the most secure from
surprise, it was decided to settle down and lead an
entirely normal life. For a while they lived at McAuliffe's
in the middle of the Greta swamp about eight miles from
the old home. As that proved satisfactory they then
moved into Mrs Kelly's old home itself, where Maggie
and the children made them very welcome. The police
had harassed the inhabitants of the home for months,
even to the extent of laying baits for their dogs, which
Maggie solved by muzzling them, but it was a relief to
switch from police attention to outlaw protection and the
fact that the boys put a new bark ceiling in the house
added to the comfort of all. On Christmas Day a hearty
time was had with a pleasant reunion, even though
funds had begun to run low and it was time to look again
for a source of money.[9]

While the four were managing to sustain themselves
in frugal comfort at Greta, two other actors in the events
that had led to the circumstances which induced them
to be there were not quite as relaxed. Constable McIntyre had left Mansfield in the wake of Stringybark Creek
with only a minimal hold on his faculties. Arriving in Melbourne he was hospitalized for a period, during which
he took copious notes of the transactions in which he
had figured prior to his escape on Kennedy's horse. He

was fully aware that eventually he would have to give utterance under oath and publicly to the things engraven in his memory. After a period at a desk, signing debentures for Berry, he was sent down to the wharves to watch the shipping movements in case the outlaws were attempting escape from Melbourne. His life there was rendered miserable. Black looks met him everywhere and he never left home in the mornings without the sinking feeling that he would assuredly overhear some chance remark in respect of a wombat hole before his return at night. His apprehensions were seldom disappointed, but he showed some spirit by reminding and silencing a taunting Jem Mace, the world champion boxer, that Ned had offered to fight and lick him if a meeting could be arranged. But it all wore him down, especially when, as the months dragged on, his advice to shoot rather than capture Ned proved incapable of execution and he realized that the day would surely come when he would again meet those cool, hazel flecked eyes across a courtroom. He took to drink, behaved in the office of the Victoria Building Society in a manner which Standish considered 'very scandalous to the force', was severely reprimanded, but survived in the Queen's uniform because it was necessary to preserve him for one final act of duty in her name.[10]

The same did not apply to Constable Alexander Fitzpatrick in the sense at least that his one, all important deed had been done and it was clear to his superiors that any further scrutiny by those who tended to think that an element of foulness clouded the whole affair would be dangerous. Hence Alexander was expendable and even the most detached observer had to concede that the young Constable had pushed to the limit the tolerance of his masters, and had continued to do so upon his return from Sydney. At his new posting, Lancefield, he appears to have fallen into his old habit of molesting young women, and although this added nothing to the official estimate of his character because he was long since regarded as a 'liar and a larrikin', it became necessary to act when the Senior Constable in charge of Lancefield made a report on him. To Senior Constable Mayes, Alexander was the most useless and unreliable subordinate with whom he had ever been obliged to deal. He could not trust him to behave in a becoming fashion unless he kept constant vigilance over him and even then Alexander was exceedingly difficult to control, in particular in his behaviour with young women. He was lazy, devious, incompetent and insolent, and although much of this had not become evident to some citizens of Lancefield who admired his dash and style, it had all become too vexing for Standish, Hare, Chomley and Berry. At last the upper echelons of Victorian officialdom actually did something decisive – they sacked Fitzpatrick, thus ending a relationship and a representation which had become so sordid as to be no longer regarded as either warranted or tolerable.[11]

By late January 1880 it had become evident to Ned, and those joined with him, that action was necessary if anything were to be done to initiate the beginning of a new order in the northeast. It was a question of tactics, both as to method and timing, and in respect of the latter there was clearly some urgency. It was now over a year since Jerilderie, during which time nothing whatever had been done, either to keep the cause of Ellen Kelly's imprisonment before the public, or to further the wider cause spoken of at the Sunday meetings. The public had grown to accept as clearly proven the supremacy of the outlaws in their conflict with the police, but that did nothing to convince the centre of authority in Melbourne that some terms of settlement had to be reached with the four scoundrels and with their misguided or disaffected allies in those remote wildernesses of the northeast. There were also the simple human matters: the drag on frayed nerves, the awful loneliness of an existence cut off from the places of men, the increasing tendency to bicker amongst themselves, the longing for a future free of fear and even the determination never to spend another winter like that of 1879 when the children of Mansfield had skated on the frozen waters of Fords Creek. Finally there was the need for the outlaws to replenish the coffers as it had proved difficult to maintain the measure of generosity made so easy by Euroa and Jerilderie, and yet it was imperative for the sake of morale to so do.

What was needed was some form of stratagem that would combine the achieving of a truce, if not a pardon, for the four, the release of Mrs Kelly and her companions, and money – which, under the circumstances, would not be won by legal means. To do any of this, some form of protection was necessary because if one thing was clear, it was that any appearance of the outlaws in or about the northeast, with such numbers of armed police present, would bring upon their persons a hail of unremitting fire until they were reduced to bone and gore. With this salutary thought in mind, Ned and the others began experimenting with various materials in an attempt to make armour. When that ever present accompaniment of the settlers' existence, sheet iron, proved ineffective, they turned to steel which was not available in the same abundance and, indeed, apart from the mould board of the single furrow plough at home at Greta, was scarcely to be had at all. It was in

such circumstances that several farmers in the district
began to report a strange phenomenon, for they noticed
that their ploughs were beginning to be denuded of their
mould boards, and although ploughing was still some
time away they were sufficiently concerned as to report
the fact.[12]

Situated immediately behind the Greta homestead
there was a primitive blacksmith's shop with the requisite equipment, and especially a large forge and bel-
lows. There the armour was made, using four mould
boards for each set, and it proved a simple enough
matter to shape them, join them at the shoulders with
heavy leather and at the bottom with bolts. It was obvious
that the first mover, and therefore the prime target, in
any engagement with the police would be Ned, for whom
a headpiece was made. It had a slit for the eyes, and
Maggie lined it for comfort and made a woollen skull
cap to protect her brother's head, as the helmet had to
rest on a strap drawn across the top of the skull. Thus
equipped Ned was both a grotesque and hilarious sight.
The armour weighed ninety-five pounds, or nearly seven
stone, clanged as he moved and made him look huge
and feel awkward, but when fully tested it proved
capable of resisting penetration by a bullet from a
Martini-Henry rifle at ten yards. It was an apparition to
frighten the dogs around the homestead, to cause the
cattle to run milling in the paddock, to put the crows
to flight from the gums. But to men who knew its use and
purpose it brought comfort, for it promised sanctuary
except for the feet, legs and arms which would have to
remain free to provide minimal movement. Ned knew
that a man could stand up in armour and face the world,
clothed within a symbol of impregnable virility. He also
knew that such a man needed mobility and there lay

its weakness, for the outlaws were not assuming that they would fight for their causes from within some citadel of rock up in their mountains, but that such a conflict would occur in the villages or towns held now by the enemy.[13]

Although the Assistant Commissioner of the Victoria Police, Charles Hope Nicolson, was regarded as 'a cranky Scottie' by his superior, Standish, his time in the northeast was effective in one way at least. He had set out to lull the outlaws into a sense of security which he fondly hoped would be false. That they felt secure was certain, for in the ten months that Nicolson had been in charge not one definite step had been taken by him to capture them, even though they had resided comfortably within eleven miles of his residence at Benalla. His inactivity had been successful in that it had resulted in their own activity and at the end of May, they were ready to break out and confront the police. It is scarcely to be expected that Nicolson could have been aware of this fact with any precision, but he was understandably appalled that, at the very time when he hoped to see some positive results from his policy, he was told that he was to be supplanted by a reluctant Hare. Standish perhaps had done no more than acquiesce to this 'change of bowlers' because the government had decided that the length struck by Nicolson was simply not good enough. There was no real evidence to suggest, on performances at least, that Hare would prove more penetrating, but perhaps the batsmen after such a long innings would prove incautious and success would come his way.

It was in vain that Nicolson went to Robert Ramsay, newly installed as Chief Secretary of Victoria, and pleaded that he be left in charge. Ramsay pointed out that no reflection was meant on his character, but that, as in cricket, it was no more than a change of bowlers. Astounded, Nicolson remonstrated that chasing the Kellys was a serious affair and that the analogy limped as a consequence, but the change was ratified and Nicolson was sent to inspect the country districts while 'My dear Frank', as Standish called Hare, went to Benalla to take the new ball, little realizing how much on the aggressive the opposing batmen were prepared to go. No one seemed to think that the obvious choice for the job was Sadleir, who at least knew the district (and had proved that he could bowl when he took nine wickets for forty-eight runs in a game against Alexandra in 1875).[14]

At all events Standish was delighted to see Nicolson out of the way because the Captain had decided that his second in command laboured under a 'mental aberration' and fully expected that he would forthwith 'go quite cranky'. Being a 'vainglorious lunatic', he had made a great hash of the chances he had of capturing the outlaws. His concluding remark to Hare in respect of Nicolson was that, as he was 'a dangerous sneak' he would not trust him any further than he 'could throw a bull by the tail'.[15] In this atmosphere of acrimony and invective the hunt for the four was again undertaken, while on their own part they had a problem which tended to create tensions of loyalty regarding both their past associations and their present proceedings. The problem was called Aaron Sherritt.

On Boxing Day 1879 Aaron had finally taken the step that he had contemplated taking either with Miss Byrne or Miss Kelly. Thwarted in both these attempts, he had rapidly courted and won the hand of Miss Ellen Barry whom he took home after their marriage on 26 December to a two-roomed house on the Eldorado Road, at the foot of a gracious hill with a view of that valley called the Woolshed. In that lovely place the young couple settled to an unusual form of domesticity in that the bread-winner's main source of income was that paid to him as a police spy and indeed their very home belonged to the police. Nonetheless, for a time, they were happy and their union was quickly blessed, for Ellen became pregnant. The situation of their dwelling for Aaron's work was ideal, because he was only seven miles from Beechworth and within half a mile of a home in which he had a special interest because it was occupied by Mrs Byrne, and Joe was known to visit there frequently for such things as a sleep, a meal and a change of clothing.

Aaron was a simple soul who liked nothing better than a glass of porter, a bag of lollies or even a ride on the merry-go-round, for there on the Woolshed a varied community still existed, and such commodities were readily available, even though the gold had mostly gone. But Aaron was not content with things that comforted only his body. He was the kind of man who also needed solace for his spirit and such was singularly lacking in his life in recent months, despite the acqui-sition of a young bride. He seemed to have fallen out with every one of his former companions, and some of those inhabitants of that new world in which he moved looked upon him coldly, for amongst the police there were those who very much doubted whether he was earning his pay. But it cut Aaron to the quick that the Byrne family seemed to have turned against him – as if they were expected to be tolerant of his new role in society, directed, it appeared, at the apprehension of Joe. He found too that members of his own family had turned their faces from him for they were staunchly of the Protestant persuasion, in that part of it at least that was convinced of the harlotry of Rome, and Miss Barry was a Catholic and hence posed a threat to the very security of Aaron's integrity. Deep down however was the burning in his spirit because of his jealousy of Joe. Ned he hated, the other two he scorned, but Aaron loved Joe with a love unbounded and Joe had been taken from him. Joe had given him his chance to join them for the Jerilderie raid, and even later with his 'few stolen lines' had pleaded with him to join them in the bush. But Aaron had found the web cast by Hare and Ward too strong to break, and marriage had closed forever the possibility of breathing again the keen air of the mountains, with Joe riding wildly beside him. Here he was settled to the tedium of domesticity, surrounded by the despised police, reviled by all about him and branded as a spy, while Joe rode free, lionized by all, feted in the newspapers, a hero of the young people of the Woolshed, including Aaron's sister Anne Jane. It was enough to turn the mind of a man, especially when he knew that, despite the fact that he had taken the pay of the police, he had really done nothing whatever to betray Joe.[16]

It was with this in his heart that one day in May Aaron met the widow Byrne. She knew that four policemen were stationed in Aaron's house and that they watched her home at night. It was reasonable for her to ask poor Aaron whether he had pondered upon what Joe would be thinking of his old friend, now turned traitor. It was all too much for Aaron, who was driven to utter an odious threat and promise, for he spat out to the mother of the outlaw words that rang as horror in her ears. 'I'll kill him and before he's cold I'll fuck him,' he said. They were words that sealed his doom.[17] Within a few days Joe called at the widow's home, and she recounted what

had transpired between herself and Aaron. Anne Jane
Sherritt was there and she heard Joe say that he would
kill Aaron first, and hence put paid to any chance the
traitor would ever have of indulging his foul fancy.[18]

Back home at Greta Ned spelt out a plan that would,
if realized, culminate in achieving his wild hopes. Perhaps Henry Parkes and his advisers in New South Wales
unwittingly led Ned to envisage the genuine possibility
that a form of truce between the outlaws and the government of both colonies was possible. Henry had written
to Robert Ramsay suggesting that at a predetermined
time the joint reward be withdrawn and the public be
apprised of that fact. The date for the withdrawal was
20 July, and Henry thought that such a step might be
sufficient to induce any would-be traitors to act before
the possibility of financial gain eluded them.[19] Possibly
this step was interpreted by Ned as a sign of weakness
on the part of the authorities, because by Friday 26 June
the outlaws were ready to break out from Greta.

It was no part of Ned's plan that Aaron be done to
death, and when Joe said, 'We'll ride over and shoot
him', Ned replied, 'No, you can't have that. You are not
going to shoot him.' But Dan too was set in his mind to
aid and abet Joe and the two brothers came to blows
over it, with Dan both losing and seeming to acquiesce
in the determination of the elder. As far as Ned was concerned the making of the armour and plans for its subsequent use were intended to avoid blood-letting,
including their own. But a cold hatred of Aaron had
come into Joe, and when he and Dan departed from
Greta on Saturday, he knew in his heart what he would
do to the friend of his boyhood and youth. To Ned the
visit of Joe and Dan to Aaron's was intended as a move
to lure the police in as large numbers as possible to

Beechworth, via the railway line from the south. The mere appearance of the two outlaws there would suffice to achieve this aim, because no member of the Victoria Police had actually laid eyes on any one of the four since the moment McIntyre rode away from Stringybark Creek almost two years before. There were four policemen in hiding at Aaron's, and any kind of disturbance would warrant their raising the alarm and causing a whole contingent of police to come hurtling to the Woolshed in pursuit of those ghostly figures.[20]

On that Saturday evening Aaron was a man in deep disturbance. His hold on reality was such that, in desperation for certainty of some kind, he had intended to take out a horse and go into Beechwotth that very day to the Catholic chapel, and seek there a sanctuary, for his soul at least. He had not done so, and hence an unshriven Aaron heard with terror in his heart a knock at his door. The policemen heard it also and they were quick to scamper to the safety of the bedroom. But Aaron had to go and answer the knock because it was only that old nuisance of a neighbour Anton Wicks, lost and probably drunk, trying to find his way home. Aaron was not to know that Joe and Dan were there with Anton, for they had brought him as living bait to the door. In fact Aaron was to know only one thing else in this world, for his beloved Joe, the boy of their playtimes in that very valley, stood there, grown to fierce and menacing manhood. In a moment Aaron, with no words spoken between them, lay dead at a blast from Joe's gun, while the wife with child quickening screamed, and her mother wailed. The four poltroons of police proved worthy of their prudence, if not their mettle, for while the women remonstrated with the killer, while the two outlaws ranted and taunted them to come out, the protectors of that hearth huddled under a bed, to emerge hours later when their quarry had long since fled.[21]

Joe and Dan rode from that place and set out to the south, as Aaron stiffened on the earthen floor of his home while his dog mourned in the nearby bush. For the traitor, neither the killer nor posterity spared a thought, and some even saw justification for the slaying. But Aaron had done no foul deed except in word, and in his weakness for the money that Hare so readily provided him. He had died amongst those he had chosen, and even his dress spelt ignominy, for his pitiful frame was clad in the cast-off clothing of Detective Michael Ward. His patron, Hare, showed his gratitude to his spy by writing a personal epitaph for Aaron, in which he said that it was fortunate that Joe shot him, because he was beyond 'reclaim' and would have spent his life in gaol.[22] Aaron left a grieving father who laid his remains to rest in an unmarked grave in Beechworth cemetery, nearby to those men who had come far from China to seek a meagre fortune in that place, but had remained forever. The two outlaws rode away from all this, strong, vital and young, with their horses under them. They were going, for a while, to a place called Glenrowan and they too were unshriven.

A Still, Cold Night   14

The Irish have always been singularly unfortunate both in the manner in which they have conducted their uprisings and in their outcome. For over a thousand years they, at intermittent intervals, had fought to throw off the English yoke. But, like oxen, their struggle had served to tighten the yoke further, so that rebellion became increasingly an act of desperation rather than hope. As oxen do, they had gradually settled to accept the prick and the goad as normal. In the new country, at Castle Hill and Eureka, the rising of the Gael had been muted, because there was the consciousness that to fight against the Crown was dark treason, which blackened them and all belonging to them with the badge of infamy. Such events and such deep matters had to be whispered of in muted and tortured strains. In those homes, and about those hearths, where men of gaelic blood forgathered, the hell holes of Port Arthur, Norfolk Island and Port Macquarie were remembered with eternal bitterness because it seemed that the hunger, cold and misery of Ireland had merely been transported beyond the seas to a land that ought to have promised better.

In the northeast the promise had been the land itself and some there were who said that the Irish were ungrateful curs, for was it not a fact that they had land? But for them, coming late and with little, they saw it happen that those who had, gained more, while they themselves struggled on their selectors' plots or if, as had been known in these recent times, they showed an inclination to be recalcitrant, they were denied even the selecting of the land. It was enough to make the blood of true men boil, and once more such men, most of them of the Gael across the seas, had begun to converge on the quiet hamlet and railway stop called Glenrowan to make another throw, and perhaps at this stand to prove that the Irish were capable of an act of transcendence which, if not for them, at least for others, would win a better future.

As Ned rode those few miles from Greta and closed in on Glenrowan on the night of Saturday 26 June, the burden on his shoulders was lightened by the fact that at last the field of action had been chosen. He had come out from the mountains and the marshes, cutting off all sources of protection, and had chosen to fight on the ground hitherto held by the adversary. It was not the case that Glenrowan was closely held, for that village of two pubs had only one policeman to guard it. Constable Hugh Bracken, ex-policeman of his own choice, and now policeman again to assist capture the outlaws, was ill and confined to his bed with his pregnant wife and child about him. He heard the nine o'clock passenger train pass through, and he knew from experience that nothing more would occur in the town that night unless the local lads caused a disturbance at Mother Jones' hotel, or at McDonnell's on the other side of the line. In such an event the Constable had no intention of rousing himself, and he went to sleep. Meanwhile, Ned, having likewise heard the train pass through, moved into Glenrowan. He was accompanied by Steve and a few others of those who had decided to take a stand with him. They brought four spare horses, the armour in a buggy, a pack-horse with two drums of blasting powder, rockets, two coils of fuse, weapons and ammunition. The others moved back into the bush once the horses were tethered behind McDonnell's and the blasting powder safely hidden.[1]

It was about 9 p.m. on Saturday when Joe and Dan left Aaron's, and they had twenty-five miles to ride across the hills and through the valley of the Ovens to Glenrowan. Ned, unaware of the nature of the deed they had done there, fully expected that word would immediately be carried to Beechworth that two of the outlaws had been positively identified in the area. As a result of such news, breaking as it did a drought of nearly two years, it was reasonable to suppose that even Standish would bestir himself and that a strong contingent of police and black trackers would set out immediately by train from Benalla to Beechworth. Two things were not known to Ned. Firstly, he was unaware that O'Connor and his black trackers were no longer in the northeast but in Melbourne, where they were awaiting a passage back to Queensland. O'Connor had finally decided that any further purpose to be served by them in Victoria was negated by the constant humiliation and frustration to which they had been subjected by Standish and Hare. In order to return to the field those men from the tribal grounds of the far north, who mentally at least had caused so much turmoil to Ned, many hours would have to elapse. Much more important however was the effect Joe and Dan's slaughter of Aaron had on the police at the Woolshed. Had the two outlaws obeyed Ned's orders, and merely created sufficient disturbance there as to give the police certain evidence as to their presence, then word would have been rapidly passed to the higher authorities. As a result a train would have left Benalla within a few hours after word was received there, and would have passed through Glenrowan within another hour. In that case, before dawn on the Sunday morning, the battle of Glenrowan would have been joined.[2]

Such of course was not the case because the police at Aaron's dwelling had decided that, whoever else was to be shot or molested in this affair, it was assuredly not going to be themselves. Alternatively lying under and about the bed, pushing Mrs Barry under with them and pondering anxiously on how next to confront the problem, they managed to pass the whole night and do exactly nothing. As a result of all this, a less than resolute Constable Armstrong arrived in at Beechworth at one in the afternoon on Sunday when, some eighteen hours after Aaron's death, other upholders of the law besides the bed-ridden officer, were apprised of what had occurred.[3] The news was then sent by telegraph to Hare at Benalla who, taken with the seriousness of the matter, sent it on to Melbourne where, after some delay due to it being Sunday, it finally came to the attention of Captain Standish. Hare had asked for the black trackers and O'Connor to help in the search, so Standish, meeting O'Connor at the Melbourne Club, sheepishly had to request that they return to the fray. By 10.15 that night all was in readiness and a special train set out from

Melbourne at the demand of Chief Secretary Ramsay,
though it was the inclination of Standish to wait for the
morrow. O'Connor and five trackers, Mrs O'Connor and
her sister joined the train at Essendon, but for reasons
best known to himself Standish remained in the city. The
men of the press were also aboard with the *Age*, *Argus*,
Daily Telegraph and *Australasian Sketcher* all represented, the latter by the artist Thomas Carrington.
Speeding along in the night, the fact that the gates were
closed at Craigieburn went unnoticed, which caused the
brakes of the engine to be ruined, but after a brief stop
the intrepid party set out again, arriving at Benalla at
1.30 a.m. on Monday. It left again at 2.30 with Hare, seven
mounted constables and their horses, and a male civilian added to the complement. Rumours were thick and
fast about the railway station that the line had been torn
up somewhere between Benalla and Beechworth, so the
precaution was taken of sending a pilot engine ahead
of the main train in case such a desperate deed had
been done. Nevertheless it was a reasonably happy
party that set out on that cold Monday in the middle of
the night, breaking the silence of the bush as they
clanged along the line. Their destination was Beechworth where the ladies were to enjoy a few days recreation while the menfolk hunted the four. By 3 a.m. they
were less than two miles from Glenrowan and Aaron
had been dead now for thirty-two hours.[4]

In that hamlet a good deal had taken place since the
ordinary passenger train had passed through on Saturday evening. Once Ned had assured himself that all was
quiet he bailed up a group of men who were sleeping
in tents near the station-master's house, as he thought
there were detectives amongst them. When this proved
not to be so, he proceeded to that other suspect source

in the village, the inn run by Mrs Anne Jones to which, by reports, the police, and in particular the local constable Hugh Bracken, were fond of resorting. Mrs Jones being easily persuaded to accompany the rapidly growing cavalcade, Ned then paid a call on Mr Stanistreet, the station-master. He had a very simple request: he asked that the master stop a special train that Ned expected to pass through Glenrowan in the next few hours. Mr Stanistreet declared that he was unable to guarantee the stopping of a special, which placed Ned in a quandary. It was imperative for the success of the plan that the special be stopped at Glenrowan, and if the station-master was unable to ensure that such were possible by normal means then abnormal ones had to be sought. Before long Ned had aroused several plate-layers and at pistol point persuaded them to lift a couple of segments of the line. The place was well chosen in that it was on the edge of a steep embankment where the line took a sharp curve about three hundred yards beyond the station on the northern side. It meant, quite simply, that no train could proceed beyond Glenrowan without endangering the lives of those aboard it. It meant also that the method of stopping the train was not one which involved the use of that handy instrument of destruction which Ned had brought to Glenrowan – blasting powder.[5]

It was getting on towards dawn when these arrangements were complete, and by then Ned was already almost frantic with anticipation. Joe and Dan had arrived after a long and wet ride through the night, but Ned was not told of the bloody deed enacted at the Woolshed, except that enough had been done to cause the police to come out hunting them. Neither the hunters nor the hunted were aware of the fact that the rules of

the chase were altered, for on the very day of Aaron's
death the Victorian parliament had been prorogued.
As a consequence the Act, by which the four had been
proclaimed as outlaws, lapsed. They were no longer to
be hunted down and shot like mad dogs, but they were
once more part of the company of citizenry who enjoyed
the protection of the Queen herself, and thus of the officers upholding her laws. Certainly they were citizens
for whom arrest warrants had been sworn out but, as
others in similar jeopardy, they had to be proven guilty
before the law could enforce its penalties. No man could
take up arms against them, no man could steal upon
them and do them to death, no one could rightfully shun
them as outcasts on the face of the earth, and it was no
longer an offence to harbour, feed and even comfort
them. In short it was as if, albeit briefly, they had returned
to the womb of civilization and when Annie Jones, aged
sixteen, allowed a sick, unhappy boy called Steve Hart
to rest his head awhile on her lap it was almost a symbol
of their welcome amongst men and women. Her mother,
Mrs Jones, comprehended nothing of proroguing and
such niceties, and she too welcomed them, to partake
of breakfast at her house called the Glenrowan Inn,
where a sign proclaimed that 'Best Accommodation' was
to be had.[6]

Ned's plans in respect of the long-awaited special
and its occupants were simple. The intention was to keep
the station-master under Steve's guard, and make him
flash a danger signal as the train approached the
station. Once there, its occupants were to be informed
of the situation they were in, and that no retreat was
possible because a tin of blasting powder was positioned behind them which would be used to blow up
the line were they to attempt to go back. In such a manner

Ned proposed to capture Hare and any other leading
police, together with such others as were in their company, take them into the bush and hold them there until
a truce was proclaimed. He also thought that he would
thereby guarantee the release of his mother, Brickey
and Bill.

Banal such a plan may have been, but it did not
involve murder and its success depended upon surprise,
the effectiveness of the armour and Ned's hopes that the
police would accept the futility of resistance. As dawn
turned to full day, and Sunday wore on, the likelihood
of such a proceeding being feasible wore thin. There
seemed to be so many people in and about Glenrowan
on that particular day of rest. No whistle or sound of an
impending special train was heard, Steve and Stanistreet sat waiting while Mrs Stanistreet wondered
whether her husband had chosen a suitable profession
in life, and Ned stretched Mrs Jones' best accommodation to its limits by bailing up all and sundry and invit-
ing them to partake of her hospitality. Amongst the
guests, who numbered sixty-two at the highest tally, was
Thomas Curnow, the local teacher who, on being discovered taking a pleasant Sunday drive in the company
of his family, was detained and lodged with the rest.
Indeed it became increasingly apparent to Ned that the
first plan was in jeopardy and by nightfall, after a day
spent in merriment, singing, dancing, sporting contests,
card playing and sundry other light-hearted pastimes,
he concocted another.

His second plan was, if anything, less likely of success
than the first because it involved even a greater degree
of compliance, if not sheer stupidity, on the part of the
police, but, given his previous experience of that body
of men, Ned was perhaps justified in his assumption.

What had to be done was to bait a trap for them and while they devoured it he planned to capture the train, together with the police horses, go back along the line and rob the banks, and perhaps even, for fantasy had overcome facts, kidnap the Governor of Victoria and hold that personage to ransom until logic and decency persuaded him that right was on the side of the Kellys rather than on that of the law. The bait, or supposed bait, was at hand in the persons of the four themselves whose presence, it was natural to expect, would draw the immediate attention of the police. The trap itself was also available because the barracks, from which the police had until recently kept a watch on Greta, was a 'strong brick building' conveniently situated about a mile on the Benalla side of the station. Ned thought that a man positioned there would be able to stop the train, inform the police that the Kellys were in that most likely of places, the barracks, watch them surround it, fire off the Mansfield parson's double-barrelled fowling piece and await the outcome. The police would have to send the train on to the platform, because the horses could not be unloaded anywhere else, and there Ned would be waiting to go off on his lark of bank raiding and playing host to the Governor.

This plan again was limpid in its simplicity, and furthermore it envisaged no loss of life. There was no lack of suitable appointees for the position of informer, especially as Ned had somehow got it into his head that it was sufficient merely to be an informer to gain the reward. The chief obstacle to the successful outcome of the new strategy was that so many people were aware of the presence of the four in the village that one or other of them might manage to get the word to the police before Ned's man was able to do so. That possibility had, however, to be left out of calculations and meanwhile there was work to be done.[7]

It appears that throughout the whole day, during which little Glenrowan had been subjected to a vast amount of unlawful dealings, Constable Bracken had been aware of nothing unusual or suspicious. In any case it is clear that until 10 p.m. on that Sunday night Ned had shown no interest whatever in the presence of an officer of the law in the town. But as he now intended to use the barracks as his trap it became necessary to persuade Bracken to join the party at the Glenrowan Inn, lest perchance he stir himself sufficiently as to inform Hare, upon the arrival of the train, that the true prize lay elsewhere. Ned went down to the police station where he told Bracken infamous things such as that he would like to catch hold of Mr Graves M.P., who reportedly said that it would be capital and wise to poison the wells and burn the grasses of the Kelly country, and that men like Graves and Bracken were damned fools to bother their heads about parliament and all its works and pomps, 'for this is our country'. While Constable Bracken was not persuaded by this line of argument he quickly accepted Ned's invitation to come to the hotel.[8]

Ned, feeling secure in the oft professed loyalty of the schoolmaster, Curnow, permitted him to return to his home and lived awhile to regret it. He did this despite the fact that the schoolmaster's house was even further from the station than the barracks, and at that also on the Benalla side from whence the train was expected. It all indicated a degree of trust in his fellow man on Ned's part that the events of the past two years had done little to shake. That it was misplaced trust had been apparent to the inner being of Curnow throughout the whole afternoon and evening, and immediately he returned home he took a red llama scarf, candle and matches and ran as fast as his game leg would permit him; he met the first engine about a mile and half from the station, and hence well beyond Ned's man in wait at the barracks. He blurted out his tale of impending destruction to life and limb on the track beyond the town, identified the miscreants as the Kellys, and fled home to the bosom of his petrified wife. To Hare and his men the news that the line was torn up was mere confirmation of what they expected – after all why had they provided themselves with a pilot engine to blaze the trail before them? What was new in all this was the word that Glenrowan had been chosen by the Kellys as the place to return to the world of normal men and their day-to-day affairs. After many minutes delay, during which the police walked up and down the line, conferred with each other and shunted the pilot back to couple it to the main engine, Hare ordered the train to proceed slowly into the station.[9]

In the few hours since the taking of Bracken nothing of great moment had occurred at Mrs Jones' place. Young master Jones who was just thirteen had entertained the company with a wild Scottish air and brought a note of relevance into the proceedings with the rendering of 'The Wild Colonial Boy', and a man sang a Kelly song. Mrs Jones had been a very busy person indeed, even though her guests had dwindled to about forty as Ned had been dispensing favours and permitting chosen souls to return to their homes, with the admonition to stay abed and asleep. The night was very cold so fires were burning in profusion, to the alarm of the licensee, who thought that the mantelpieces might get so hot that they, and the frail wooden building with its hessian walls, could become a blazing inferno with the consequent loss of all her possessions. Despite the fact of it being an hotel, very little was drunk during the long wait and Ned himself touched not a drop. His wildest moment was when he rounded on Denis Sullivan, a line repairer, and wanted to know whether he was that infamous cur, Sullivan, the New Zealander who was both murderer and traitor, but whose false testimony had saved himelf and condemned others. Denis was fortunate in that he was quickly able to placate Ned, otherwise matters may have gone ill with him. The hours wore on and finally it was decided that all except the men could go to their homes, but one last act had to be performed by Ned before their departure. As at Jerilderie, so at Glenrowan, the old urge to vindicate himself in words came over him and thus he had to give a lecture before parting with his prisoners. He had scarcely launched himself into his theme, when, it being about three o'clock in the Monday morning, the sound of the train was heard.[10]

At this precise moment Mr Curnow, safely within his home, was able to contemplate the heroism of his deed. After all had not that murderous villain Kelly told him during the day that his purpose in coming to Glenrowan was to slaughter in cold blood every soul, including any innocent civilians, who travelled on that train? Lest any of them were perchance to escape the carnage consequent upon derailment, Ned was to be there at the ready so as to shoot them down as they scrambled from the wreck. But as Curnow nursed his righteousness, what was the fiend doing? Surely one bent so determinedly on slaughter as Ned supposedly was ought to have positioned himself long since at that place of intended carnage some four hundred yards away, ready to gloat over his victims and do the living to death.

It seems however that Ned, being so abruptly inter-
rupted in the midst of his lecture, calmly proceeded, with
Dan and Joe, to don his armour and the rattling and
tinkling was heard by the platelayer, James Reardon,
who thought it took them about twenty minutes to put
it on. In short Ned was behaving in exactly the manner
of a man who saw no cause for haste, because he
expected that the train, rather than go hurtling into the
bend on the other side, would proceed quietly to the
station after having let the police off at the barracks.
The train had indeed stopped near the place where he
had expected, but it had done so at Curnow's bidding
rather than that of Ned's own man, and that cast an
entirely different light on the whole affair.

Soon after the train came to a halt, Constable Bracken,
having acquired the key to the hotel, went out, locking
the door behind him. He ran to the station, met the train
with Hare aboard, told him that the Kellys were at Mrs
Jones' and to surround the place to prevent their escape.
Hare and others began to move towards the hotel and
the firing commenced, so that the peaceful vale of Glenrowan was transformed into a front line as if it were a
battleground, and the night was rent with noise and
light, screaming and groaning and shouted orders. It
was the night of a full moon and the dark shape of Morgan's Lookout stood up behind the hotel, brooding over
the farce enacted by men below. As the guns blazed
their second volley from the police, two rockets arched
high into the sky from between the station and McDonnell's Hotel. To those who had watched and waited in
the valley near Greta they signalled the end of their
dream of a free northeast for the plans had all gone
awry.[11]

Within minutes Ned who had been delayed in arriving

at the station because a bolt broke in his armour, was wounded in the foot and arm, proving that armour prevailed not unless it clothed a man's whole frame. Hare, who came within fifty to eighty yards of the hotel, although it seemed to him like five, was wounded in the wrist and had to retire from the field, leaving O'Connor and his trackers to take cover in a ditch. From there they blazed away at the frail structure where women screamed, children cried and men covered them with their bodies to protect them from the hail of lead. Constable Bracken, having locked the inmates in, had failed to mention to his fellows that the hotel contained others besides the Kellys, so that in no time at all two children were shot, an old man called Cherry fell mortally wounded, Joe received a wound in the leg and the place was transformed into one of carnage rather than hospitality.

Thus the night wore on with more police arriving, amongst them Sadleir, until eventually it dawned upon the trigger-happy lunatics that quite possibly the innocent were dying in the company of the guilty. Women and children tried to escape, with Sergeant Steele doing his best to gun them down in cold blood, Mrs Jones screeching at what she deemed the cowardice of the police and Constable Arthur threatening to shoot Steele if he tried to kill any more women and children. Ned managed to approach the back of the hotel where he found that he could not persuade the injured Joe to join him outside. He deemed it imprudent to go within and hence make it clear to the younger two that their leader was badly wounded. Having gone back further to tell those who lingered on amongst his following that it was all up and that they were to go home, he returned and tried to stem the blood with his skull cap, but eventually it fell, together with his rifle, to the ground and he wandered off into the bush where he lay in semi-conscious agony. In a last desperate gesture of flamboyance, Joe went to the bar and, raising a glass of brandy to his lips, he toasted the Kellys. He fell dying from a bullet in the groin crying on his Saviour to show him mercy. In a lull in the firing others heard his life blood gush out on the dusty boards.[12]

As the first, faint smudges of dawn broke in the east, Ned roused himself and began shuffling back towards the hotel. A mist was rising from the soft earth and to those who held the ground there this huge figure with an overcoat over his armour appeared as a madman, a ghost, an old Aboriginal, a bunyip or the very devil himself. They began to fire away at him, and their horror was consummated when they found that the bullets merely whipped and pranged from him. Mindful still of the years when the police had acted uniformly as a mongrel breed to him and his, Ned taunted them and called them 'bloody cocktails', but his weaponry was useless now to him, with maimed arm and hand, and they suffered no injury from him. Steele looked to his legs to bring him down and directing his aim there he filled them with shot, so that Ned sank quietly to the earth behind a big, broken log and they fell upon him. For a few moments they seemed as if they would tear him to pieces or that Steele would shoot him dead as he lay with a wild and wasted look on his face. Dwyer, who was a madman, a liar and a policeman, kicked him as he lay but Bracken, mindful of some common humanity between them, saved him from death in that place and they took him to the station. It was seventeen minutes past seven when he fell.[13]

The hotel was now a veritable sieve held together with

nails, and protecting no one. A white flag was raised at the urging of Dan who wanted the people there to escape, and who gave his promise that neither he nor Steve would fire until they had done so successfully. But white flags were of no avail to such as Steele, O'Connor and the trackers.[14] Was it not the case, long since established, that the northeast was a nest of traitors, miscreants and worthless people who could sympathize with such curs as the Kellys and all such ilk? What right-minded person then could be expected to show mercy to such as these, so the guns boomed away while people fled or crawled from the building; Mrs Jones' son who was the singer of ballads was taken off to die, young Reardon carried a bullet beneath his ribs fired by Steele, while Martin Cherry lay in agony in the hotel. No one knew when the firing stopped from within, because the police now surrounded the building and they were incapable of distinguishing their own fire from that of the others.

After the escape of the last prisoners at 10 a.m. no shots were fired, but the problem remained of how best to ensure the slaughter of Dan and Steve without loss of police lives. Sadleir thought up the idea of sending for a piece of field artillery to blow the hotel and its remaining inhabitants to smithereens, and with such a weapon at his disposal Standish was emboldened to issue forth from his club and proceed to Glenrowan to take up a position of command at the front lines. The cannon never came beyond Seymour, because fire itself seemed the better and safer means to ensure destruction. In vain Maggie tried to get to the hotel to beg the boys to surrender, but the police threatened to shoot her if she ventured to do so for they wanted blood, or at least some of them did. O'Connor rested in his ditch reading the

Argus while his trackers amused themselves with constant volleys, and Sadleir stood about smoking. These last moments were a spectacle indeed, for between five and six hundred people had gathered to watch it all, amongst them some of those whose hearts and hopes had burned high.[15]

But it was the inn of Mrs Jones that burned and into it ran a certain Father Gibney who was a passenger on a passing train. He had given the last rites to the apparently dying Ned and asked him to say 'Lord Jesus have mercy on me', and the outlaw had roused himself, said it and added 'It's not today I began to say that.' The priest wanted to extend the great courtesy of his ministry to those other wild ones in the hotel and he went into the building as it was engulfed in flames from the fire lit by the police. He saw the body of Joe, and then those of the young ones, Dan and Steve. They were peaceful now and close together with the armour at their sides and their heads raised on rolled up bags, as if pillows. At their feet lay the body of a dog, and the flames were beginning to lick at the room. The priest felt them, and found them cold, and thought by it all that they had taken singly, their own young lives, but he did not know that another had been there during those hours after the escape of the prisoners. This loyal one found them dead, killed by that hail of fire which had penetrated the whole place in almost every inch of its very parts. He had laid them out quickly, but gently, and placed the dog at their feet, as if they were kings of a northern race rather than simple bush boys. He had known them in better and happier times and he stole away saddened. When the police came they brought out Joe's body and the shattered frame of Cherry, who shortly expired.[16]

The wailing of Maggie and Kate rent the keen air of those mountains as they knelt over the charred and unrecognizable bodies of their youngest brother and that of Steve, his companion in their act of impetuous rebellion. Sadleir let them take the bodies, and it was out to Greta they went where, in the manner of their for-bears and those who followed their strange customs in a new land, a wake was held. It is said that Ettie Hart was hysterical with grief but no one dared to ask her whether she mourned for Steve alone or for the dark leader and loved one of days now gone. Before dawn the men who had planned to follow the elder Kelly gath-ered, while the thin ground was opened, and the remains of Dan and Steve were put down behind Mrs Kelly's home nearby to Annie who had lain there since it all began. That done they hitched horses to logs and flattened out the ground above them, so that no trace would be seen of that resting place. With Joe it was differ-ent, for it was deemed a goodly thing by the police to string his body up at the gate of the gaol in Benalla, for the edification of the curious, and the benefit of the photographers. They put him down at the local cem-etery, because the police refused to give up his body. No one came to mourn him for Joe's loves had been fleet-ing, except for the person of his leader, who battled back to life at Glenrowan with the help of Dr John Nicholson. Much care was lavished on Ned for he had one purpose left to fill in order that the inexorable abstraction men call law might grind on to its finality.[17]

The Son of his Mother   15

The number of a man's days upon the earth is finite, and with the criminal condemned to death they can be counted to the very minute. In a civilized society such a one is precious for he is the symbol of its mortality. Men know that his doom is theirs, but to safeguard their own hold on the quicksilver of life he must be cut out from amongst them. Yet it is not good and fitting to lead the criminal to his end broken in body or even in spirit for, until that final act, he must stand as one who is whole amongst them. His expiatory deed has to be such that its awful magnitude penetrates the core of his mind, to which purpose it must be sane. His body has to bloom in order to speak to all of life in its fullness which in him will be cut off in an instant and cast aside. The steps that lead to that end need to be measured, precise, and full of meaning, as befits the enormity of what is afoot so that, again, men who deem themselves as ones risen beyond barbarism will suffer no disquiet at it all. They hence ensure that the proceedings are all carefully formulated and surrounded with ritual, because only thus can the fact be disguised that the collective is itself a killer. Not for them the actual doing lest it may perchance come upon their minds that blood is upon their hands. The one to be slain is passed from place to place, from functionary to other official actors, all of whom take their authority from the collective by whom they are empowered to act. But it cannot be said that, in the end, any of them did it, because each acted for all and, when it is done, good and upright men can go to their dinner tables and thence to bed, justified because what was done was by another or, if they are men given to philosophy, they can content themselves with the thought that it was not done by men at all, but by the law itself. As for the one who actually does the thing he can expect to be reviled, and some will even curse him because he took money to do his thing, as if it were the case that he should kill for the collective without reward. All in all it is not a pretty thing to be about, and that section of civilized society known as the colony of Victoria began to be about it when Ned Kelly, once an outlaw but now only a citizen under arrest, was brought low at Glenrowan on 28 June 1880.

For a man with three severe bullet wounds to his right elbow, hand and foot and numerous others of a minor nature, Ned proved himself 'fit to run in the Cup' although it was not for that particular contest that he was so carefully prepared in the weeks following Glenrowan. Brought to Melbourne on Wednesday, he was removed from the train at North Melbourne in order to avoid the crowds waiting for him at Spencer Street, the main terminus for trains arriving from the country. Taken immediately to the Melbourne Gaol he was lodged there under the care of J. B. Castieau, the governor of that institution. Castieau was a gentleman who took his duties very seriously indeed, and the lodging of Ned Kelly in his care was the pinnacle of a career as a gaoler that now spanned twenty-six years. In those years he had suffered only one severe set back in his chosen profession when, on 19 April 1873 at 1.45 a.m., he was observed by a young constable sitting on the doorstep of the chemist shop at the corner of Bourke and Stephen Streets. Castieau, clearly a man of great respectability, was violently drunk and sporting a companion in the person of a harlot. The young constable was mindful of his responsibilities in respect of worthy citizens whom he found consorting with ladies of ill-repute. Indeed, being a member of a force some of whose senior officers were well-known frequenters of brothels in their role as private citizens, he had reason to fear for the reputation of this particular gentleman, so he forthwith ordered the woman to hie herself elsewhere. She did so and Castieau, being aroused, ordered her return. Other citizens gathered, the governor assaulted the constable, much unpleasantness ensued, Castieau was fined 10s and was demoted to the bottom of his class. Yet by 1880 he was back in favour, and when Mrs Kennedy asked permission to visit Ned so as to inform herself of the last moments of her beloved husband at Stringybark Creek, Castieau was able to bring his considerable knowledge of men, and women too, to bear in advising Standish to refuse the request. Ned, in the opinion of those upright fellows, would merely behave in the manner to which he was born as one by nature given to foul, abusive and low conduct to which no respectable female ought expose herself. Mrs Kennedy's 'devout wish' remained unfilled, while Ned lost his last chance to show something of that gentility, remarked upon universally by women, to one whom he had so grievously deprived.[1]

Over the next few days Ned struggled back to better
health, though a bullet remained in his ankle, while his
right thumb was shattered and henceforth he could only
write in the manner of his forbears and sign with his
mark. It was, however, imperative to start the machinery
of the law moving; although, if the judgements of some
editors were to be accepted, no such formality was
needed because Kelly was a white-livered poltroon, a
man-wolf for whom the grave even then yawned, while
the nation was eagerly clamouring 'for the life so long
and bloodily forfeited to its outraged laws'.[2] Nevertheless it was not deemed appropriate to act on such sen-
timents yet awhile, and after an aborted remand to the
Melbourne City Court on 5 July, it was decided that he
had to be taken back to the jurisdiction of his crime for
a hearing. To this purpose an assembly gathered in the
kitchen attached to the prison's hospital and Ned,
unrepresented, was brought there on 31 July. He insisted
that no trial take place without Fitzpatrick present and
while stating firmly that he did not want to live he refused
to die until they got to the bottom of the whole matter.
That of course was the exact intention of the authorities
but no one, except Ned, saw the need to interrogate Fitzpatrick. McIntyre was heard and on his evidence Ned
was remanded to Beechworth. Once more he set forth
on that journey with McIntyre, Steele and Bracken
amongst his guards. He pointed out the place of his birth
as they passed by Wallan, he sang several Kelly ballads
in a soft tone, and, when they came in sight of the Strathbogies, the old longing to roam free as a brumby welled
up, and he wondered aloud whether he would ever be
there again. The proceedings at Beechworth were rendered vexatious by the difficulties placed in Ned's way
of making any proper arrangements for his defence, and
David Gaunson, M.L.A. for Ararat, who accepted the

brief when requested to by Maggie, was able to do little
to prevent the already foregone conclusion by which
Ned was committed to stand trial at Beechworth on
14 October for murder.

After all that fruitless pursuit of the four in the northeast
it was not unreasonable for the officers of the law to con-
clude that a jury picked from amongst those who had
for so long refused to betray Kelly might fall short of its
desired objective, so on 10 August he was on his way
back to Melbourne for trial and the northeast saw him
no more. But before his departure from those places, he
met Tom Lloyd for a fleeting moment and in one sentence
he summed up what Glenrowan and their struggle had
all been about. To Tom he said, 'If they will give you
land let it all be over', for Ned knew that for himself it
was indeed all over but the battle for land remained
to be won by them.

He spoke little on the journey but at Wangaratta he
looked at the large crowd which had gathered at the
station and said, 'There's a lot of colonials.' Ned himself
was no longer a mere colonial boy, despite the ballads
and their plaintive themes. Outlaw no longer but 'an
accused person awaiting trial', he was being treated,
according to David Gaunson, in a 'grossly illegal' manner which was furthermore 'a violation of the rights of
common humanity'. Such protests were as nothing to that
champion of the colonial underdogs, Graham Berry, to
whom the document was addressed. Kelly had cost the
colony a great deal of money, he was a severe embarrassment to Berry's administration and, while the sem-
blance of the formalities were to be observed, nothing
further would be done to protect Ned's rights. Berry told
Gaunson he would be given no co-operation by the government in the conduct of any proceedings in respect
of Ned. In any case political affairs with an election

pending overrode any other trivia such as former outlaws.[3]

While Ned was gaining his strength under the careful medical attention provided assiduously by the state, his erstwhile adversaries in the police force were engaged in a welter of recrimination, denunciation, resignation and continued futility. For reasons which remain obscure they possessed themselves of a lust to obtain ownership of the armour and to ascertain exactly who made it, as if the latter piece of knowledge would add a cubit to their stature as sleuths. As was to be expected, they were consistent in that their enquiries in and about Greta proved as futile as their previous efforts to capture the four had been.[4] It does not appear that they were minded to ask the one person in a position to have certain knowledge in the matter, Ned himself. But then anything that Ned said, unless he actually chose to incriminate himself, was of necessity suspect; yet if he opted to make an alleged admission of guilt, then his word had to be accepted with complete confidence. Indeed Constable John Kelly, who was no relation to the clan, and Constable Cornelius Ryan were happy to be able to report that, as he lay stupefied with the whisky plied to him by the police at Glenrowan, and his spirit wandered through his daze of agony, Ned admitted that he had indeed shot Fitzpatrick. It took them two months to communicate this choice piece of information to their superiors, but its significance was possibly lost on them in the heat of those moments below old Morgan's Lookout.[5]

In respect of the suits of armour, immediate interest had been shown by the wider community with requests that they be loaned to agricultural shows and such like worthy causes, frenetic application of the hammer to the anvil by eager blacksmiths wishing to duplicate same, and a determination by the police to share the real sets up amongst each other, resulting in acrimonious and jealous exchanges, as Hare in particular claimed his spoils of war, while Standish remained disdainful and distressed because to him it was all an example of disgusting exhibitionism leading to further hero worship of Ned.[6]

The thing that distressed the police most was the rapidity with which the taste of glorious victory over the four boys turned bitter in their mouths. Congratulated so promptly they were reviled as promptly, and not only in Victoria where many had battened fat on their ineptitude. In the New South Wales parliament that tempestuous lawyer and fighter for justice, to those whom he regarded as downtrodden, David Buchanan, flayed them as men who acted with 'insane recklessness', ruthless, cowardly and scandalous, upon whom nothing but downright 'unequivocal condemnation' ought be passed. Indeed were they tried for manslaughter, in his judicial opinion, there could be no possibility of their escaping a verdict of guilty. Henry Parkes was goaded to a gauche reply on behalf of his own government. He said that the boys had been able to secrete themselves in an area where a thousand policemen could not capture them, due to its terrain and the fact that 'the whole population were in a criminal confederacy to save them.' Excusing his own force for its ineptness during and after Jerilderie, he claimed that they were up against a group of young men whose 'courage, precaution and military genius' far surpassed that of any bushrangers the country had seen. From further away, in Queensland, the same opinions were expressed and the Premier excoriated O'Connor and his trackers for participating in the bloody affair at Glenrowan. O'Connor himself,

when it came to his ears that Hare was claiming that
he had spent his time at the front hiding in a ditch, began
to clamour for an investigatory commission to look into
the whole matter. Harassed to distraction by it all, Captain Standish did the only sensible thing left open to a
gentleman who could read the signs of bureaucracy,
whatever was his knowledge of the signs in the bush.
He resigned in September to live henceforth on his pen-
sion and devote himself to the leisurely and uninterrup-
ted pursuit of the turf. It was no cause for satisfaction
to him that his temporary replacement as Chief of Police
was the subordinate whom he considered both inept
and cranky, Nicolson.[7]

Saturday 2 October 1880 was a Melbourne grey day,
but the city and a large part of its quarter million inhabitants throbbed with excitement because they were the
hosts to a great exhibition designed to prove that, if Australia itself were to become 'A greater Britain,' neath
these 'Southern Skies', then the city on the little Yarra
was worthy to be its capital. Banners flew, Monsieur
Caron conducted his one-thousand-person choir, the
Marquis of Normanby, representative of Her Majesty in
the colony of Victoria, opened the exhibition with great
aplomb and little sense, guns boomed, and generally
there was much pride and jollity.[8] One citizen, at least,
did not participate, even in spirit, in these proceedings.
Just a short, brisk walk from the new edifice with its tower-
ing dome called the Exhibition Building, in a cell of the
Melbourne Gaol, Ned lay quietly. The bullet had been
removed from his ankle, but his legs were still causing
pain, his left arm had begun to shrivel while his hand
had 'a wasted and crushed appearance'.

Ned had been permitted a visit from his mother, Maggie and Kate, but it all seemed so futile. Between them

they could raise no money because, on the advice of
the police, the scrubby bit of land of Ellen's pride on
the Eleven Mile had been taken back by the Lands
Department without compensation, while nothing
remained of the Euroa and Jerilderie riches except the
threepence found on Ned at Glenrowan. Furthermore
it was nigh impossible to talk in any sensible or even
affectionate manner, for Castieau had taken upon himself responsibility to ensure that Ned's body was handed
over to whatever fate lay before it, sound and as entire
as could be arranged. He was haunted by the thought
that in some ingenious way Ned might achieve a means
of escape, but having concluded that only by death
could death be thwarted, he hovered anxiously about
whenever Ned was visited so as to ensure that no poison
was passed. Much less was passed than poison, for the
Kelly clan were not accustomed to conducting their personal affairs in the presence of the officers of the government and, as a result, their preparations for their own
big day at Melbourne's Central Criminal Court was rendered somewhat nugatory. Ned could perhaps have
taken some consolation in the knowledge, had it come
to his ears, that the government was doing its best to
ensure that the court was in proper order, for in anticipation of a larger than normal attendance gas lighting
was put in and extra accommodation provided.[9]

The other chief actor in the drama was a man who
was also plagued with worries. Gone were the days of
his virile manhood when Sir Redmond Barry, senior
puisne judge of the Supreme Court of Victoria, could
indulge his sexual fantasies with learned disquisitions
on the aberrations of medieval barons with the virginal
daughters of their dependent vassals. His warm friend
and confidant, Curtis Candler, resident with Standish

at the Melbourne Club and functioning publicly as the
city coroner, no longer delighted in writing to the judge
on the training, both mental and bodily, required by
those ancients so that they might engage in the pro-
longed performance of such a delicate function as penetrating a maidenhead with nimble agility. Such matters
were far behind, for the judge was desperately in debt
and accordingly much straitened, so he could not understand why his beloved Mrs Barrow would so grossly
annoy him as to purchase a piano – an acquisition
emphatically beyond his slender means. That he loved
her with a love unbounded was unquestionable, as his
letter revealed and he was 'most penitent and contrite'
whenever he offended her and ready to submit to 'any
amount of scolding' she had in store for him. But the
years had taught his Honour that it was a very expensive
matter to keep up two establishments, his own at Carlton
Gardens and another for his lady, with their four children, in Fitzroy. He had been generous also to the needy,
and his many benefactions to public causes had
drained his purse, while his long-suffered diabetes had
weakened his constitution. Added to all this was the
affair of this awful Kelly fellow whose mother even now
resided in the same gaol as her precious son. While it
was improbable that the matter could be neatly
arranged by a long sentence in prison, as was in prospect in 1878 had Ned come before him at Beechworth,
there were other solutions. Perhaps Barry remembered
the waggish joke he had clipped from a newspaper and
pasted in his scrapbook amongst his love poems. It was
a singularly apposite joke for a man engaged in such
activities as his Honour before whom more than two hundred capital charges had come and it went like this.
'Why does the operation of hanging kill a man?'

inquired Dr Whateley. A physiologist replied, 'Because inspiration is checked, circulation stopped, and blood suffuses and congests the brain.' 'Bosh,' replied his Grace. 'It is because the rope is not long enough to let his feet touch the ground.' And that indeed was a witty thing to come from the lips of an Archbishop.[10]

As a consequence of the inability of the family to raise funds, combined with the impossibility of preparing any adequate defence due to the refusal by Berry to allow proper access to Ned, an attempt was made on 15 October, a mere three days before the date set for the trial, to get a postponement of one month. At this stage, Mr H. Molesworth had been retained for the defence, and he pleaded the case for postponement. Ned was not present, but Barry could see no grounds whatsoever for delay. He was certainly prepared to concede that in the normal course of events an application of this nature was 'never refused except on substantial grounds', but he would not regard lack of money or access as reasons 'founded on justice or principle'. In his opinion, if the government had seen fit to deprive the Kelly family of the one thing they held of even minimal value, the land at Greta, it was done with fit and proper reasons. It was also pointed out by Mr Smyth, prosecutor for the Crown, that the prisoner could apply for funds of the state to pay for his defence. What was not made clear to the uninitiated was that government payment precluded the very lawyer who knew most about the case from undertaking it. David Gaunson knew a great deal about the whole affair but he was the member for Ararat in the Legislative Assembly and he risked his parliamentary position if he took a fee from the state. Hence were he to take any part in the case he had to do so in a secondary capacity as attorney, and it was unlikely that any competent counsel would consent to appear, given that the Crown would only pay £7 7s for his work. Even more importantly the defence was, at this stage, very seriously hampered by the fact that, with only three days to go, it was unlikely that an adequate case could be prepared, given the amount of work required to become familiar with the facts, prepare witnesses and generally make some reasonable attempt to prevent the whole thing collapsing into a judicial farce. Barry's refusal forced them into that very position, but David Gaunson spent a frantic and useful weekend because he was as determined as was Barry to have his way in the matter.[11]

On the Monday morning, 18 October, a very large crowd of several thousand had gathered both within and without the court to witness the proceedings. Amongst those down from the northeast were Maggie, dressed in black as the occasion warranted, Tom Lloyd who kept a low profile, and other unidentified sympathizers. Kate was not present as she had to stay at home to mind the children including young Alice who had been taken home from Melbourne to Greta. The Crown had taken great pains to ensure that no mishap occurred because of a lack of appropriate jurors, and eighty persons had been subpoenaed to that purpose, with a consequent overcrowding of the court. Indeed it was necessary for the Victorian authorities to ensure a meritorious display because the Attorney-General of New South Wales together with his High Sheriff, were there to witness all that transpired. Much interest was evinced in the person of McIntyre, resplendent in full uniform, for it was generally known that he had collapsed from nervous debility at the Beechworth trial and had spent some time in hospital recovering. It was a source of very considerable satisfaction to see that he appeared fully

recovered. Barry seated himself at ten sharp, and Ned
was produced. At Glenrowan, to the surprise of Dr
Charles Ryan, Ned had been found 'as clean as if he
had just come out of a Turkish bath' and his whole person
still conveyed a scrupulous attention to his toiletry with
hair and beard neatly arranged, clothing likewise, and
over it all Gaunson's overcoat. Before departing from
the gaol Ned pointed out the shabbiness of his own and
David had been quick to lend him his. So attired Ned
stood, smiled slightly at Maggie and listened while they
charged him with having 'wilfully and of malice aforethought murdered Thomas Lonigan'. He pleaded 'Not
guilty', but not loudly or brashly, so they then charged
him with having done the same in respect of Michael
Scanlan. At that moment a barrister-at-law named Bindon pleaded for a postponement, so all settled down
to hear the legal niceties therein involved.[12]

Put very simply, it appeared that, while David Gaunson could not take the case, equally Mr Molesworth was
not prepared to do so. He was most unwilling to under-
take a matter involving the possibility of a conviction
for murder at such short notice, he deemed it a miserly
act to ask him to accept such a slender fee given his
eminent standing, especially as two charges were prof-
fered and he had already accepted a case to be heard
at Bendigo. None of this seemed to be of any consequence to the Attorney-General of Victoria, one William
Vale, admitted to the Victoria Supreme Court in 1879 and
who had held his high legal office for less than three
months. He wrote plainly, 'To me the prisoner E. Kelly
is simply a prisoner for trial for murder.' Mr Smyth also
saw no need for a postponement, but as he did not want
anyone to think that the prisoner was being treated
harshly, he was prepared to compromise on a week at

the outside, although he thought it all a 'sham' on the part of the defence. It was thus up to Judge Barry to decide whether he would deprive of their promised entertainment those who had fought their way into the court on that Monday or whether he would proceed with the matter. His Honour pointed out that he too would be up the country on legal matters until the 28th of the month and though he thought it 'very becoming on the part of the Crown' to grant clemency of a week's post-ponement, his own engagements made ten days a necessity. The court was closed, Ned walked quietly back to prison accompanied by three armed warders and it was noticed that he no longer limped. People cried 'hats off' as he passed, which some interpreted as an act of sympathy and others as a means of ensuring that those behind saw the chief actor. He disappeared into the prison to be seen no more in public until the 28th.[13]

By Monday 25 October, three days before the trial, it was apparent to David Gaunson that there was no possibility of obtaining the services of Hickman Moles-worth as counsel. Molesworth had been absent from Melbourne on a case of attempted murder tried before Barry at Bendigo in the previous week and hence could not be briefed. Gaunson then made a fatal choice in the person of Henry Massey Bindon, perhaps on the grounds that he, at least, knew a little of the affair. But three days were perilously short to brief a man as inex-perienced as Bindon, whose background was sound in that his father had been a County Court judge, but whose admission to the Victorian bar dated only from the previous December and who was absent from the colony when the matter to be judged took place. Now aged thirty-seven, it had taken him three attempts at matriculation before passing at the age of twenty-seven,

after which he betook himself to London where he was
welcomed to the Inner Temple in the same year as that
other legal luminary, the Attorney-General, William
Vale. The main thing in his favour was his willingness
to work for £7 7s, so on the morning of 28 October he
appeared in court, with Ned who was on this occasion
dressed in William Gaunson's chesterfield overcoat,
and pleaded for a further extension of time. Barry, back
in town after his stint in the bush, was determined to con-
clude the whole sorry affair so he promptly refused, a
jury was sworn in and proceedings began. The *Bulletin*
reporter was struck by Ned's 'handsome and essentially
manly features', his height, his large pale blue or steel
grey eyes and his heavy eyebrows. He concluded that
'no one could see in his face the ferocity with which he
is credited . . .' But then again no one could see anything
of those with whom it had all begun, for neither Flood
nor Fitzpatrick were called to give an account of their
dealings with those whom Kelly loved.[14]

For a time in that court the two chief participants were
overshadowed by the performance of another, for there
was one there on whose word the outcome hinged. Of
those eight who stood clothed in their flesh at Stringybark Creek in the Wombat ranges on 26 October 1878,
only two stood now, the one on trial for his life, the other
for his conscience. Thomas McIntyre's word would seal
the issue for evermore, for only he could tell whether Ned
had feloniously, wilfully and of his malice aforethought,
killed and murdered Thomas Lonigan. It was all quite
simple really and the question was whether Ned stole
up upon them, set in his mind to kill, or whether he killed
in order to prevent his own killing. On the day after his
night in the wombat hole, Thomas had sat down at Mansfield, within twenty-four hours of the death of Lonigan,

and had written the words, 'Constable Lonigan made
a motion to draw his revolver.'[15] But two springs had
passed over those ranges since that day and here stood
Thomas, and he was a man whose mind was turned,
for on his own admission the days between had been
filled with such torment that he believed that by the time
he came to the court 'I must have been several times
upon the brink of insanity.'

And thus it was that McIntyre swore that Ned shot
Lonigan down, poor defenceless Lonigan who made no
move to shoot Ned down, after he had been called upon
to surrender. No mention was made of the weapons the
police took out to arrest two young men, of the reward
offered for them, of the surprising fact that such a cold-
blooded brute as Kelly had not gunned McIntyre down
too. And stupid, bemused, inept and overawed Bindon
asked nothing that mattered a whit, so McIntyre went
back to his place justified because he had told the truth,
but not the truth that mattered. After his testimony all
that happened in the shape of a long list of persons who
swore that Ned had told them he shot Lonigan, was a
mere charade – for Ned had never denied that he shot
him. It had to be gone through for the sake of the thing,
but the judge was anxious to get the whole tedious business over because Cup week was coming upon them,
and he was not prepared to have those worthy citizens,
to whose care the fate of Edward Kelly had been committed, locked up while such festivities went on about them.
At 5 p.m. on Friday 29 October, it was nearly over, and
Barry told the jury to go away and deliberate, but not
to return with any mention of manslaughter, for it had
to be guilty of murder or an acquittal. It only took half
an hour for the others to overcome the scruples of one
juror who was uneasy about his role in a verdict that

would lead a man to the gallows. By 5.40, as men came
in for a drink at the local pubs, Ned Kelly was found
guilty of the wilful murder of the man, Thomas Lonigan.
After a few preliminary remarks by Ned, who was asked
politely whether he had anything to say, the judge performed the obligatory, black cap ritual and spoke the
set piece about Ned's body and his neck which meant
that he was to die.[16]

Yet it happened that something real took place in that
room in Melbourne which somewhat disturbed the
smooth course of awful ceremony with which the colony
of Victoria clothed itself when dealing in death. The
people in the court heard an interchange between two
men, neither of whom was to speak to the public again,
and each of whom represented the world that made
them. No angry words passed, no curses were hurled,
nothing lowered the tone of that awesome place, for
these men had things to say to one another, and it mattered not to them that in galvanized silence they were
heard, for the only sound was the faint scratch of pencils
as the reporters took it down. Ned told Judge Barry that,
had he decided to speak earlier, he could have cleared
himself of all the things said against him, and proclaimed solemnly, 'I declare before you and my God that
my mind is as easy and clear as it possibly can be.' To
the hearers, this statement was stupendous; some mur-
mured, while others cried out. To Barry, the mention of
his God by such a craven monster was blasphemy, and
he said so. As if their roles were reversed, and Ned stood
there as arbiter of the man before him, he reminded
Barry that they would 'all have to go to a bigger court
than this' where both would see the right and wrong of
things. He spoke tenderly of his mother, and he listened
calmly while Barry told him how enormous a crime was

his, because he had risen up to strike at the very heart of civilized society. The judge partly explained the reason for them all being there when he reminded Ned that his career had cost the colony £50,000. And then, having spoken the death words, he was minded to ask his God to have mercy on Ned's soul. From the lips of the man in the dock came a sentence which sent a shudder through the room. 'I will go a little further than that, and say I will see you there where I go.'[17]

On the following Tuesday, the favourite, Grand Flaneur, won the Cup at two-to-one from Progress, possibly in the presence of some of those who had so expeditiously discharged their duties as jurors on the preceding Friday. For David Gaunson, his brother William, and leading members of the Society for the Abolition of Capital Punishment, for Maggie, Kate, Tom Lloyd and others, it was a week in which racing was not uppermost in their minds. They busied themselves in the matter of the life of Ned whose days were slipping by, faster it seemed than the furlongs under the feet of the thoroughbreds at Flemington. He had been permitted a visit from Maggie and a few others on Saturday after the trial, and in the afternoon his mother was alone with him although Castieau insisted that their conversation take place through an iron grate. On Wednesday the Governor met with his Executive Council and heard Barry, who stated that he saw no reason to recommend against carrying the sentence into execution. The nine personages there assembled equally saw no cause but to agree with him, so Ned had eight nights to lie on his bed. Other citizens, to the number of 32,000, did not agree and signed a petition to the Governor requesting that his life be spared. Ned himself wrote two letters to His Excellency endeavouring to explain why things had come to this pass. It

was all to no avail. Even Kate with her winsome ways
could not move that representative of the Queen, who
had been importuned by a certain lass who called herself Lucy Dashwood, and who wrote that Ned was not
a 'cruel monster' but 'true and brave as the day'. When
Castieau told him on 6 November that his death day was
to be the eleventh of that month Ned said it was 'a very
short notice'. On the tenth he wrote again to the Governor, and he and his gentlemen sat down for their third
Executive Council meeting and had the letter read to
them. They remained impassive, even when they heard
the last words Ned wrote in life:

There is one wish in conclusion I would like you to grant me,
that is the release of my Mother before my execution, as detain-
ing her in prison could not make any difference to the Government now for the day will come when all men will be judged
by their mercy and deeds. And also if you would grant permission for my friends to have my body that they might bury
it in consecrated ground.

    That evening the woman whose womb had borne him,
and whose life had been so entwined with his own, held
him for the last time in her arms. It is not recorded what
passed between them, but of her son, who had told Barry
in the court-room a few days before that he feared death
as little as he feared the drinking of a cup of tea, she
asked one thing. She reminded him of his origins and
the longer history of his race by asking him to die like
a Kelly. Meanwhile, across the city another lay in the
illness that was to be his last, for death had already
begun to stretch forth its fingers into the frame of Redmond Barry.[18]
    The person chosen by the state to execute its last deed
on the body of Ned was a fellow prisoner, the cruelly

misshapen Upjohn who had much to attend to on that Wednesday. The rope had to be well oiled, tested for strength and measured according to Ned's weight, for were it too short it might not do its work, while too great a drop could result in messy decapitation. The bolts had to work to perfection, leather straps and a white cap provided, and, above all, care had to be paid to cleanliness for was it not the case that for a little time at least the Melbourne Gaol was to be transformed into the official abattoirs of the state? By evening all was in readiness, down to the hand trolley provided to take the body away to the dead house, and thence to the lime pit for this body was not to lie in blessed earth. Meanwhile Ned took his last meal because, after midnight, he could neither eat nor drink for, in the morning, he was to receive the wafer under the form of which he believed His Saviour was present. After his meal he lay down to rest.[19]

Beveridge, Avenel, high Glenmore, little Greta, itself now almost a ghost town, the ranges and the plains across the mother river were all gone now, and so too were many he had known, but the dead have ways of living and Lonigan, Scanlan and Kennedy were there, because the spirits of Stringybark Creek were soon to be expiated. As in the act of life, blood begets blood, so too in death, and Ned in that dark place in the Wombat Ranges had dealt in death, which was now at his door. The dreams of freedom from subjugation to a legal tyranny had reached their final, ironic climax, for all around him stood the ultimate symbols, with their grim reality, by which killing was rendered legal. What could it matter if Fitzpatrick, Flood, Mullane, poor lame Curnow and even he who was gripped by death, called Redmond Barry, still lived? They too were nearer now to the

dissolution that stood before Ned, even as he lay his
young limbs on his bed. In not granting him that last
wish of the release of his mother, the state had been kind,
for she was close by in that place, and there was a certain
fitness in the thing for mother and son had been caught
up in a common bond that removed them from the walks
of men. Only one legacy remained of that dark heritage
of the hovels and cottages of Ireland and her woes that
mattered now to Ned. That legacy would have its symbol
too in the charnel house of the morrow, for a cross with
another broken body would stand beside him.

In the end he slept, and when Edward Adams, a war-
der who had befriended him, looked in at 5 a.m. he was
on his knees praying. He slept again, rose at eight, sang
ballads of the bush and of the old days, and had his
irons removed. It was time to shift to the death cell and
on the way he passed the death trolley, but he chose
to look at life, and remarked on the flowers in the little
garden. 'They are beautiful,' he said. Father Donaghy,
chaplain of the prison, and Dean O'Hea, who had known
Ned in his earliest years, came with the sacrament and
stayed to pray with him. Shortly before ten, Castieau
indicated that the time had drawn nigh, so Upjohn
inspected his tools and came to tie Ned, who protested,
saying in the lilting brogue which stayed to the end,
'There's no need for tying me,' but the executioner
thought otherwise. Ned turned and said to Adams, 'Well,
it has come to this,' as indeed it had. The two priests
went before him, one reading the litany of the dying,
although it was Barry who was dying at that moment,
rather than Ned. As Upjohn tied the knot, Ned looked
at the crucifix steadily, stood in the full vigour of the
health to which it had been deemed proper to restore
him, and said 'Such is life.' The light of late spring played

through the windows of the gaol; outside a crowd had assembled amongst whom some knelt in silent prayer, while below the scaffold society's representatives stood to witness his being cast from them. With the agility of a cat Upjohn pulled the white hood down, stepped aside, released the bolt and Ned fell, living. In a very little while he rested. It was 10.00 a.m. 11 November 1880, and a man whose calling was healing pronounced him dead, as the priests with their oil anointed his stilled senses.

Epilogue

For a time death had its way and at Greta and the places
thereabouts the grass grew over graves and all was
quiet. Those who had joined with Ned in deed or spirit
showed briefly that the cause was not done for, but
gradually they too were permitted to become part of
society, with small holdings growing larger and moderate comfort replacing penury. Memories became muted
and men talked only in whispers of the purpose of Glenrowan but in loud voices of its causes of hunger for land
and hatred of police suppression. No monument was
raised to the leader for they had taken the mortal
remains of Edward Kelly, cut off the head and consigned
the rest to a pit which became in time the car park of
the police. The head itself was loaned to a gentleman
learned in the ways of foolishness called phrenology
who declaimed upon it. He passed it back to the police
who used it as a paper weight. In our own day some
gentle person had the decency to remove it from its resting place on a shelf in the prison where Ned was execu-

ted. One can only hope that, even if not in consecrated
ground as he had wished, his head has been returned
to the earth at last.

The police did moderately well in respect of the £8,000
reward money for it could clearly be proved that they
were indeed present when Ned fell amongst them. They
reaped over £6,000, of which the black trackers received
£50 each, while Hare, as was his due, took the lion's
share of £800 and the Royal Commission of 1881 recom-.
mended that his services be dispensed with. Even those
gentlemen who fled under the bed at Aaron's place were
granted £42 12s 6d each and Sergeant Steele who shot
innocent persons at Glenrowan received £290 13s 9d.
He was recommended by the Royal Commission for
reduction to the ranks for cowardice. Thomas Curnow
was the civilian most generously rewarded with £550 but
when he died at Ballarat in 1922 the newspaper obituary
made no mention of his role at Glenrowan.

All in all it was a sordid business which had the
cleansing effect of making Victorians aware of the short-
comings of their law enforcement system and resulting
in the reformation of the force. That a hundred years
later the members of that same force could have celebrated the deaths of their men at Stringybark Creek
with dignity, restraint and generosity to all the dead says
a great deal for the development of a higher code
amongst them since 1878.

The little ones of Greta remained in obscurity despite
the forays of the gentlemen of the press, who through
the years tried to invoke the memories of former days
and probe the motives that activated those close to the
four. Ellen Kelly lived on until 1923 lovingly cared for
by Jim who died in 1946. She never forgot the two wayward ones whose lives and manner of death had broken

her spirit and blighted her hopes. Kate behaved misera-
bly after Ned's death and she is still spoken of with
shame amongst her people, although the loneliness of
her death in New South Wales mitigates the bitterness.
She lies next to Ben Hall in the Forbes cemetery and
hence forges a bond between the two legends of the
colonies whose names are remembered amongst the
bushrangers.

As for Ned his spirit was never at peace. The one fact
that stood out was his return from the bush to try to save
the two younger ones at Mrs Jones' hotel. On the battle-
fields of Flanders and along the Kokoda trail this game-
ness was held up as a torch to others. Some tried to
blacken him and Candler of the Melbourne Club told
Hare that Ned died a craven, which all others present
called a foul lie. Others tried to forget that he had killed
in the Wombat as if the killer was not gripped by the
guilt of blood, or worse, as if it did not matter that men
died because they were only the police. Ned did not forget the open flesh and staring eyes and the grieving
of the women and children. Time helped to heal, but
the wounds are there yet and so too is the mystery of
the making of the legend.

Three men, two of the pen, the other of the brush, have
done more than all others to keep the legend in noble
flight. With his poems on Ned and the northeast, David
Campbell brought to the legend the gentle touch of a
mind sinewed in strength and loving purpose that all
who knew him revered. Douglas Stewart came from his
own New Zealand mountains to those lesser but no less
beautiful ones and peopled them with the spirits of the
'four dead trees in a sunset', the boys who lived in a
barrenness but left a legacy to surpass flesh. His play,
like the 'gum tree's country', will be there 'when we're

gone'. The man of the brush has never ceased his quest and the legend pursues him as a hound of another heaven. In another age men will still stand before Sidney Nolan's Ned and go away saying 'Such is life.' Somehow Nolan has understood that Ned spoke on behalf of many with that sentence of final acceptance as he felt the roughness of the rope.

The seasons of a century have come and gone and some men speak again of rights to the land, of resisting those who rape its heritage and of raising a republic of the free. To many, such ones are visionaries, dreaming like prophets of an Australia still to be born. The legend that is Kelly stands with them. Ned shared their vision, dreamt their dream and, with them, loved the native land.

Notes

Abbreviations used in the notes

V.P.R.O. : Victorian Public Record Office.
A.O.N.S.W. : Archives of New South Wales.
L.C. S.L.V. : La Trobe Collection, State Library of Victoria.
P.D.C. : Police District Correspondence.
C.C.P. : Chief Commissioner of Police.
A.D.B. : *Australian Dictionary of Biography*.

1 The Making of a Man

1.   The most graphic account of the potato famine, which reduced the Irish to 'a rag of a nation', is by C. Woodham-Smith, *The Great Hunger; Ireland 1845–9*, London, 1962. See also N. Coughlan, 'The coming of the Irish to Victoria', in *Historical Studies: Australia and New Zealand*, vol. 12, no. 45, October 1965, pp. 68–86; J. B. Were. *A Voyage from Plymouth to Melbourne in 1839; the shipboard and early Melbourne diary*, Melbourne, 1964, pp. 247, 249; W. Westgarth, *Personal Recollections of Early Melbourne and Victoria*, Melbourne, 1888.

2.   For details on the Quinn family see Lists of assisted immigrants

on *England* 1841, Series 14, vol. 1, V.P.R.O.; Death certificate of James Quinn, district of Oxley, no. 58, Government Statist, Melbourne. Mary Anne, aged 11 in 1841, does not appear on the shipping records but her name and age are given on this death certificate. She is there stated as the eldest daughter. See also *Port Phillip Patriot and Melbourne Advertiser*, 15, 19 July 1841.

3.   1841 saw the largest influx of migrants into N.S.W. before the gold-rushes with 22,483 entering, of whom 20,103 were assisted. For a discussion of the Bounty system see: R. B. Madgwick, *Immigration into Eastern Australia, 1788–1851*, Sydney, 1969, chs. VIII & IX; R. C. Mills, *The Colonization of Australia 1829–42; the Wakefield experience in empire building*, London, 1915, ch. X. For the population of Melbourne see W. H. Archer (ed.), *The Statistical Register of Victoria, from the Foundation of the Colony*, Melbourne, 1854; *Kerr's Melbourne Almanac and Port Phillip Directory*, Melbourne, 1842. The population at any given time of the year is difficult to establish, given the influx of immigrants. By the end of 1841 there were 20,000 people in Port Phillip, 11,000 of them in Melbourne.

4.   P. Ryan, 'Sir Redmond Barry (1813–80)', in *A.D.B.*, Carlton, Vic., 1969, vol. 3, pp. 108–11.

5.   For the birth records of William, Margaret and Grace Quinn see N.S.W. Roman Catholic Baptisms Solemnized in the Parish of Melbourne in the County of Bourke for 1843, 1845, 1847, Government Statist, Melbourne.

6.   For information about James Quinn's Wallan property see Parish of Wallan map, Crown Lands and Survey Department, Melbourne; Land conveyance particulars, Registrar General's Office, Melbourne.

7.   For John Kelly's baptism see Baptisms 2 January 1814–10 August 1827, Register of the Parish of Killenaule and Moyglass, Diocese of Cashel and Emly, National Library of Ireland, Dublin.

8.   For details of John Kelly's crime see Registered Papers, 1840, first division, file: 27/19877, The State Paper Office, Dublin Castle, Ireland; *Tipperary Free Press*, 13 January, 20 February 1841. For Regan see Registered Papers, 1840 and 1841, first division, files: 27/19103, 181, 237, 469, 471 and C2033, 2251. See also H. A. White, *Tales of Crime and Criminals in Australia*, London, 1894, p. 167.

9.   For details of John Kelly's time in Van Diemen's Land see Con 33/15, Archives of Tasmania, Hobart.

10. Marriage certificate of John Kelly and Ellen Quinn: N.S.W. Roman Catholic marriages solemnized in the Parish of St Francis in the County of Bourke 1850, Government Statist, Melbourne; Birth of Mary Jane Kelly: Baptism Register, Volume with records 24 April 1849–26 May 1861, St Patricks Roman Catholic Church, Kilmore, Victoria.

11. Birth of Anne Kelly: Baptism Register, St Francis Roman Catholic Church 1854–5, Melbourne. For the birth of Edward Kelly: Notebooks of Inspector G. W. Brown, Education Department of Victoria Library, Melbourne. Death certificate of his father, John Kelly, filed 27 December 1866, district of Avenel, no. 85, Government Statist, Melbourne. Ned was very probably born at his grandfather's home at Wallan.

2   The Gentle Years

1. For general background to Beveridge see J. W. Payne, *The History*. Dr William Bland came to Australia as a convict consequent upon a duel and lived to contribute greatly to its cultural, political and social life, see J. Cobley, 'William Bland (1789–1868)' in *A.D.B.* vol. 1, pp. 112–5. Mt Bland was changed to Mt Fraser in the late 1860s. See also C. M. Tudehope, ' "Kalkallo" a link with the past', *Victorian Historical Magazine*, no. 126, vol. 32, 26 November 1961, pp. 99–115.

2. Township of Beveridge, Parish of Merriang map, Crown Lands and Survey Department, Melbourne.

3. J. W. Payne, *The History*, p. 7.

4. Parish of Wallan map, Crown Lands and Survey Department, Melbourne.

5. The Jerilderie letter I have used the copy in Law Box I, Kelly Papers, V.P.R.O. This copy, made between February 1879 and November 1880 is unpaginated but as it was taken from the original it is the best available document.

6. Baptismal record in Register of Baptisms, volume with records 24 April 1851–21 July 1870, St Pauls Roman Catholic Church, Coburg, Victoria.

7. ibid. Margaret was born on 15 June 1857 and baptized on 11 August 1857. James was born 31 July 1859 and was baptized on 5 August 1859. Daniel was born on 1 May 1861 and baptized 28 August 1861. All three were baptized at St Pauls, Coburg – Margaret and James by Father Lorenzo J. O'Mara.

8.   Lists of assisted immigrants on *Maldon* 1857, Series 14, vol. 11, V.P.R.O.

9.   Victoria, *Papers Presented to Both Houses of Parliament*, Session 1881, vol. III, no. 22. 'Second Progress Report of the Royal Commission of Enquiry into the circumstances of the Kelly Outbreak and the present state and organisation of the Police Force', p. vii. Hereafter cited as *Police Commission 1881*.

10.   ibid., Appendix 10, p. 699.

11.   *Examiner and Kilmore and McIvor Journal*, 4, 11, 25 October 1860.

12.   *Police Commission 1881*, Appendix 10, p. 699.

13.   ibid.

14.   ibid. and *Examiner and Kilmore and McIvor Journal*, 4, 11, 25 October 1860, 27 March, 3, 24 April, 15 May 1862.

15.   *Examiner and Kilmore and McIvor Journal*, 23 April 1863.

16.   *Advocate*, 13 November 1946; Baptismal record in Register of Baptisms, volume with records from 15 November 1860–7 May 1896, St Patricks Roman Catholic Church, Kilmore, Victoria; Birth certificate in the district of Kalkallo, no. 394 – 1863, Government Statist, Melbourne.

17.   The small allotments in Beveridge raised a total of £51 10s when they were sold in 1857 and 1861 respectively. See Memorial no. 815, Book 48, Registrar General's Office, Melbourne.

18.   The precise date of the departure from Beveridge is uncertain but it was after July 1863 when Catherine was baptized at Kilmore and prior to March 1864 when Maggie and Ned were enrolled at the Avenel School.

19.   R. P. Whitworth (comp.), *Bailliere's Victorian Gazetteer and Road Guide*, Melbourne, 1865.

20.   Some of the factual material relating to the residence of the family at Avenel comes from the excellent article by L. J. Blake, 'Young Ned', in *The Educational Magazine*, Melbourne, vol. 27, no. 8, September 1970, pp. 350–5.

21.   *Ovens and Murray Advertiser*, 2, 9, 14 January, 23 February 1864; *Examiner and Kilmore and McIvor Journal*, 23 February 1860.

22.   R. V. Billis and A. S. Kenyon, *Pastoral Pioneers of Port Phillip*, Melbourne, 1974, p. 214.

23.   Conveyance of portions 38 and 39, Parish of Wallan, 20 July 1864, Registrar General's Office, Melbourne.

24.   Information on Avenel School is taken from the notebooks of

Inspector G. W. Brown 1864–6; teachers' records compiled by Research Officer Bryan Simm, James Irving's record no. 1086; L. J. Blake, *The Educational Magazine*. Irving was reported as being 'addicted to drink' in 1874 and dismissed from his position at Byrneside in 1882. See record no. 1086 noted above.

25. Margaret Burrows failed to satisfy Brown in all matters except attendance. See Inspector's notebook 1864.

26. L. J. Blake, *The Educational Magazine*, p. 353. In 1865 at Wangaratta Roman Catholic School, Brown met another lad – Stephen Hart, ibid.

27. This event is preserved both in Avenel folklore and in the personal traditions of the Shelton family. Ned is said to have worn the sash at Glenrowan.

28. Inspector Brown's notebooks for 1865 and 1866.

29. Birth certificate, district of Avenel, no. 241 – 1865, Government Statist, Melbourne.

30. Avenel Petty Sessions Cause List Book, 20 June 1865–28 July 1870, Series 287, V.P.R.O.

31. F. Clune, *The Kelly Hunters*, Sydney, 1954, pp. 50 and 342. Clune states (p. 342) that his evidence comes from the Charge Book at Avenel courthouse. It is no longer available either there or at the V.P.R.O. but all Kelly tradition is unanimous on the actual event although confused as to details. There is no record that Red served a sentence in Kilmore which indicates that the fine was paid.

32. Inspector Brown's notebooks 1864–6.

33. Memo of Inspector G. W. Brown to the Secretary of the Board of Education, 22 May 1865, suggests that the committee of the school resign because its members lacked any personal interest in it. William Campion, John Mutton and Esau Shelton were among its members. Avenel School No. 8, Building file, Series 795, V.P.R.O.

34. Avenel Petty Sessions Cause List Book, 20 June 1865–28 July 1870, Series 287, V.P.R.O.

35. Ned's reference to Van Diemen's Land in Jerilderie letter.

36. Ned's words in the Jerilderie letter.

37. Death certificate, district of Avenel, no. 85 – 1866, Government Statist, Melbourne.

3   *Greta by the Creeks*

1. Some of the information of Greta and its early history is contained in S. E. Ellis, *A History of Greta*, Kilmore, Vic., 1972.

2.   Much the best contemporary account of the rush to the Ovens is contained in W. Howitt, *Land, Labour and Gold*, London, 1855.

3.   The best study of Victoria in the 1860s and 1870s is that by G. Bartlett in his unpublished Ph.D. thesis, Political organization and society in Victoria 1864–83, A.N.U., Canberra, 1964. Because of the amount of 'cackle' rather than action in the Victorian Parliament it was called 'A Goose Parliament', *Mansfield Independent*, 31 July 1869.

4.   D. M. Whittaker, *Wangaratta*, Vic., 1963, p. 152.

5.   S. E. Ellis, *History*, pp. 7–10.

6.   *Ovens and Murray Advertiser*, 24 October 1865.

7.   Avenel Petty Sessions Cause List Book, Series 278, V.P.R.O., especially for 28 May 1867, when three charges were heard; in two Ellen Kelly claimed assault and damage of property against Thomas Ford, and in the other Ford claimed abusive and threatening language against Ellen. The damage charge was dismissed, the assault charge caused Ford to be fined £5 or six weeks gaol in default, while Ellen was fined 40s or seven days for the language.

8.   Victoria, *Police Gazette*, 4 October 1866, 6 June 1867.

9.   The site of the camp is part of Avenel tradition.

10.   I am indebted to the Tadaro family, present occupants of Glenmore, for permitting me to inspect the house which has changed little in over a century.

11.   See the account of the trial in *Ovens and Murray Advertiser*, 21 April 1868.

12.   The exact details of Mrs Kelly taking up the selection at the Eleven Mile will not be known until, and if, her missing file is located. The exact location, size and other minor details of the selection can be established from the map of the Parish of Lurg in the County of Delatite, Crown Lands and Survey Department, Melbourne. Mrs Griffith, who presently owns the land and who lived as a young bride in the old home, kindly showed me over its remains.

13.   See the details of the Isaacs' mother and son relationship in Z. Cowen, *Isaac Isaacs*, Melbourne, 1967, ch. I. Isaac Isaacs became the first Australian born Governor-General in 1931, fifty-one years after Ned's death.

14.   Capital Case files, Series 264, Box 5, V.P.R.O.; *Ovens and Murray Advertiser*, 21 April 1868.

15.   *Benalla Ensign and Farmers' and Squatters' Journal*, 22, 29 October 1869. Amongst other things, Ah Fook swore that Ned had

assaulted him with a stick eighteen feet in length! There were 17,705 Chinese in Victoria in 1871, only thirty-six of whom were women, *Mansfield Independent*, 5 May 1871.

4   *Harry's Cub*

1.   *Ovens and Murray Advertiser*, 21 September, 5, 21 October 1871 for an account of the maintenance case brought by Ellen Kelly against William Frost.
2.   Death certificate, district of Oxley, no. 58, registered 25 August 1869, Government Statist, Melbourne; Register of Wills and Administration papers, 11/332, V.P.R.O. Quinn died intestate but the property was sworn at £655 with debts and expenses of £658 13s 6d.
3.   For details on Henry (Harry) Power see: I. F. McLaren, 'Henry Power (1820–91)' in *A.D.B.* vol. 5, p. 454; *Argus*, 3, 10 March 1877. All sources agree on Harry's amiable nature. After serving fifteen years between 1870–85 he worked for a time with the Clarke family and was later drowned in the Murray near Swan Hill. See also Male Prison Register, vol. 13, p. 159, no. 2643, Series 515, V.P.R.O.
4.   *Benalla Ensign and Farmers' and Squatters' Journal*, 18 March, 6, 13 May 1870; *Kyneton Guardian*, 11 May 1870. For the Frost-Ellen Kelly infant see Birth certificate dated 6 July 1870, district of Benalla, no. 867, Government Statist, Melbourne. The child was called Ellen and shame or some other emotion so overtook the mother that she gave the father's name as John Kelly – her husband long dead and buried at Avenel.
5.   *Kyneton Guardian*, 27 April, 11, 14, 21, 28 May 1870; *Kyneton Observer*, 4 June 1870.
6.   *Benalla Ensign and Farmers' and Squatters' Journal*, 10 June 1870; F. A. Hare, *The Last of the Bushrangers; an account of the capture of the Kelly gang*, London, 1894, pp. 55–76.
7.   Standish to Chief Secretary, 19 August, 27 September 1870, Chief Secretary's Correspondence, Series 1189, Box 573, V.P.R.O. James Quinn is named in the text and margin as the informant. The *Age*, 4 December 1880, said John Lloyd was the informant but the official records are clear on the point.
8.   W. Howitt, *Land*, pp. 180, 213, 217; J. S. Legge, 'Frederick Standish (1824–83)' in *A.D.B.*, vol. 6, pp. 172–3; manuscript copy of Frederick Standish Diary, MS9502, L.C. S.L.V.
9.   Frederick Standish Diary, entry for 25 November 1868, MS9502, L.C. S.L.V.

10.   See remarks of Superintendent Wilson of Beechworth on Record of Service of Edward Hall, 16 February 1870, P.D.C., Series 937, Box 412, and other correspondence dated 17 February, 26 April, 6, 14, 15, 16, 25, 31 January, 4 February, 31 May 1870. The latter letter refers to the instructions, but that particular Memo book of the C.C.P. outlining the instructions is missing from the archives.

11.   Superintendent Nicolas to C.C.P., 12 July 1870, and note by Standish on same, P.D.C., Series 937, Box 49, V.P.R.O.

12.   *Mansfield Guardian*, 10 September 1870; Male Prison Register, vol. 11, nos. 7371, 7372, Series 515, V.P.R.O. Thomas was released on 19 March and John on 31 July 1869.

13.   *Ovens and Murray Advertiser*, 15, 18 October 1870; Hall to Superintendent Nicolas, 28 August, 6 September 1870, P.D.C., Series 937, Box 49, V.P.R.O.

14.   Hall to Superintendent Nicolas, 17 November 1870, Kelly Papers, 'Kelly Gang' Box 5, V.P.R.O.

15.   Jerilderie letter.

16.   ibid.

17.   *Ovens and Murray Advertiser*, 10, 12 November 1870; *Benalla Ensign and Farmers' and Squatters' Journal*, 28 October, 4 November 1870; Hall's report in Kelly Papers, 'Kelly Gang' Box 5, V.P.R.O.; Ned's account in Jerilderie letter.

18.   Hall to Superintendent Barclay, 22 April 1871, memo at end in which Hall asks Barclay to send on his report of Ned's arrest to Hare because he would wish to let Mr Hare see that he kept his promise, P.D.C., Series 937, Box 49, V.P.R.O.

19.   G. Morris, *Devil's River Country; selections from the history of the Mansfield district*, Shepparton, Vic., 1952.

20.   See details of Isaiah Wright in extract from Glenrowan Watch House Book, Victoria Police Archives, Russell St, Melbourne.

21.   Victoria, *Police Gazette*, 25 April 1871. Other details for these and the subsequent events are taken from the Jerilderie letter; *Ovens and Murray Advertiser*, 27 April, 2, 4, 5, 6, 13, 23, 25 May, 5 August 1871; Hall's account, P.D.C., Series 937, Box 49; Memo to Dr N. McCrae, Medical Department, 15 July 1871, P.D.C., Series 937, Box 413, V.P.R.O.

22.   The revolution was spoken of in an editorial entitled, 'Alleged Communist Conspiracy to Burn London', *Mansfield Guardian*, 11 August 1871.

5 *The Passing of Boyhood*

1. For the details of Ned's period of imprisonment see Male Prisoner Register, vol. 17, p. 287, no. 10926, Series 515, V.P.R.O. At the age of eighteen he was 5 foot 10 inches, weighed 11 stone 4 pounds, could both read and write and bore four scars to his head!

2. ibid. On 21 July 1873 Ned handed two rations of tobacco to a fellow prisoner on the *Sacramento* and received seven days further detention. The *Sacramento* held 112 male prisoners, the great majority of whom were taken ashore daily for hard labour. Report of Penal Establishments and Gaols, Victoria, *Statistical Register*, 1873.

3. See K. W. Turton, *The North East Railway; a lineside guide, Melbourne to Wodonga*, Melbourne, 1973.

4. The purpose of setting up the station is clear in the police correspondence regarding Glenmore 1870 to late 1875 when the station was transferred to Hedi.

5. Comment of Standish on Barclay to Standish 19 April 1872, P.D.C., Series 937, Box 414, V.P.R.O.

6. James Quinn's record is in the Male Prison Register, vol. 15, no. 9757, p. 521, Series 515, V.P.R.O. He served five years and five months on these charges and was released on 23 July 1877. For the court cases see *Ovens and Murray Advertiser*, 3, 6 February, 17 April 1872 and 21 April 1873.

7. *Ovens and Murray Advertiser*, 6 February 1873.

8. In respect of the character of Flood, see anonymous letters to Superintendent Wilson of Beechworth, and to Standish, 27 May 1869, and Flood to Wilson, 5 June 1869, P.D.C., Series 937, Box 412, V.P.R.O. Also Police Muster Rolls, Series 55, vols 1–9, V.P.R.O. The anonymity was allegedly rendered necessary because Flood told the writer 'that he would have it in for me if I wrote about it but what I say is true'.

9. Greta and Glenrowan Occurrence Book, 9 September 1871, Victoria Police Archives, Russell St, Melbourne; *Ovens and Murray Advertiser*, 14 September 1871.

10. *Ovens and Murray Advertiser*, 4 May 1870 and 3 February 1872; William Williamson in Male Prison Register, vol. 14, p. 228, no. 9441, Series 515, V.P.R.O.

11. James Short to Standish 29 January 1872, Standish to Barclay 21 February 1872, P.D.C., Series 937, Box 414, V.P.R.O.; Birth certificate, district of Greta, no. 3, 11 November 1872, Death certificate, district of Greta, no. 1, 11 November 1872, Government Statist,

Melbourne; G. Wilson Hall, *The Kelly Gang; the outlaws of the Wombat Ranges*, Mansfield, 1879, p. 28. The writer of this contemporary pamphlet, himself editor of the *Mansfield Guardian*, was clearly well aware of the grave dishonour done to Annie by Flood and by extension to the whole family.

12.   *Ovens and Murray Advertiser*, 18 April 1873.

13.   James Kelly in Male Prison Register, vol. 17, p. 221, no. 10861, Series 515, V.P.R.O. James was 5 foot 4 inches on entry and weighed 8 stone 13 pounds. A Stock Protection Society was set up at Mansfield in 1873 because of the infestation of 'bad characters' locally. It rarely met and found it difficult to get a quorum when it did. In the early 1870s every week saw upwards of sixty horses impounded in the northeast indicating how many animals simply roamed free. *Mansfield Guardian*, *passim* and 4 July 1874.

14.   Jerilderie letter.

15.   McBean to Standish, 8 May 1872, P.D.C., Series 937, Box 414, V.P.R.O.

16.   Birth certificate, district of Benalla, no. 1244, 19 February 1874, Government Statist, Melbourne. George's name was given as Keane and his place of origin California in South America but three months later Mr George Louch, the registrar, rectified both mistakes. See also Marriage certificate, district of Benalla, no. 23, 17 September 1873, Government Statist, Melbourne. William Skillion (spelt Skilling) was twenty-four while Maggie was sixteen.

17.   In the Jerilderie letter Ned mentions Brown by name and the truth of his statement is borne out in the official records. J. A. Brown to Standish, 12 February 1874, Standish to Superintendent Barclay, 10 March 1874, Chief Secretary's Correspondence, Series 1189, Box 354, V.P.R.O. In another letter to Standish of 6 April 1874, Brown threatened to kill Flood if he were not moved — a threat which, had it been made by a Kelly, would probably have resulted in imprisonment.

18.   See Marriage certificate, district of Benalla, no. 32, 19 February 1874, and Birth certificate, district of Benalla, no. 1244, 19 February 1874, Government Statist, Melbourne; for the Benalla football club see *North Eastern Ensign*, 21, 24 April 1874.

19.   *Police Commission 1881*, evidence, Q.12609. In his evidence Flood admitted that he was a source of 'continual annoyance' to the whole clan, Q.12611.

20.   Jerilderie letter; *Wangaratta Dispatch*, 3 March 1875; *Ovens and Murray Advertiser*, 21 December 1878.

21.   Marriage certificate, district of Benalla, no. 20, 1 April 1873, Government Statist, Melbourne. I. Jones, 'The years Ned Kelly went straight', *Walkabout*, June 1962, pp. 16, 17.

22.   Jerilderie letter; Birth certificate, district of Benalla, no. 1397, John born at the Eleven Mile with Maggie in attendance as 'nurse', 18 March 1875, registered 27 April 1875, Government Statist, Melbourne.

23.   *Ovens and Murray Advertiser*, 21 December 1878.

24.   Male Prison Register, vol. 11, p. 12, no. 7371 for John Lloyd and vol. 17, p. 221, no. 10861 for James Kelly, Series 515, V.P.R.O.

6   *From Clan to Mob*

1.   For information on the Woolshed and the district generally I am indebted to Rev. Leo Lane, *A History of the Parish of Beechworth, 1854–1978*, Beechworth, Vic., 1978; E. J. Dunn, 'The Woolshed Valley, Beechworth', *Bulletin of the Geological Survey of Victoria*, Melbourne, no. 25, 1913; B. Wynn, 'Woolshed revisited', *Holy Name Monthly*, Melbourne, 1 June 1962, pp. 3–4.

2.   Notes made by G. W. Brown in his notebooks 1864–6. John James Sherritt, Aaron's youngest brother, was in the under-sevens in 1866 and Elizabeth Sherritt was ten years old. Both were at the nearby Reid's Creek School, No. 525. Reid's Creek was a Church of England establishment set up in 1857. The Sherritts were members of the Church of England. Aaron Sherritt does not appear in the notes but James Wallace asserted to the *Police Commission 1881* that Aaron was a 'school fellow' of his. See Q.14477.

3.   *Ovens and Murray Advertiser*, 1 June 1876; Male Prison Register, nos 13890 and 13891, Series 515, V.P.R.O. Both were born in Victoria, Aaron in 1856 and Joe in 1857. Joe's complexion was fair, his eyes blue and his height 5 foot 9½ inches; Aaron had a fresh complexion with hazel eyes and stood 5 foot 10 inches.

4.   Information on the Hely killing comes from Brooke Smith to Standish, 24 August, 12 September 1876, P.D.C., Series 937, Box 418, V.P.R.O.; *Ovens and Murray Advertiser*, 3 March 1877; *Wangaratta Dispatch*, 7 April 1877; W. Ebsworth, *Pioneer Catholic Victoria*, Melbourne, 1973; T. J. Linane, 'With revolver and breviary', in *Footprints*, Melbourne, vol. 3, no. 7, 1979.

5.   *Ovens and Murray Advertiser*, 14 October 1876, 15 February, 1, 3 March 1877.

6.   Oxley Shire Council to Standish, 4 June 1877, note on back by

Standish. Brooke Smith to Standish, 15 June 1877; Standish to Nicolson, 5 July 1877; Standish to Brooke Smith, 24 July 1877. All in P.D.C., Series 937, Box 419, V.P.R.O.

7. Nicolson read out his report in reply to questions 1020–36 at the *Police Commission 1881*.

8. Kelly Special Bundle SZ843, A.O. N.S.W.; N.S.W., *Police Gazette* 13, 27 June 1877; *Wagga Wagga Advertiser*, 20, 30 June 1877.

9. I obtained the information regarding the Hart family and the relationship between Ned and Esther from Mr Thomas Lloyd – son of Tom Lloyd and Rachel Hart and himself a member of the Victoria Police as their chief horse-breaker for thirty years. Mr Lloyd's information, gleaned from his father as a youth, was in all respects most reliable and I remain very much in his debt for his courtesy and helpfulness.

10. G. W. Brown's notebooks. Wangaratta Roman Catholic School, No. 679, 21 September 1864. Stephen Hart was in the under-sevens on that date while Richard and Esther Hart were in the under-sevens on 23 October 1865; Stephen Hart in Male Prison Register, no. 14823, p. 106, Series 515, V.P.R.O.; *Ovens and Murray Advertiser*, 26, 31 July 1877.

11. R. H. Croll, 'Before I forget', ch. 3, in Croll Papers, MS8910, L.C. S.L.V. Croll obtained his information from a state member of parliament who was a near neighbour of the Kellys and often visited the home. I. Jones, *Walkabout*, pp. 16–17; *Wangaratta Dispatch*, 17 February, 3 March 1875; *Mansfield Guardian*, 24 March 1877.

12. The Jerilderie letter and the Cameron letter both of which recount the same series of events.

13. *Police Commission 1881*, Q.9764–5 for Ned's statement that he would have it out with Lonigan; Benalla Court of Petty Sessions Cause List Book, MS8572 L.C. S.L.V. When Constable Thom reported to his superior Brooke Smith on 12 September 1877, he began with 'in reference to the criminal class' and then spoke of the whereabouts of the clan – noting *inter alia*, that the Kelly family were 'at home'. See P.D.C., Series 937, Box 419, V.P.R.O.

14. Report of trial in *Ovens and Murray Advertiser*, 20 October 1877; Thom to Smith, 1 November 1877, P.D.C., Series 937, Box 419, V.P.R.O.; Benalla Court of Petty Sessions Cause List Book, MS8572, L.C. S.L.V.

15. Manuscript copy of Frederick Standish Diary, entry for 8 December 1877, MS9502, L.C. S.L.V.

7 *Tea and Scones*

1. Record of Conduct and Service of Alexander Fitzpatrick, no. 2867, Victoria Police Archives, Russell St, Melbourne.
2. Letter of Miss Jessie McKay, 28 February 1879, P.D.C., Series 937, Box 145, V.P.R.O.; Jerilderie letter.
3. Mrs S. M. Savage to Standish, 1 July 1878, P.D.C., Series 937, Box 144, V.P.R.O.
4. Warrant to apprehend Edward Kelly issued by A. McCleary J.P. at Chiltern 15 March 1878 and Warrant to apprehend Daniel Kelly issued by C. C. Darvall J.P. at Chiltern 5 April 1878, Kelly Papers, Police Box VI, V.P.R.O.
5. *Police Commission 1881*, A. Fitzpatrick's evidence, Q.12822.
6. See articles by Samuel James Jamieson in *Dubbo Liberal*, 23 September to 30 November 1933. Jamieson was born at Wallan in 1856 and later worked in the northeast. He knew the Kelly family well. Jamieson repeats the universal family tradition that Fitzpatrick forcibly attempted to make love to Kate, whereupon Ellen, discovering him so acting, struck him with the fire shovel.
7. See Alexander Fitzpatrick's evidence: *Police v. Ellen Kelly, William Williamson, William Skillion* given on 17 May 1878 at Benalla Police Court, Kelly Papers, Law Box I, V.P.R.O.; see further evidence in Item 4, Law Box I for evidence as to Brickey being armed while splitting wood.
8. See John Nicholson M.D. evidence: *Police v. Ellen Kelly, William Williamson, William Skillion* given on 17 May 1878 at Benalla Police Court, Kelly Papers, Law Box I, V.P.R.O.
9. Warrant to apprehend Edward Kelly for attempting to murder Constable Fitzpatrick issued by F. McDonnell J.P. at Benalla on 16 April 1878; warrants to apprehend Daniel Kelly, William Skillion, William Williamson and Ellen Kelly for aiding and abetting Edward Kelly in his attempt to murder Constable Fitzpatrick issued by F. McDonnell J.P. at Benalla on 16 April 1878, Kelly Papers, Police Box VI, V.P.R.O.
10. *Police Commission 1881*, A. Steele's evidence, Q.8817–21.
11. Warrants as in note 9.
12. *Mansfield Guardian*, 12 January 1878; *Police Commission 1881*, evidence, Q.8817–21; transcript of trial, *Police v. Ellen Kelly, William Williamson, William Skillion*, Kelly Papers, Law Box I, V.P.R.O.
13. Transcript of trial, *Police v. Ellen Kelly, William Williamson,*

William Skillion and Strahan's evidence given on 27 September
1878, Kelly Papers, Law Box I, V.P.R.O.
14.   In all subsequent accounts by Ned of the 15 April incident he
asserted that he was many miles from his mother's home on that evening. In the Jerilderie letter Ned wrote, 'I heard nothing of this transaction until very close on the trial I being then over four hundred
miles away from Greta.' Such a distance can place him in the Dubbo
area. From this and other evidence there is no reason to accept Fitzpatrick's account rather than Ned's who at the time of writing the
Jerilderie letter had no reason to lie about the said 'transaction'. For
Pennycooke, see article by John Ritchie from an undated newspaper
clipping held in the Dubbo Historical Society archives.
15.   N.S.W., *Police Gazette*, 2 October 1872, 23 July 1873, 22 May,
4, 12 September 1878; Entrance Book, Parramatta Gaol 1870 entry
for Thomas Law, no. 1045, ref: 4/6487, A.O.N.S.W.; Superintendent
Lydiard from Bathurst to Inspector General, Sydney, 8 November
1878, Inspector General to Principal Under Secretary, 13 November
1878, ref: 1/2424, A.O.N.S.W. Gibson, Reynolds, Bowman, Wilson and
White were some of the 'aliases' for Law.
16.   Wagga Wagga Police station telegram to Sub-Inspector Med-
ley, 31 October 1878; Inspector General, Sydney, to Colonial Secretary, 13 February 1879, reports that Ned was in the Murrumbidgee
district in August 1878. He went on to say that the 'outlaws have a
good knowledge of N.S.W.', Colonial Secretary's Correspondence
file no. 79/10148, A.O.N.S.W. For William Kelly see N.S.W., *Police
Gazette*, 25 September, 6 November 1878.
17.   For Sergeant Wallings' death see *S.M.H.*, 23, 24 September 1878;
Death certificate, 20 September 1878 for Thomas Edward Wallings.
18.   *S.M.H.*, 26 September 1878; N.S.W., *Police Gazette*, 25 September 1878.
19.   Supplement to the *Central Australian and Bourke Telegraph*,
Colonial Secretary's Correspondence file no. 78/9150, A.O.N.S.W.;
N.S.W., *Police Gazette*, 30 October 1878.
20.   Report from Superintendent of Police, Bathurst, to Inspector
General, Sydney, 8 November 1878, Inspector General to Principal
Under Secretary, 13 November 1878, Colonial Secretary's Correspondence, file no. 78/9777, A.O.N.S.W.
21.   Thomas Alexander Browne identifies Midnight or Starlight in
his manuscript diary, but carefully omits to carry the identification
further to Law. Mitchell Library manuscript, Ab. 98/2.

22.   McIntyre's deposition at trial of Kelly, Brief for the Prosecution, Kelly Papers, Law Box I, V.P.R.O.

8   *A Killer*

1.   The visit to Jerilderie was reported in March and April 1879 as taking place in early October 1878. See Fitzpatrick to Detective Office, 25 March 1879 and report from Jerilderie police station, 5 April 1879, Kelly Special Bundle SZ843, A.O.N.S.W. Two men were spoken of as having visited the pub, one of whom resembled Dan. C. A. Raeuber, proprietor of the Turn Back Jemmy wrote to McIntyre saying that the Kellys had visited the hotel ten weeks previously; see: Thomas Newman McIntyre, A narrative of my experience with the Kelly gang and a short account of other bushrangers, MS6343, L.C. S.L.V. p. 89.

2.   The hut is described in *Federal Standard*, 17 November 1880; Ned later said Dan was making 'good wages' there, and two men who worked the area a few months afterwards also made 'good wages' from the gold in the creek. *Mansfield Guardian*, 5 April 1879.

3.   See account of hearing in *Federal Standard*, 25 May 1878. Fitzpatrick had sworn that although he knew Kate he had never attempted 'to take any liberties with her'.

4.   *Police Commission 1881*, evidence of Wyatt, Q.2262–78. This offer must have been made before the trial because making it after sentence was passed would have been futile. For the police harassment see the Jerilderie letter.

5.   The complications in this affair are numerous but they can be partially unravelled in the accounts of the trial in the *Ovens and Murray Advertiser*, 17, 24, 27 November, 6, 8, 11, 22 December 1877, 2, 5 March, 2 May, 12 October 1878. For Ned's version, probably the truthful one as it implicates both himself and George King fully, see the Jerilderie letter.

6.   Letter by 'Six Victorian Gold Miners' to *Federal Standard*, 16 October 1878.

7.   For a prison description of Ellen Kelly, known as such to the law despite the King alliance, see Female Prison Register, no. 3520, p. 197, Series 516, V.P.R.O.

8.   Entry in Mansfield Occurrence Book, 7 October 1878, Victoria Police Archives, Russell St, Melbourne.

9.   Marriage certificate, district of Mornington, Alexander Fitz-

patrick and Anna Frances Savage, 10 July 1878, no. 5, and Death
certificate of Alexander Fitzpatrick, 6 May 1924, no. 3382, Government
Statist, Melbourne; Susanne Mary Savage to Standish, 1 July 1878,
Standish to S. M. Savage, 4 July 1878, P.D.C., Series 937, Box 144,
V.P.R.O.; Brooke Smith to Standish, 8 July 1878, P.D.C., Series 937,
Box 364, V.P.R.O.

10.   See account of trial in *Ovens and Murray Advertiser*, 10 October
1878. The name William Chadwick appears on the final jury list; for
his police record see: Police Muster Rolls, Series 55 and P.D.C., Series
937, Box 135, V.P.R.O. Ned took note of Chadwick's role and wrote
in the Jerilderie letter 'It seems that the jury was well chosen by the
police as there was a discharged sergeant amongst them, which
is contrary to law. . .' I am aware that at the trial Ned's relative Joseph
Ryan was alleged to have produced a paper purporting to be a bill
of sale for a horse bought by Ned on 15 April. Some have concluded
that such a document proved Ned was present at his mother's home
on the day in question. The point of course is that Ryan was endeavouring to prove that Ned was with him and not at Greta shooting
Fitzpatrick. The jury did not accept the bill as proof of anything nor
indeed do I.

11.   *Ovens and Murray Advertiser*, 15 October 1878.

12.   I am prepared to accept that Redmond Barry passed a remark
regarding Ned's imprisonment when sentencing Ellen. The twenty-
one years is mentioned by G. Wilson Hall, proprietor of the *Mansfield
Guardian* in his *The Kelly Gang; the outlaws of the Wombat Ranges*,
Mansfield, 1879, p. 15. Hall wrote only a few weeks after the trial
and was both in a position to know the facts and to report them accu-
rately. For the opinion of the editor of the *Ovens and Murray Advertiser*, see 30 May 1878 issue.

13.   Female Prison Register, vol. 7, no. 3520, p. 197, Series 516,
V.P.R.O. Brickey served until 11 October 1882 when he was released
'for rendering service to Police', Male Prison Register, vol. 14, no.
9441, p. 228, Series 515, V.P.R.O. Bill Skillion apparently did not prove
sufficiently amenable as he remained a prisoner until 11 June 1883
and hence served his full six years; see Male Prison Record, vol. 28,
no. 15905, p. 272, Series 515, V.P.R.O. It is curious that, although all
three were charged, and found guilty, with aiding and abetting an
attempt to murder, the offence on their prison records reads
'wounding with intent to prevent lawful apprehension'.

14.   *Ovens and Murray Advertiser*, 22 October 1878. Superintendent

Sadleir acted as an umpire and did it efficiently.

15.   Salaries of the Victoria Police, P.D.C., Series 937, Box 136 and 464, V.P.R.O.

16.   Brooke Smith to Standish, 5 July 1878, Kelly Papers, Police Box II, V.P.R.O.; Brooke Smith probably found it convenient to have his expenses paid as he was habitually in debt. He was imprisoned, briefly, for fraud in 1870 and in May 1878 he came before the County Court for debts incurred in the northeast. See Castieau to Standish, 20 June 1870 and Joseph Wertheim to Minister of Justice, 30 May 1870, in Chief Secretary's Correspondence, Series 1189, Box 570 and P.D.C., Series 937, Box 364, V.P.R.O.

17.   Edward Kelly to His Excellency the Governor, 3 November 1880, Edward Kelly Capital Case File, V.P.R.O.

18.   Ward to Secretan, 10 May 1878, Kelly Papers, Police Box IV, V.P.R.O.; Flood to Chomley, 27 May 1878, ibid.

19.   See affidavit of Patrick Quinn of Greta in the *Argus*, 10 November 1880. Superintendent James in a letter to John Sadleir, 24 June 1898, confirms this story and remarks that Strahan's threat 'would, in a measure, account for the murder of the police . . . Strahan's ill-judged speech caused the mischief', H 2909, L.C. S.L.V.

20.   For this and the rest of the Stringybark Creek episode see: McIntyre to Pewtress, 27 October 1878, Kelly Papers, without citation, V.P.R.O.; Deposition of McIntyre, Prosecution Brief, Kelly Papers, Law Box I, V.P.R.O.; T. N. McIntyre, A narrative, MS6342, L.C. S.L.V.; *Mansfield Guardian*, 2 November 1878; Jerilderie letter; Edward Kelly to the Governor, 3, 10 November 1880, Kelly Capital Case File, V.P.R.O. The weapon Ned used was so old it was bound up with string or wire. Statement by Edwin Living, undated but 1880, Kelly Papers, Miscellaneous Box V.P.R.O. The *Advocate*, Melbourne, was the Catholic paper but took a detached attitude to the Kellys. On 2 November 1878 it wrote, 'The bushrangers upon surprising the camp, said, "We don't want to take life, what we want is ammunition".' The spelling of Scanlan rather than Scanlon has been adopted, as the former is used on his grave at Mansfield and on the Mansfield monument.

9   *Wombat Hole*

1.   The conflicting account in all the literature on the flight and events in the immediate aftermath of Stringybark Creek leaves clar-

ity only on the visit to Greta, the passing by Beechworth, the attempt to cross into New South Wales and the return via Wangaratta to the Warby ranges. The weather was atrocious in the few days after Stringybark Creek, with 'lightning all night' and deafening thunder. *Ovens and Murray Advertiser*, 31 October 1878.

2.   T. N. McIntyre, A narrative, MS6343, L.C. S.L.V.

3.   *Federal Standard*, 6 November 1878. Superintendent John Sadleir was even more explicit on Lonigan's attempt to use his revolver. He spoke with McIntyre two days after the affair and recorded the following words, 'Lonigan was sitting on a log, and on hearing the call to throw up his hands, he put his hand to his revolver at the same time slipping down for cover behind the log on which he had been sitting. Lonigan had his head above the level of the log and was about to use his revolver when he was shot through the head.' See J. Sadleir, *Recollections of a Victorian Police Officer*, Melbourne, 1913 (Penguin facsimile edition, 1973), p. 187. In the Jerilderie letter Ned said Lonigan 'put his head up to take aim when I shot him that instant or he would have shot me as I took him for Strahan the man who said he would not ask me to stand he would shoot me first like a dog.' James Tomkins, shire president of Mansfield, was one of the party that found Kennedy's body. He makes no reference to mutilation or of the body being strapped to a tree. He saw one wound only – 'a jagged hole right through his chest'. See G. Morris, *Devil's River*, p. 41. It is my conviction based on all the available evidence that the story of Kennedy pleading with Ned for life, that Dan actually shot him, that the body was mutilated and tied to a tree are all fictions, propagated in the aftermath of the event to engender hatred of Ned.

4.   Pewtress to Sadleir, 29 October 1878, Victoria Police Archives, Russell St, Melbourne; *Police Commission 1881*, evidence of T. Meehan, Q.17643–87. A double-barrelled fowling piece and a woollen cartridge belt for holding twenty cartridges were loaned to the police by Rev. Mr Sandiford of Mansfield. See Supplementary Report, 11 November 1878, Kelly Papers, Police Box VI, V.P.R.O.

5.   Standish to Chief Secretary, 28 October 1878, Kelly Papers, Miscellaneous Box, V.P.R.O.

6.   T. N. McIntyre, A narrative, MS6343, L.C. S.L.V.; *Ovens and Murray Advertiser*, 31 October 1878; reports of inquests taken at Magisterial Enquiry before Mr Kitchen J.P., Mansfield, 29 October, 1 November, Kelly Papers, Miscellaneous Box, V.P.R.O. Contrary to the reports that circulated about the alleged 'mercy killing' of Kennedy,

Detective Ward made a contemporary report to testify that, 'Ned fired at him and struck him in the chest. Kennedy immediately fell, Ned went up to him, it is then he felt sorry for shooting him, such a good man. They then covered him over with his cloak. Ned said he only wanted their arms and ammunition, he did not want to shoot them.' See document signed by M. E. Ward, Kelly Papers, Miscellaneous Box, V.P.R.O. The fantastic fabrication of Kennedy's last moments in which he allegedly pleaded for his life was supposed to have come from Dan who told it to a 'confederate', who passed it to the Mansfield correspondent of the *Argus* which then printed it. *Mansfield Guardian*, 14 December 1878. Dr Moorhouse's sermon is in *Mansfield Guardian*, 9 November 1878.

7.   See description of the murderers of Scanlan and Lonigan, Benalla police station, October 1878, Kelly Papers, Police Box VI, V.P.R.O.; J. Sadleir, *Recollections*, pp. 183, 185; *Mansfield Guardian* 9 November 1878.

8.   For the Legislative Assembly see G. Bartlett, Ph. D. thesis; for the Legislative Council see G. Serle, 'The Victorian Legislative Council, 1856–1950', *Historical studies: Australia and New Zealand*, vol. 6, no. 22, May 1954, pp. 186–203; for Berry, see G. Bartlett, 'Sir Graham Berry (1822–1904)', in *A.D.B.*, vol. 3, pp. 151–6.

9.   Victoria, *Parliamentary Debates*, Session 1878, vol.29, Legislative Assembly, pp. 1534, 1535, 1560–3, 1588–92, 1595 and Legislative Council, pp. 1593, 1594. The 'Felons Apprehension Act' which was given assent 1 November 1878, is 42 Victoria no. 612. The Governor, G. F. Bowen, deemed it necessary to send a dispatch to the Colonial Office explaining the need for adopting 'the stringent provisions of the "Felons Apprehension Act" of N.S.W., which was found very efficient in putting a stop to bushranging in the adjacent colony'. Bowen to Sir M. E. Hicks Beach, 31 October 1878, Despatches of the Governor to the Secretary of State, Series 1084, vol.9, no.206, V.P.R.O.; Kelly Special Bundle SZ843, A.O.N.S.W., where the N.S.W. Attorney-General points out the discrepancy in the descriptions of Joe and Steve.

10.   *Ovens and Murray Advertiser*, 29 October, 16 November 1878; *Mansfield Guardian*, 9 November 1878.

11.   Lists of civilians and police offering services, Kelly Papers, Police Boxes, V.P.R.O.; Standish to Palmer, Standish to Inspector General, Sydney and Brisbane, 21 October 1878, Standish to Nicolson, Standish to Superintendent of Police, Sale, 29 October 1878,

Standish to Sadleir, 30 October 1878 (3 telegrams), Standish to Nicolson, 1 November 1878, Memo Book of C.C.P., Series 678, V.P.R.O.; Williamson statement made 29 October 1878, in Kelly Papers, Police Box VI, V.P.R.O. It served him little good as he was not released until 1881. *Ovens and Murray Advertiser*, 7 November 1878; *Advocate*, 16 November 1878, was scathing of police officers with 'nothing to do but air themselves at social gatherings'.

12.   Standish to Sadleir, 31 October, 4 November 1878, Memo Book of C.C.P., Series 678, vol.180, file x1931; *Police Commission 1881*, evidence, Q.12355–509, 13059–81, 17280–400, 17456–586; Jerilderie letter.

13.   Michael Woodyard's statement made 1 November 1878, Kelly Papers, Police Box II, V.P.R.O.; Sadleir to Standish, 4 November 1878, Victoria Police Archives, Russell St, Melbourne; *Melbourne Punch*, 31 October, 14, 21 November 1878. The story of the Siege or Charge of Sebastopol, as it became known, is so tedious as not to warrant repetition here. It was written up at length in the papers. See for example, *Argus*, 8 November 1878. It is also referred to in the *Police Commission 1881*, p. xii where the commissioners called it 'an utter fiasco, calculated simply to excite ridicule'.

14.   For the Sherrit transaction see *Police Commission 1881*, evidence, Q. 405a, 1773, 1784–1813. For Monk see *Federal Standard*, 13, 27 November 1878; Pewtress to Standish, 9 November 1878 telegram, Standish to Pewtress, telegram, no date but probably same day, Kelly Papers, Police Box IV, V.P.R.O. Ninety years later Segeant K. Holden, Public Relations Officer for the Victoria Police contributed a segment to *Ned Kelly; man and myth*, Melbourne, 1968. His chapter was entitled 'Kelly – the criminal', pp. 190–9. At p. 194 he reproduced the letter to Monk as proof of the deep criminality of the brothers. One can only assume that he was not conversant with the prosecution and sentencing of Lynch for the offence.

15.   Statement by Brickey Williamson made to Inspector Winch at Pentridge, 6 November 1878, Kelly Papers, Police Box VII, V.P.R.O.; Standish to Nicolson, 13 November 1878, Nicolson to Standish, 14 November 1878, Victoria Police Archives, Russell St, Melbourne; John Thomas (William Donnelly) to Sadleir, 11 November 1878, Kelly Papers Police Box VII, V.P.R.O.; *Police Commission 1881*, J. Sadleir's evidence, Q.1887–93.

16.   Albury police to Inspector General, Sydney, 7 November 1878, Kelly Special Bundle SZ843, A.O.N.S.W.; Standish to Inspector General, Sydney, 15 November 1878, Memo Book of C.C.P., Series 678,

vol.180, file x1985; *Federal Standard*, 20 November 1878; article from *Sydney Echo*, 15 November 1878 in *Ovens and Murray Advertiser*, 23 November 1878.
17.   James Gillon to Hare, 16 November 1878; Irwin to Pewtress, 17 November 1878; Standish to Sadleir, 19 November 1878; Pewtress to Standish, 21 November 1878; Sadleir to Standish, 21 November 1878; Standish to Sadleir, 22 November 1878; Hare to Purcell, 26 November 1878; Alfred Boddington to Palmer, 28 November 1878; Nicolson to Standish, 29 November 1878; Sadleir to Standish, 30 November 1878; Standish to Nicolson and Sadleir, 30 November 1878. All items in Kelly Papers, Police Box IV, V.P.R.O. Standish memo, 6 December 1878, Memo Book of C.C.P., Series 678, vol.180 file x2091, V.P.R.O.; Standish to Under Secretary, 3 December 1878, Memo Book of C.C.P., Series 678, vol.180, file x2070; G. E. Buckmaster to Hon P. Lalor, Brisbane, Kelly Papers, C.S.O. Box I, V.P.R.O,; Bourke police to Bathurst police, 7 December 1878, Kelly Special Bundle SZ843, A.O.N.S.W.; *Federal Standard*, 20, 27 November 1878; *Ovens and Murray Advertiser*, 19 November 1878.

10 Happy Christmas

1.   *Historical Records of Australia*, Series I, vol.XIX, Sydney, 1923, pp. 398, 400, 510, 807; A. Andres, *The First Settlement of the Upper Murray*, Sydney, 1920, pp. 61–3.
2.   The events at Faithfull's Creek and Euroa are recorded in the *Ovens and Murray Advertiser*, 12, 14 December 1878; Macauley's statement to Wyatt, Kelly Papers, Police Box VI; William Fitzgerald's affidavit 20 September 1880, Kelly Papers, Miscellaneous Box; list of prisoners at Faithfull's Creek station, 3 July 1880, Kelly Papers, without citation; George Stephens' statement to Detective Ward, Kelly Papers, Police Box VII, V.P.R.O.
3.   *Melbourne Punch*, 19 December 1878; *Police Commission 1881*, evidence of Wyatt, Q.2132–320; Percival to Sadleir, 11 January 1879, Kelly Papers, Police Box VII, V.P.R.O.; letter of Henry Wyse (Joe) to John Quinn, December 1878, Kelly Special Bundle SZ843, A.O. N.S.W. The letter is undated except for the month but a note on it identifies it as the letter which sent Nicolson and Standish to Albury.
4.   *Police Commission 1881*, evidence of Standish, Q. 21–3; Standish to Chief Secretary, 15 December 1878, Kelly Papers, Miscellaneous Box; Scott to Chief Manager, National Bank, Melbourne, 13 December 1878, Kelly Papers, Police Box V, V.P.R.O.

5. For Moorehouse's speech see *Ovens and Murray Advertiser*,
12 December 1878; Standish to Chief Secretary, 15 December 1878,
Kelly Papers, Miscellaneous Box V.P.R.O. For Standish 'rusticating
peacefully in Benalla' and reading novels, see *Police Commission
1881*, p. xvi and Q.1091–2.
6. See the engraving in *Illustrated Australian News*, 28 November
1878, p. 193 of Stringybark Creek with the caption 'Murderous Attack
on Victorian Police by Kelly and his Gang'. At p. 196 the Kelly
brothers are depicted with a clear attempt to emphasize visually their
criminality. There is considerable evidence that the outlaws were
liberally supplied with newspapers while in the bush. See for
example *Ovens and Murray Advertiser*, 23 January 1879, where it
was reported that Maggie came to Benalla daily and purchased
a Melbourne paper.
7. Clerk's copy of Edward Kelly to Donald Cameron, posted Glenrowan 14 December 1878, Kelly Papers, 'Kelly Gang' Box 2, V.P.R.O.;
Advocate, 14 December 1878; *Ovens and Murray Advertiser*, 19 December 1878; Victoria, *Parliamentary Debates*, Session 1878, vol.29,
Legislative Assembly, p. 1793; Standish to Chief Secretary, 18 December 1878, Kelly Papers, Miscellaneous Box; Chief Secretary memo
on his note to Standish, 3 December 1878, Kelly Papers, C.S.O. Box
1, V.P.R.O.; Marriage certificate, district of Mornington, Alexander
Fitzpatrick to Anna Savage, 10 July 1878, no.5, Government Statist,
Melbourne.
8. *Ovens and Murray Advertiser* prior to the Euroa raid had nothing
but scorn for the Kellys as a pack of worthless criminals. In its editorial
of 14 December 1878 it took a less rigid line and wrote 'the love the
Kellys are known to have for their mother borders almost on worship',
while Fitzpatrick was described as 'an inexperienced, vain, con-
ceited boy'.
9. *Ovens and Murray Advertiser*, 14, 17, 24, 26 December 1878;
Advocate, 14, 21, 28 December 1878; *Federal Standard*, 28 December
1878, 6 January 1879; Victoria, *Government Gazette*, 13 December
1878; Memo on Artillery Corps, Kelly Papers, Police Box VI; Sadleir
to Secretan, 27 December 1878, Kelly Papers, Police Box VI; Nicolson
to members in charge various stations, 14 December 1878, Kelly
Papers, Police Box IV; O'Shannassy to Officer in Charge, Bourke
District, 19 December 1878, Kelly Papers, Police Box IV; reports from
Bundoora and Whittlesea, 27 December 1878, Kelly Papers, Police
Box IV; Nelson to Superintendent of Police, Richmond, 28 December

1878, Kelly Papers, Police Box IV; Baber to Nicolson, 30 December 1878, Kelly Papers, Police Box IV, V.P.R.O.
10. *Mansfield Guardian*, 29 March 1879; *Federal Standard*, 8 January 1879; *Ovens and Murray Advertiser*, 31 December, 4, 7, 9, 14, 18, 23, 28 January, 4, 8, 11 February 1879. The name Hearty – more commonly Harty – is so spelt in the police records. Standish to Acting Chief Secretary, 23 January 1879, and Acting Chief Secretary to Lake Rowan residents, Kelly Papers, C.S.O. Box I; Report of Constable Percival, Euroa, Kelly Papers, Police Box V, V.P.R.O.
11. Ned's letter was published in C. Osborne, *Ned Kelly*, London, 1970, pp. 63–4.

11   Wilderness of the Heart

1. The accepted meaning of the name Jerilderie is reedy place. Rev. H. C. Lundy, *History of Jerilderie*, Jerilderie, 1958, p. 1.
2. ibid., p. 64.
3. D. H. Harris, *The Teams of the Blacksoil Plains*, Camberwell, Vic., 1977, p. 39.
4. A good deal of the purely factual narrative in this chapter is based on those sections which, after comparison with other sources, prove reliable in Rev. H. C. Lundy, *History*, pp. 14–120. Recorded originally by William Elliott in his diary, these pages first appeared in serial form in the *Jerilderie Herald* in 1913. Details come from Diary of Duty and Occurrences at the Jerilderie Police Station, 9–16 February 1879, 4/5573, A.O. N.S.W.; Statement of Senior Constable Devine, Jerilderie, Colonial Secretary's Correspondence, 79/1239, A.O. N.S.W.; Statement of Constable Richards, Jerilderie, 19 February 1879, Kelly Special Bundle SZ843, A.O. N.S.W.
5. Jerilderie letter.
6. T. J. Linane and F. A. Mecham (eds), *The Men of '38 and Other Pioneer Priests*, Kilmore, Vic., 1975, p. 186. The visiting priests were in the habit of taking breakfast after Mass with the Devines.
7. At Longreach, Queensland, in 1954, Andrew Nixon, then aged ninety-two, made a recording of his experiences on that Monday in Jerilderie in 1879. Miss Jean Batten of Jerilderie kindly loaned me her copy of the recording while Mr Eddy Cully, President of the Chamber of Commerce, showed me the historical sites of his town.
8. See the letter of J. E. Rankin to Duncan Rankin, Jerilderie 1879, in a publication entitled *The Jerilderie Letter*, Finley, N.S.W. n.d.,

p. 16, produced by the Jerilderie and District Historical Society. James Ewen Rankin was assistant to Henry Jefferson, the postmaster. Both were put in the lock-up by Ned to ensure they did not telegraph news of the raid. See also S. Gill, 'The Kelly gang at Jerilderie', *Life*, Melbourne, 1 March 1910, p. 264.

9. This episode is recounted in M. Brown, *Australian Son; the story of Ned Kelly*, Melbourne, 1948, p. 133. The actual theft and return of the mare by Ned is well documented although Superintendent Hare, with customary malice, asserted that Ned took the mare 'and promised to return it in three weeks which of course he never did'. See F. A. Hare, *The Last*, London, 1894, p. 152.

10. J. E. Rankin to D. Rankin in *The Jerilderie Letter*, p. 16.

11. The last line of the Jerilderie letter.

12. The meeting between Kelly and future General Monash is based on oral tradition. Ned's description of Fitzpatrick, so consistent with that of the estimate of the Constable by his superiors, is in Rev. H. C. Lundy, *History*, p. 88. For Ned's speech see *Mansfield Guardian*, 15 February 1879.

13. Edwin Living's statement, undated but 1880, Kelly Papers, Miscellaneous Box, V.P.R.O.; Deniliquin police to Inspector General, Sydney, 14 February 1879, Kelly Special Bundle, SZ843, A.O. N.S.W.

14. William Elliott devoted the final chapter of his account of the happenings at Jerilderie to a defence of his fellow citizens against the criticism levelled at them 'from all quarters, especially from the Southern State'. See Rev. H. C. Lundy, *History*, p. 18. By 12 February 1879 Devine was already ill. See Jerilderie police to Inspector General, Sydney, 13 February 1879, Kelly Special Bundle, SZ843, A.O. N.S.W.

15. Rev. H. C. Lundy, *History*, p. 18.

16. J. Ryan, 'Ned Kelly: the flight of the legend', *Australian Literary Studies*, vol.3, October 1967, pp. 98–115.

12   Shadows in the Ranges

1. The account of the deputation to Longmore, Commissioner for Crown Lands, is in the *Advocate*, 15 February, 12 April 1879.

2. *Sun* (Sydney), 14 September 1911. The fence line, the Bowdern property and the sites of the Kelly and police camps were pointed out to me by Councillor John Nolan of Glenrowan, whose grand-

father held land nearby and who recounted the story of the visits to the Bowderns.

3.   H. Moors for Assistant C.C.P. to Standish, 11 February 1879, Memo Book of C.C.P., Series 678, vol.183, file ȳ227, V.P.R.O.; Parkes to Victorian Chief Secretary, 14 February 1879, Kelly Papers, C.S.O. Box 1, V.P.R.O.; N.S.W., *Government Gazette*, 18 February 1879; Victoria, *Government Gazette*, 18 February 1879; *Ovens and Murray Advertiser*, 20 February 1879.

4.   Secret Service expenditure, 1 November 1878 to 31 June 1880, Memo Book of C.C.P., Series 678, vol.190, file A1699–A1700, V.P.R.O.

5.   Standish to Seymour (C.C.P. Brisbane), 15, 17, 19 February 1879 and Seymour to Standish, 17, 28 February 1879, Kelly Papers, Police Box I; Statements of O'Connor and King, 10 March 1879, Kelly Papers, Police Box VI, V.P.R.O.; *Herald*, 4 March 1879; *Ovens and Murray Advertiser*, 8 March 1879; *Federal Standard*, 15 March 1879. Sadleir records Sambo's death in his diary entry of 19 March 1879; see John Sadleir Diary, H2948, L.C. S.L.V. In 1871 there were only 516 male Aborigines left in Victoria, *Mansfield Independent*, 5 May 1871.

6.   *Argus*, 10 February 1879; *Mansfield Guardian*, 11 January 1879; *Ovens and Murray Advertiser*, 15, 18, 22, 25, 27 February, 27 March 1879; *Federal Standard*, 8, 15 March 1879; Crown Law Correspondence, file no. 79/1029, 79/1735, Series 266, V.P.R.O.

7.   *Argus*, 10 February 1879; *Ovens and Murray Advertiser*, 18 February 1879; Standish to Acting Chief Secretary, 22 April 1879, Kelly Papers, C.S.O. Box 1, V.P.R.O.

8.   Nicolson to Miss Jessie McKay, 3 March 1879, P.D.C., Series 937, Box 145; Nicolson to Fitzpatrick and private note on copy of same, 26 April 1879, P.D.C., Series 937, Box 145, V.P.R.O.

9.   Fitzpatrick to Inspector General, Sydney, 5 March, 30 April 1879 and to Standish, 7 May 1879; Standish to Inspector General, Sydney, 12 May 1879 and to Nicolson, 25 May 1879; Fosberry to Standish, 20 May 1879; Detective Camphin to Inspector General, 30 April 1879 (two separate communications); K. T. Pogonowski to Sub-Inspector Rush of N.S.W. Police, 6 May 1879; Sub-Inspector Rush to Superintendent Read of N.S.W. Police, 6 May 1879. All in Kelly Papers, Miscellaneous Box, V.P.R.O. James Wilson alias Kelly, prison record in N.S.W., Kelly Papers 'Kelly Gang' Boxes 2 and 3, V.P.R.O.

10.   *Police Commission 1881*, evidence of Hare, Q.1281 and 1282.

11.   ibid., Q.1284–5.

12.   Anonymous letter to Hare, 6 April 1879 and anonymous letter to Nicolson, 30 April 1879, in Kelly Papers, 'Kelly Gang' Box 6, V.P.R.O.
13.   'Veritas' to Chief Secretary, 30 December 1878, Chief Secretary's Correspondence, Series 1189, Box 121, V.P.R.O.

13 Captain of the Northeast

1.   'The book of Keli' ran over thirteen weeks in the *Mansfield Guardian*, 13 February to 28 June, 1879. Standish – called Dishstand – was captain of the King's guard. Printed as a pamphlet, it sold for 6d. Standish to Secretan 12 March 1879, Kelly Papers, 'Kelly Gang' Box 2, V.P.R.O.; Sadleir's diary entry for 6 February 1879, John Sadleir Diary, H2948, L.C. S.L.V.; C. H. Chomley, *The True Story of the Kelly Gang of Bushrangers*, Melbourne 1907, p. 106; J. M. Tregenza, *Professor of Democracy; the life of Charles Henry Pearson, Oxford don and Australian radical*, Carlton, Vic., 1968, pp. 148–9; Standish to Sadleir, 17 June 1879, H2916, L.C. S.L.V.
2.   *Police Commission 1881*, Appendix 7, p. 697; McMannery to Secretan, 13 June 1879, Detective Letter Books, Series 1198, vol.30; Conolly to Secretan, 14 June 1879, Kelly Papers, Police Box V; Secretan to Nicolson, 16 June 1879, Detective Letter Books, Series 1198, vol.30; Nicolson to Officer in Charge, Benalla, 16 June 1879, Memo Book of C.C.P., Series 678, vol.182, file y902; Sadleir to Secretan, 18 June 1879, Kelly Papers, Police Box VI; Report of Detectives Dowden and Hayes, 20 June 1879, Kelly Papers, Police Box V, V.P.R.O.; Standish to Sadleir, 17 June 1879, H2916, L.C. S.L.V.; *Advocate*, 21 June 1879; *Ovens and Murray Advertiser*, 17 June 1879. In early 1880 the police still considered escape by sea from a Victorian port was possible. It came to nothing, if indeed it was ever contemplated by Ned. See Battye to Inspector General, Sydney, 17 March 1880, Kelly Papers, Miscellaneous Box; James to Standish, 19 April 1880, Kelly Papers, Police Box II, V.P.R.O.
3.   For references to these matters see *North Eastern Ensign*, 20 February 1874, 24 March 1877; *Federal Standard*, 2 August 1876, 13 January, 29 September, 10, 27 October 1877; *Wangaratta Dispatch*, 28 August, 8 December 1875, 8 March 1876, 10 January 1877. For the population figure see Victoria, *Statistical Register*, 1878–80.
4.   Mr Thomas Lloyd told me that as a boy he had seen the 'exercise books' containing the 'minutes' of these meetings. The meetings were held at three-monthly intervals, and according to Mr Lloyd, Mr David

Gaunson attended one of them. *Police Commission 1881*, evidence
of Mrs Byrne, Q.13166–8.
5. J. Sadleir, *Recollections*, pp. 215, 220; *Police Commission 1881*,
Appendix 5, p. 693.
6. *Police Commission 1881*, Appendix 7, p. 697; Standish to Chief
Secretary, 30 June 1879, Memo Book of C.C.P., Series 678, vol.182,
file y1002, V.P.R.P. As there is no place called Coloopna, I have opted
for Mooroopna as the sighting took place near Shepparton.
7. C. H. Chomley, *The True Story* says, p. 112, that Maggie soon
put a stop to Aaron's courting of Kate.
8. In 1978, Research Officer Lloyd Cropper of the Victorian Education Department compiled an account of Wallace's career. See
also Education Department files for Yea School, No.699, Series 640,
V.P.R.O. Wallace was sacked by the Department in May 1882 for
his alleged assistance to the Kellys. He later worked as an insurance
agent in Queensland. 'Diseased Stock' gets frequent mention in the
Police Commission 1881, Q.755, 1516, 2597, 2663–6, 2764, 2804, 2880,
and also in Sadleir, *Recollections*, p. 217, where he is identified as
a professional man. He was probably Dr John Nicholson of Benalla.
For the names given to the outlaws, see entry for 21 and 22 March
1879 in Sadleir's diary, H2948, L.C. S.L.V.; Wallace was known as
Bruce and Aaron as Moses or Tommy or Sheet.
9. See *Advocate*, 20, 27 March, 24 April, 15 May 1880; *Federal Standard*, 27 March, 2 June, 17 July, 1880; B. W. Cookson article, *Sun* (Sydney), 13 September 1911; Chomley, *The True Story*, p. 111; J. J.
Kenneally, *The Complete Inner History of the Kelly Gang and Their
Pursuers*, Melbourne 1955, p. 173; *Ovens and Murray Advertiser*, 20
April 1880.
10. T. N. McIntyre, A narrative, MS6343, pp. 14, 21, 48a, L.C. S.L.V.;
Standish to Hare, 21 July 1879, Memo Book of C.C.P., Series 678,
vol.182, file y1116, V.P.R.O.
11. The complete file on Fitzpatrick's discharge is in Chief Secretary's Correspondence, Series 1189, Box 325; Standish to Hare, 14
February 1880, Memo Book of C.C.P., Series 678, vol. 185, file z215,
V.P.R.O.
12. *Mansfield Guardian*, 21 June 1879; *Police Commission 1881*, evidence of Nicolson, Q.746; *Argus*, 30 June 1880. Five farmers noticed
their mould boards missing at Easter 1880.
13. On the making and testing of the armour see 'Diseased Stock'
to Nicolson, 20 May 1880, in *Police Commission 1881*, Q.755; J. J.

Kenneally, *The Inner History*, pp. 174–8; Secretary of Shire of Oxley Council to Standish, 12 May 1880, Kelly Papers, Police Box II, V.P.R.O.
14.   I am indebted to the Commissioners for drawing my attention to the use of the expression 'a change of bowlers' by Ramsay. They used it in their Report, the *Police Commission 1881*, p. xxi, and it is further detailed by Nicolson in his evidence in Q.933–4, *Mansfield Guardian*, 11 December 1875.
15.   The attitude of Standish to Nicolson is revealed in the recently discovered Hare Personal Papers now deposited in the Melbourne University Archives, from which the quotes are drawn.
16.   *Police Commission 1881*, Q.14166, 15365, 15699; *Federal Standard*, 30 June 1880.
17.   Oral tradition for this remark of Aaron's is found in a letter of James Ryan, brother of a sympathizer, to Kenneally, n.d. but circa 1930 in J. J. Kenneally, *The Inner History*, pp. 191, 315-6, and the *Sun* (Sydney), 5 September 1911, where Cookson reports it as coming from Jim Kelly. The latter was released from Darlinghurst in January 1880 and hence was in a position to know at first hand the events of that year. For Aaron and Joe being 'more than a brother to each other' see Enoch Downs to John Blight, Beechworth, n.d., but certainly 1880, MS10612, L.C. S.L.V.
18.   Ward to Secretan, 28 December 1880, said he received this information from Anne Jane Sherritt on 30 May 1880, Kelly Papers, Reward Box I, V.P.R.O.
19.   Fosberry to Parkes, 4 March 1880; Parkes to Ramsay, 22 March 1880; Ramsay to Parkes, 3 April 1880, Kelly Papers, C.S.O. Box II, V.P.R.O.; N.S.W., *Government Gazette*, 20 April 1880; Victoria, *Government Gazette*, 20 April 1880.
20.   Ned's refusal to countenance the killing of Aaron and his fighting Dan over such a proposal is family tradition. Mr Michael Ryan, Albury, passed it to me. The horse ridden by Dan to Sherritts, and back to Glenrowan, belonged to the Ryan family at Cashel and was returned to them. See List of property, Edward Kelly Capital Case File, V.P.R.O.; see also *Argus*, 3 July 1880 and *Ovens and Murray Advertiser*, 1 July 1880, where it is recorded that at Glenrowan, after his capture, Ned expressed ignorance of Aaron's slaying; that it was done unknown to him and that he was '. . . wild about it'.
21.   The clearest account of Aaron's death is contained in the evidence given at the *Police Commission 1881* by Mrs Ellen Barry, his mother-in-law, Q.13374–439.

22.   F. A. Hare, *The Last*, p. 322.

14 A Still, Cold Night

1.   After the events at Glenrowan, the eight horses were all accoun-
ted for, complete with saddles and other equipment. The two drums
of powder were found, one near the railway gates and the other
on a pack-horse in the bush behind McDonnell's Hotel. See List of
property, Edward Kelly Capital Case File; Bracken to Sadleir, 2 July
1880, Kelly Papers, Police Box II, V.P.R.O.; *Ovens and Murray Advertiser*, 24 July 1880; *Advocate*, 18 September 1880, p. 16; *Argus*, 30 June
1880. One of the weapons was the double-barrelled fowling piece
that belonged to the parson at Mansfield.
2.   Seymour to O'Connor, 15 June 1880, Kelly Papers, Police Box VI,
V.P.R.O.; Standish to Hare, 25 June 1880, Hare Personal Papers, Melbourne University Archives.
3.   *Police Commission 1881*, evidence of Armstrong, Q.12162, 12189
and evidence of Ellen Barry, Q.13405, 13409.
4.   *Argus*, 29 June, 5 July 1880; Hare to Standish, 2 July 1880, Kelly
Papers, C.S.O. Box III, V.P.R.O.; *Police Commission 1881*, evidence
of O'Connor, Q.1114, 1115; Standish to O'Connor, 27 June 1880, Kelly
Papers, Police Box I; Report of Guard Frank Bell, 27 June 1880, Kelly
Papers, Miscellaneous Box; Hare to Standish, 27 June 1880, Kelly
Papers, Police Box I, V.P.R.O.; P. Adam Smith, *Romance of Australian
Railways*, Adelaide 1973, pp. 169–81.
5.   *Police Commission 1881*, evidence of James Reardon, Q. 7607–10.
6.   'Felons Apprehension Act 1878', Victoria, *Acts of Parliament*, 42
Victoria 612; 'Expiring Laws Continuation Act 1879', Victoria, *Acts
of Parliament*, 43 Victoria 648. For the proroguing of parliament, see
Victoria, *Government Gazette*, 1880, pp. 1661–5; *Police Commission
1881*, evidence of Hare, Q.1485; *Federal Standard*, 3 July 1880.
7.   Ned's plans are stated in his letters, E. Kelly to Governor of Victoria, 5 November 1880, 10 November 1880, Edward Kelly Capital
Case File, V.P.R.O. An account of Sunday's activities is given in the
'Minutes of evidence taken before the Board of Enquiry into claims
for the compensation of Mrs Ann Jones', Kelly Papers, C.S.O. Box
IV, V.P.R.O.; *Age*, 29 June 1880. The Township of Glenrowan map,
Crown Lands and Survey Department, Melbourne, places both barracks and Curnow's house in the position stated by Ned.
8.   Evidence of Hugh Bracken given at 'Board of Enquiry into claims

for the compensation of Mrs Ann Jones', Kelly Papers, C.S.O. Box
IV; Report of Bracken, 15 December 1880, Reward Board Box I,
V.P.R.O.

9.   Thomas Curnow's statement, 20 July 1880, Kelly Papers, Police
Box I; Hare to Standish, 27 June 1880, Kelly Papers, Police Box I; Hare
to Standish, 2 July 1880, Kelly Papers, C.S.O. Box III, V.P.R.O.

10.   The Sullivan affair was written up at length in the *Mansfield
Guardian*, 6 May 1876; 'Minutes of evidence taken before the Board
of Enquiry into claims for the compensation of Mrs Ann Jones', Kelly
Papers, C.S.O. Box IV, V.P.R.O.; *Police Commission 1881*, evidence
of Curnow, Q.17598. Bracken said none of the outlaws had 'the slight-
est appearance of having been drinking nor drunk anything to my
knowledge', Bracken Report, 15 December 1880, Kelly Papers,
Reward Board Box I, V.P.R.O.

11.   *Police Commission 1881*, evidence of James Reardon, Q.7628;
Hare to Standish, 2 July 1880, Kelly Papers, C.S.O. Box III; Gas-
coigne's report, 28 June 1880, Kelly Papers, Reward Board Box I,
V.P.R.O. For rockets, see *Federal Standard*, 4 August 1880; *Police
Commission 1881*, evidence of James Arthur, Q.11190.

12.   E. Kelly to Governor of Victoria, Edward Kelly Capital Case
File, V.P.R.O. A set of armour in the old Melbourne gaol, which is
identifiable as that worn by Ned, has a broken bolt thus helping
to verify Ned's story to the Governor. *Police Commission 1881*, Hare
to Standish, 28 June 1880, Q.11861; Mr Mortimer's statement in *Federal
Standard*, 3 July 1880; *Police Commission 1881*, evidence of James
Reardon, Q.7663–70; for Joe's death see *Police Commission 1881*,
1141–2, 11426–7, also T. N. McIntyre, A narrative, MS6343, p. 75, L.C.
S.L.V.

13.   There are many accounts of the capture of Edward Kelly at
Glenrowan. Those used include: Report of Steele to Sadleir, 6 July
1880, Kelly Papers, Police Box VI; Report of Arthur Sadleir, 2 July
1880, Kelly Papers, Police Box VI; Jesse Dowsett to Traffic Manager,
2 July 1880, Kelly Papers, Miscellaneous Box, V.P.R.O.; *Police Commission 1881*, evidence, Q.9034, 9232, 9514, 9561, 9677, 10043, 10356,
10763, 10772, 10936.

14.   *Police Commission 1881*, evidence, Q.7654–60, 9679.

15.   Sadleir's report to Standish, 1 July 1880, in *Police Commission
1881*, Q.2880. George Metcalfe, a stonebreaker, died in the Melbourne Hospital on 15 October 1880, after receiving a severe eye
injury whilst lying on the hotel floor at Glenrowan, see Grey to Stan-

dish, 1 July 1880, Kelly Papers, Police Box II, V.P.R.O.; Phillips to Standish (telegram), 28 June 1880, H2897, L.C. S.L.V.; Colonel Anderson
to Sadleir (telegram), 27 June 1880, H2898, L.C. S.L.V.; *Police Commission 1881*, evidence, Q.2821, 2864, 7208, 9190, 10841.
16.   *West Australian Catholic Record*, 29 August 1880; *Argus*, 29 June
1880. For Steve and Dan's deaths see Sadleir to Standish, 28 June
1880, Kelly Papers, without citation, V.P.R.O. *Police Commission 1881*,
evidence Q. 7383. Tom Lloyd of Broadmeadows passed on the tradition about Dan and Steve's bodies being laid out by an old friend
– probably his father.
17.   *Argus*, 1 July 1880. Father Batchelor of Moyhu told me the details
of the burial of Steve and Dan. As he knew Jim Kelly well, his recollec-
tion of oral tradition in this and other matters is reliable.

15   *The Son of His Mother*

1:   Saxe to Standish, 28 June 1880, Kelly Papers, C.S.O. Box II; Ramsay to Standish, 28 June 1880, Police Box I, V.P.R.O.; T. N. McIntyre,
A narrative, MS6343, L.C. S.L.V.; *Argus*, 30 June 1880; Bridget Kennedy to Standish, 30 June 1880; Castieau to Standish, 8 July 1880;
Standish to Mrs Kennedy, 8 July 1880, P.D.C., Series 937, Box 145;
Report on Castieau by Constable Healy, 2 May 1873, Chief Secretary's Correspondence, Series 1189, Box 72, V.P.R.O. Castieau's
diary for 1880 is missing from those held by the National Library,
Canberra.
2.   *Melbourne Punch*, 1 July 1880; *Argus*, 29 June 1880. While taking
no stand for Ned the *Advocate* asked that the police of the Glenrowan fray be brought before the court and charged with manslaughter, *Advocate*, 2 July 1880.
3.   *Argus*, 9 July, 2 August 1880; Shields to Standish, 2 July 1880, Kelly
Papers, without citation; Standish to Harriman, 2 July 1880, Crown
Law Correspondence, Series 266, Box 336, V.P.R.O. Reports on the
Beechworth trial from T. N. McIntyre, A narrative MS6343, L.C. S.L.V.;
Federal Standard, 14 August 1880; Gaunson to Chief Secretary (telegram), 7 August 1880, Kelly Papers, C.S.O. Box II, V.P.R.O.
4.   See letters P. Meade and Alex Dick, 1, 13, 14 July 1880 and Sadleir
to Secretan, 17 July 1880, Edward Kelly Capital Case File, V.P.R.O.
5.   Ryan to Officer in Charge, Benalla 28 August 1880, Kelly Papers,
Miscellaneous Box, V.P.R.O. This admission by Ned is contrary to
all he ever asserted after 15 April 1878 and even after Glenrowan

itself. Together with the circumstances in which it was said to have been made and the interest of the police in substantiating Fitz-patrick's story, sufficient doubt is cast as to make its veracity highly suspect.

6. In the end Hare managed to get a suit which has passed on in the Rupert Clarke family with whom he stayed at Sunbury to recuperate in 1880. The Victoria Police claim to have a genuine set, while the old Melbourne gaol has two more and the Beechworth Museum a fifth. All have a helmet which is surprising given only one was made. It all constitutes a form of relic perservation, reminiscent of and somewhat more banal than the interest of medieval Christendom in the assorted heads of John the Baptist.

7. As early as April 1879 it was reported at Mansfield that the local tradesmen would be sorry to see the outlaws caught so lucrative was their trade due to the police in the area, *Mansfield Guardian*, 19 April 1979. N.S.W., *Parliamentary Debates*, Session 1879–80, vol.III, Legislative Assembly, pp. 3194–7; *Federal Standard*, 18 August 1880; Standish to Chief Secretary, 11 September 1880, Chief Secretary's Correspondence, Series 1189, Box 242, V.P.R.O. On 19 March 1883, Standish died at the Melbourne Club after a deathbed relinquishing of Freemasonry and conversion to Catholicism. He is best remembered by his memorial – the Standish Handicap on New Year's Day run over six furlongs at Flemington. See J. S. Legge, 'Frederick Standish (1824–83)', in *A.D.B.*, vol.6, pp. 172–3.

8. See the excellent account of the Exhibition in G. Davison, *The Rise and Fall of Marvellous Melbourne*, Carlton, Vic., 1978, pp. 1–16.

9. Standish to Winch, 13 July 1880, Memo Book of C.C.P., Series 678, vol. 186, file x1154. Castieau to Standish, 17 August 1880; Standish confidential note 6 July 1880; Secretan to Standish 6 July 1880; Reports of Detective O'Donnell, 6, 7 July 1880; Reports of Detective Kett, 30, 31 July and 11 August 1880; all in Kelly Papers, Police Box V, V.P.R.O. Edward Kelly to Chief Secretary, 19 July 1880, Kelly Papers, C.S.O. Box II, V.P.R.O.; *Federal Standard*, 23 October 1880; *Ovens and Murray Advertiser*, 16 October 1880.

10. Barry to Barrow, 26 September 1860, n.d. December 1879, 12 July n.d. but 1880; Curtis Candler to Barry, 7 June 1861, 13 February 1873; all in Redmond Barry Papers, MS8380, L.C. S.L.V. Candler wrote an anonymous book on these matters which he refrained from dedicating to Barry because it was all 'so horribly filthy'.

11. *The Age*, 16 October 1880; Gaunson to Attorney-General, 15

October 1880; Gaunson to Sherriff, 19 October 1880; Gaunson to
Brown, 19 October 1880; Brown to Gaunson, 19 October 1880; all in
Crown Law Correspondence, Series 266, file 80/4910, V.P.R.O.
12.   *Herald*, 18 October 1880; Dr Ryan's statement, *Argus*, 30 June
1879; Sadleir to Standish, 9 August 1880, P.D.C., Series 937, Box 366;
Baber to Standish, 9 August 1880, Kelly Papers, without citation,
V.P.R.O.; *Ovens and Murray Advertiser*, 14 August 1880; *Argus*, 13
August 1880.
13.   Gaunson to Attorney-General, 15 October 1880 (two letters), file
80/4842; Edward Kelly to the Sherriff, 16 October 1880, file 80/4910;
Smyth to Attorney-General, 17 October 1880, file 80/4833 (this letter
contains the word 'sham' in relation to the application for postponement); Gaunson to the Sherriff, 19 October 1880, file 80/4910;
Gaunson to Brown, 19 October 1880, file 80/4910; Brown to Gaunson,
19 October 1880, file 80/4910; Gaunson to Sherriff, 21, 22 October
1880, file 80/4910; all in Crown Law Correspondence, Series 266,
V.P.R.O. A.G. Vale to Sherriff, 20 October 1880, Kelly Papers, Police
Box VI, V.P.R.O.; *Herald*, 18 October 1880; J. E. Parnaby, 'William Vale
(1833–95)', in *A.D.B.*, vol.6, pp. 324–5.
14.   Matriculation Roll. Melbourne University Archives; *The Law List
of Australasia*, Melbourne, 1880; Certificate of admission as a barrister, 6 December 1879, Series 1356, Box 2, File 177, V.P.R.O.; *Bulletin*,
30 October 1880; J. A. Gurner, *Life's Panorama: being recollections
and reminiscences of things seen, things heard, things read*, Melbourne, 1930, p. 227; *Herald*, 28 October 1880.
15.   McIntyre to Pewtress, 27 October 1878, Kelly Papers, without
citation, V.P.R.O.
16.   T. N. McIntyre, A narrative, MS6343, L.C. S.L.V.; *Argus*, 29, 30
October 1880; Louis Waller, 'Regina v. Edward Kelly', in *Ned Kelly:
man and myth*, pp. 105–53.
17.   The best account of the trial is contained in the *Argus*, 29, 30
October 1880. It editorialized on 30 October that it found satisfaction
in there having been no miscarriage of justice and that 'a verdict
was arrived at without hesitation'.
18.   Petition for reprieve, Edward Kelly Capital Case File; Executive
Council minutes, 3 November 1880, Series 1080, vol.20; Lucy Dashwood to Queen Victoria, 1 September 1880 in Secretary of State to
the Governor, Series 1087, no.54; Edward Kelly to Governor of Victoria, 3, 5, 10 November 1880, Kelly Capital Case File, V.P.R.O.; Mrs
Barrow to son Nicholas, 10 November 1880, Redmond Barry Papers,

MS8380, L.C. S.L.V.; 'Kelly's defence by a lady', Kelly Papers, C.S.O. Box II, V.P.R.O.; *Argus*, 1, 10 November 1880; *Age*, 6, 8, 9, 10, 11 November 1880; *Federal Standard*, 6 November 1880; *S.M.H.*, 8 November 1880. Redmond Barry died on 23 November, twelve days after Ned.

19.   For the account of Ned's last hours, I have followed in the main that of Edward Adams, prison warden, contained in R. Testro, *The Testro Story*, Melbourne, 1970, pp. 90–2. Adams was in attendance on Ned and signed his letter to the Governor of 5 November 1880, as Ned's injured thumb still did not permit him to write. I am indebted to Mr Ian Fitchett, Canberra, for drawing my attention to this source.

Bibliography

BOOKS, PAMPHLETS, THESES and ARTICLES

Adam Smith, P., *Romance of Australian Railways*, Rigby, Adelaide, 1973.

Andrews, A., *The First Settlement of the Upper Murray*, D. S. Ford, Sydney, 1920.

Archer, W. H. (ed.), *The Statistical Register of Victoria, from the Foundation of the Colony*, Government Printer, Melbourne, 1854.

Bartlett, G., Political organization and society in Victoria 1864–83, unpublished Ph.D. thesis, Australian National University, Canberra, 1964.

——,'Sir Graham Berry (1822–1904)', in *Australian Dictionary of Biography*, vol. 3, Melbourne University Press, Carlton, Vic., 1969, pp. 151–6.

Billis, R. V. and Kenyon A. S., *Pastoral Pioneers of Port Phillip*, Stockland Press, Melbourne, 1974.

Blake, L. J. (ed.), *Vision and Realisation: a centenary history of state education in Victoria*, 3 vols., Education Department of Victoria, Melbourne, 1973.

Blake, L. J., 'Young Ned', *The Educational Magazine*, Melbourne, vol. 27, no. 8, pp. 350–55, September 1970.

Brown, M., *Australian Son; the story of Ned Kelly*, Georgian House, Melbourne, 1948.

Carroll, B., *Ned Kelly, Bushranger*, Lansdowne Press, Dee Why West, N.S.W., 1976.

Chomley, C. H., *The True Story of the Kelly Gang of Bushrangers*, Fraser and Jenkinson, Melbourne, 1907.

Clune, F., *The Kelly Hunters*, Angus and Robertson, Sydney, 1954.

Cobley, J., 'William Bland (1789–1868)', in *Australian Dictionary of biography*, vol. 1, Melbourne University Press, Carlton, Vic., 1966, pp. 112–15.

Cookson, B. W., 'The Kelly gang from within', *Sun*, Sydney, 27 August–24 September 1911.

Coughlan, N., 'The coming of the Irish to Victoria', *Historical Studies: Australia and New Zealand*, vol. 12, no. 45, pp. 68–86, October 1965.

Cowen, Z., *Isaac Isaacs*, Oxford University Press, Melbourne, 1967.

Davies, J. M. S., 'The Kellys are out', *Herald*, Melbourne, 1 November–16 December 1930.

Davison, G., *The Rise and Fall of Marvellous Melbourne*, Melbourne University Press, Carlton, Vic., 1978.

Dunn, E. J., 'The Woolshed Valley, Beechworth', *Bulletin of the Geological Survey of Victoria*, Melbourne 1913, no. 25, pp. 3–16.

Ebsworth, Rev. W., *Pioneer Catholic Victoria*, Polding Press, Melbourne, 1973.

Ellis, S. E., *A History of Greta*, Lowden, Kilmore, Vic., 1972.

Evans, W. P., *Port of Many Prows*, Hawthorn Press, Melbourne, 1969.

Farwell, G., *Ned Kelly; the life and adventures of Australia's notorious bushranger*, Cheshire, Melbourne, 1970.

Fitchett, W. H., *Ned Kelly and His Gang*, Fitchett Brothers, Melbourne, 1938.

Gill, S., 'The Kelly gang at Jerilderie', *Life*, Melbourne, p. 264, 1 March 1910.

Gurner, J. A., *Life's Panorama: being recollections and reminiscences of things seen, things heard, things read*, Lothian, Melbourne, 1930.

Hall, G. Wilson, *The Kelly Gang; the outlaws of the Wombat Ranges*, G. Wilson Hall, proprietor *Mansfield Guardian*, Mansfield, 1879.

Hare, F. A., *The Last of the Bushrangers; an account of the capture of the Kelly gang*, Hurst and Blackett, London, 1894.

Harris, D. H., *The Teams of the Blacksoil Plains*, Rohan Rivett, Camberwell, Vic., 1977.

Haydon, A. L., *The Trooper Police of Australia*, Andrew Melrose, London, 1911.

Historical Records of Australia, Series I, vol. XIX, Library Committee of the Commonwealth Parliament, Sydney, 1923.

Hobsbawm, E. J., *Primitive Rebels; studies in archaic forms of social movement in the nineteenth and twentieth centuries*, Manchester University Press, Manchester, 1963.

Howitt, W., *Land, Labour and Gold*, Longman, Brown Green and Longmans, London, 1855.

Isaacs, A., *Ned Kelly: the ironclad Australian bushranger, by one of his captors*, Alfred J. Isaacs and Sons, London, 1881.

Jacobs, P. A., *Famous Australian Trials and Memories of the Law*, Robertson and Mullens, Melbourne, 1944.

Jennings, M. J., *Ned Kelly, the Legend and the Man*, Hill of Content, Melbourne, 1968.

The Jerilderie letter, Jerilderie and District Historical Society, Finley, N.S.W., n.d.

Jones, I., 'The years Ned Kelly went straight', *Walkabout*, June 1962.

Kenneally, J. J., *The Complete Inner History of the Kelly Gang and Their Pursuers*, Stevens, Melbourne, 1955.

Kerr's Melbourne Almanac and Port Phillip Directory, Kerr and Thompson, Melbourne, 1842.

La Nauze, J. A. and Crawford R. M. (eds), *The Crisis in Victorian Politics, 1879-81; a personal retrospect*, Melbourne University Press, Carlton, Vic., 1957.

Lane, Rev. L., *A History of the Parish of Beechworth, 1854-1978*, Parish of Beechworth, Beechworth, Vic., 1978.

The Law List of Australasia, Charles F. Maxwell, Melbourne, 1880.

Legge, J. S., 'Frederick Standish (1824-83)', in *Australian Dictionary of Biography*, vol. 6, Melbourne University Press, Carlton, Vic., 1976, pp. 172-3.

Linane, T. J., 'With revolver and breviary', *Footprints*, Melbourne, vol. 3, no. 7, pp. 3-6, 1979.

Linane, T. J. and Mecham, F. A. (eds), *The Men of '38 and Other Pioneer Priests*, Lowden, Kilmore, Vic., 1975.

Lundy, Rev. H. C. *History of Jerilderie*, Jerilderie Shire Council, Jerilderie, N.S.W., 1958.

McLaren, I. F., 'Henry Power (1820–91)' in *Australian Dictionary of Biography*, vol. 5, Melbourne University Press, Carlton, Vic., 1974, p. 454.

McQuilton, J., *The Kelly Outbreak 1878–1880: the geographical dimension of social banditry*, Melbourne University Press, Carlton, Vic., 1979.

Madgwick, R. B., *Immigration into Eastern Australia, 1788–1851*, Sydney University Press, Sydney, 1969.

Melville, R., *Ned Kelly; 27 paintings by Sidney Nolan*, Thames and Hudson, London, 1964.

Mills, R. C., *The Colonization of Australia 1829–42; the Wakefield experiment in empire building*, Sidgwick and Jackson, London, 1915.

Morris, G., *Devil's River Country; selections from the history of the Mansfield district*, printed by the Advertiser, Shepparton, Vic., 1952.

Morrissey, D., 'Ned Kelly's sympathisers' *Historical Studies: Australia and New Zealand*, vol. 18, October 1978, pp. 288–95.

O'Callaghan, T., *List of Chief Constables, District Constables, Police Cadets and Police Officers in Victoria 1836–1907*, Government Printer, Melbourne, 1907.

Osborne, C., *Ned Kelly*, Blond, London, 1970.

Parnaby, J. E., 'William Vale (1833–95)', in *Australian Dictionary of Biography*, vol. 6, Melbourne University Press, Carlton, Vic. 1976, pp. 324–5.

Payne, J. W., *The History of Beveridge*, Lowden, Kilmore, Vic., 1974.

Prior, T., Wannon, B. and Nunn, H., *Plundering Sons: a pictorial history of Australian bushranging*, Lansdowne Press, Melbourne, 1966.

Queale, A., 'Harrisville's link with the Kelly gang', *Royal Historical Society of Queensland Journal*, vol. 10, 1975–6, pp. 24–29.

Ryan, J., 'Ned Kelly: the flight of the legend', *Australian Literary Studies*, vol. 3, October 1967, pp. 98–115.

Ryan, P., 'Sir Redmond Barry (1813–80)', in *Australian Dictionary of Biography*, vol. 3, Melbourne University Press, Carlton, Vic., 1969, pp. 108–11.

Sadleir, J., *Recollections of a Victorian Police Officer*, George Robertson, Melbourne, 1913 (Penguin facsimile edition 1973).

Serle, G., *The Rush to be Rich: a history of the colony of Victoria, 1883–9*, Melbourne University Press, Carlton, Vic., 1971.

——, 'The Victorian Legislative Council 1856–1950', *Historical Studies: Australia and New Zealand*, vol. 6, no. 22, May 1954, pp. 186–203.

Shaw, A. G. L., 'Violent protest in Australian history', *Historical Studies: Australia and New Zealand*, vol. 15, no. 60, April 1973, pp. 545–61.

Stewart, D., *Ned Kelly; a play*, Angus and Robertson, Sydney, 1943.

Testro, R., *The Testro Story*, Hawthorn Press, Melbourne, 1970.

Tregenza, J. M., *Professor of Democracy; the life of Charles Henry Pearson, Oxford don and Australian radical*, Melbourne University Press, Carlton, Vic., 1968.

Tudehope, C. M., ' "Kalkallo": A link with the past', *Victorian Historical Magazine*, vol. 32, no. 126, 26 Nov. 1961, pp. 99–115.

Turton, K. W., *The North East Railway; a lineside guide, Melbourne to Wodonga*, Australian Railway Historical Society, Victorian Division, Melbourne, 1973.

Walker, R. B., 'Bushranging in fact and legend', *Historical Studies: Australia and New Zealand*, vol. 11, no. 42, April 1964, pp. 206–22.

Wangaratta Adult Education Centre, *Ned Kelly; man and myth* (with introduction by Colin Cave), Cassell Australia, Melbourne, 1968.

Were, J. B., *A Voyage from Plymouth to Melbourne in 1839; the shipboard and early Melbourne diary*, J. B. Were and Son, Melbourne, 1964.

Westgarth, W., *Personal Recollections of Early Melbourne and Victoria*, George Robertson, Melbourne, 1888.

White, H. A., *Tales of Crime and Criminals in Australia Based Principally upon Reminiscences of Over Thirty Years Official Experience in the Penal Department of Victoria*, Ward and Downey, London, 1894.

Whittaker, D. M., *Wangaratta; being the history of the township that sprang up at the Ovens Crossing and grew into a modern city 1824–1838–1963*, Wangaratta City Council, Wangaratta, Vic., 1963.

Whitworth, R. P. (comp.), *Bailliere's Victorian Gazetteer and Road Guide*, Bailliere, Melbourne, 1865.

Woodham-Smith, C., *The Great Hunger; Ireland 1845–9*, Hamish Hamilton, London, 1962.

Wynn, B., 'Woolshed revisited', *Holy Name Monthly*, Melbourne, 1 June 1962, pp. 3–4.

PRINCIPAL GOVERNMENT RECORDS

Victorian Public Record Office

Chief Secretary's Correspondence, Series 1189.
Crown Law Correspondence, Series 266.
Despatches of the Governor to the Secretary of State, Series 1084.
Despatches of the Secretary of State to the Governor, Series 1087.
Edward Kelly Capital Case File, without series.
Executive Council Minutes, Series 1080.
Kelly Papers, without series, but including:
 – Chief Secretary's Correspondence, 1878–82.
 – Police Department Correspondence, 1878–81.
 – Prosecution Briefs.
 – Kelly Reward Board Papers.
 – Jerilderie letter.
 – Cameron letter.
Police Department Correspondence, Series 937.
Police Muster Rolls, Series 55.
Prison Registers, Series 515.

Archives of New South Wales

Colonial Secretary's Correspondence.
Kelly Special Bundle, SZ843.

Victoria Police Archives, Public Relations Division (Russell St Melbourne)

Greta and Glenrowan Occurrence Book.
Mansfield Occurrence Book.
Record Sheets of Victoria Police Officers and Constables.

Victorian Government Statist

Birth, Death and Marriage Certificates 1843–78.

OFFICIAL GOVERNMENT PUBLICATIONS

New South Wales, *Government Gazette*, 1878–80.
New South Wales, *Parliamentary Debates*, 1878–80.
New South Wales, *Police Gazette*, 1877–80.
Victoria, *Acts of Parliament*, 1878–80.
Victoria, *Government Gazette*, 1877–80.
Victoria, *Papers Presented to Both Houses of Parliament*. Session
 1881, vol. III, no. 22, 'Second Progress Report of the Royal Com-
 mission of Enquiry into the circumstances of the Kelly Outbreak
 and the present state and organisation of the Police Force'; no.
 31, 'Minutes of Evidence taken before Royal Commission on the
 Police Force of Victoria'.
Victoria, *Parliamentary Debates*, 1878–80.
Victoria, *Police Gazette*, 1860–80.
Victoria, *Statistical Register*, 1873, 1878–80.

MANUSCRIPTS

Barry, Redmond, Papers, MS8380 La Trobe Collection, State Library
 of Victoria.
Brown, Gilbert W., Notebooks 1864–6, Education Department of Vic-
 toria Library.
Browne, Thomas Alexander, Diary, Mitchell Library Manuscripts.
Croll, R. H. 'Before I Forget', ch. 3. in Croll Papers, MS8910 La Trobe
 Collection, State Library of Victoria.
Hare, Francis, Personal Papers, Melbourne University Archives.
McIntyre, Thomas Newman, A narrative of my experience with the
 Kelly gang and a short account of other bushrangers, MS6343 La
 Trobe Collection, State Library of Victoria.
Sadleir, John, A collection of correspondence and diaries of, La
 Trobe Collection, State Library of Victoria.
Standish, Frederick, Manuscript copy of diary, MS9502 La Trobe Col-
 lection, State Library of Victoria.

NEWSPAPERS

Advocate, 1878–80, 1946.

Age, 1878–80.
Argus, 1877–81.
Benalla Ensign and Farmers' and Squatters' Journal, 1869–71.
Dubbo Liberal, 1933.
Examiner and Kilmore and McIvor Journal, 1860–63.
Federal Standard, 1875–80.
Herald, 1878–80.
Illustrated Australian News, 1878.
Kyneton Guardian, 1870.
Kyneton Observer, 1870.
Mansfield Guardian, 1872–79.
Mansfield Independent, 1869–71.
Melbourne Punch, 1878–80.
North Eastern Ensign, 1872–75.
Ovens and Murray Advertiser, 1864–81.
Port Phillip Patriot and Melbourne Advertiser, 1841.
Sun, (Sydney) 1911.
Sydney Morning Herald, 1878–80.
Wagga Wagga Advertiser, 1877.
Wangaratta Dispatch, 1873–77.
West Australian Catholic Record, 1880.

Index